PARTICIPATING IN GOD

A Pastoral Doctrine of the Trinity

PARTICIPATING IN GOD

A PASTORAL DOCTRINE OF THE TRINITY

PAUL S. FIDDES

WESTMINSTER JOHN KNOX PRESS
LOUISVILLE, KENTUCKY

First published by Darton, Longman and Todd, London, UK.

Copyright © 2000 Paul S. Fiddes

Cover design by Lisa Buckley

Published by Westminster John Knox Press
Louisville, Kentucky

PRINTED IN GREAT BRITAIN

00 01 02 03 04 05 06 07 08 09 — 10 9 8 7 6 5 4 3 2 1

Library of Congress Cataloging-in-Publication Data
A catalog record for this book is available from the Library of Congress.

ISBN 0-664-22335-4

For
Barnaby

CONTENTS

ACKNOWLEDGEMENTS

Quotation from the poem 'Tenebrae' by Paul Celan in *Poems of Paul Celan*, translated and introduced by Michael Hamburger, is by kind permission of Anvil Press Poetry Ltd and Persea Books Inc. (New York) © 1972, 1980, 1988, 1995 by Michael Hamburger.

Quotations from *The Poems of St John of the Cross*, English translation by John Frederick Nims, third edition, are by kind permission of The University of Chicago Press © 1959, 1968, 1979 by John Frederick Nims.

Except where otherwise noted, quotations are from *The Holy Bible: Revised Standard Version* copyright © 1946, 1952 by Division of Christian Education of the National Council of Churches of Christ in the United States of America, and are used by kind permission. Quotations from *The Holy Bible: New Revised Standard Version* are copyright © 1989 by Division of Christian Education of the National Council of Churches of Christ in the United States of America, and are used by kind permission.

Note: Since this book was not designed with Greek readers in mind, in the transliterations of Greek words accents are not marked and long vowels are not distinguished from short ones.

PART I

Persons and Participation

I

Introduction:
from Experience to Doctrine

Some years ago the Court of Appeal of British Columbia, Canada, was hearing a case about a man accused of arson. During his trial in a lower court a microphone had picked up something he had murmured under his breath – 'O God, let me get away with it just this once.' The judge of that court had ruled that this incriminating remark was not admissible as evidence, since it was not (in his view) a public utterance, but a private conversation between two persons – the accused and God. The Appeal Court, however, now ruled against this judgement, on the grounds that 'God is not a person'. When this story was reported in the *Guardian* newspaper,[1] the reporter added his own twist to the verdict: he suggested that Christians should agree with the judgement of the Appeal Judges since they believe that 'God is not one person but three'.

No doubt it is a good thing that lawyers and journalists are interested in theology, but this little anecdote illustrates all the confusions that can arise with the word 'person', when Christians affirm the doctrine of the Trinity by speaking of three persons in one God. The newspaper reporter clearly thought that it meant something like three individual beings, a group of people. So if the plaintiff was talking to God, he was having a conversation with three others, and his remark was quite public after all! It seems unclear *what* the judges intended to say; possibly they meant simply that God was not exactly the same as a human person and so did not come under the provisions of the legal code of British Columbia. In this they were certainly correct.

How can God be truly personal, and yet also three persons? How much can a human word like 'person' be applied at all to the infinite and unique reality of God? These are questions that confront us when we want to speak of belief in a 'personal God'. If it is Christian theology we are embarked upon, then we can only talk of a personal God in a triune way. It is not possible to conduct a philosophical enquiry simply on the question 'Is God *a* Person?' and then follow this up with a theological debate about God as Trinity. For Christian faith, it is the self-unveiling of God as Father, Son and Spirit which determines the use and meaning of the word 'person' in the first place. Of course, already in the faith of ancient Israel God is pictured concretely and actively in personal terms: God loves, is faithful, keeps covenant, is angry at sin, speaks and listens. But the Old Testament writers do not reflect on the *concept* of a person or personality with regard to God; this kind of thinking emerges from the development of the doctrine of the Trinity in the early church. Indeed, there is quite a strong case for maintaining that the notion of what it means to be a *human* 'person' received sustained attention for the first time in Western culture in the context of affirming 'persons' in God.[2]

There is no question then of the doctrine of the Trinity being a kind of numerical puzzle designed to test faith or to baffle the human mind. The doctrine is not stating the paradox that God is one being and three beings at the same time, or even that God is both 'one person' and 'three persons', as something impossible to believe but required as a proof of devotion. Unfortunately, Christian people do often think like this, as was shown by a survey conducted in 1984 by a professional sociologist and entitled 'The Triune God in Hackney and Enfield'. When church members in this area of London were asked, 'How is it that God is three persons in one?', the answers of about a third of the sample group showed that they understood the last word in the sense of 'one person', one respondent affirming typically that 'The three are one person: they're all one person'.[3] The willingness to accept a pious puzzle was well illustrated by the church member who remarked that 'two are hardly enough and four are too many. But if God decides to make one more it's all right with me.'[4]

Mathematical illustrations of the Trinity can take the same line. To the sceptical charge that $1 + 1 + 1 = 3$ and not 1, Christian apologists have sometimes replied by pointing out that $1 \times 1 \times 1 = 1$. But the doctrine of the Trinity is not an exercise in mathematics, even of the most sublime sort. It is not a juggling with numbers, for God cannot be the result either of addition or multiplication. Although the theologian Karl Barth has been accused of stressing the unity of God at the expense of three persons ('modalism'), he rightly asserts that the oneness of God is not to be confused with the 'singularity' that is connected with numerical unity. Unlike a numerical oneness, the 'revealed unity does not exclude but includes a distinction'.[5]

When the early church fathers developed the doctrine of the Trinity they were not painting by numbers; they were finding concepts to express an *experience*. That is, they were trying to articulate the richness of the personality of God that they had found in the story of salvation and in their own experience. It was not any longer sufficient to say 'the Lord' when they spoke a blessing in worship (Num. 6:24–6); they must speak of the love of the Father, the grace of the Lord Jesus and the fellowship of the Holy Spirit (1 Cor. 13:14), although they knew that the ultimate demand on their lives must come from one Lord. They began with God at work in salvation, healing human life. They had encountered God in the actions and words of a human Son, Jesus Christ; they found God revealed and active in this Son who welcomed outcasts into the Kingdom of God the Father and spoke the word of forgiveness on God's behalf. They found God in a new energy and guidance they experienced within their community, opening up relationships beyond the accepted social boundaries and opening up a hope for a future new creation; they could only speak of this in terms of the 'Holy Spirit' of God and they associated this Spirit in some way with the ongoing presence of Jesus Christ who had been crucified (2 Cor. 3:17–18).

So the early followers of Jesus had to rethink their understanding of the being of God because of their experience of God's acts among them. They took a new and revolutionary path of thought that conformed neither to strict Jewish monotheism nor to the many divine principles of Hellenism, believing that the very being of God must correspond in some way to their experience of God as Father, Son and Spirit. We notice that this experience of God is not of three personal realities in isolation from each other, but of persons in relation, always interweaving and interpenetrating each other. As people followed Christ through the experience of death to an old life and resurrection to a new one, they were baptised in the name of the Father, Son and Holy Spirit (Mt. 28:19), and the baptism of Jesus himself is portrayed as an event involving *a relationship* like that between a Father, a Son and a Spirit who opens up the heavens (Mk 1:10–11).

To put this in the technical terms that developed in theological scholarship, the early Christians moved back in thought from the 'economic' Trinity to the 'immanent' Trinity, or from the activity of God in ordering the household (*oikonomia*) of the world to the being of God within God's own self. In modern times, their conviction is mirrored by the thought of Karl Barth that 'God interprets himself' in revelation and act,[6] and by the affirmation of Eberhard Jüngel that 'God corresponds to himself'.[7] The God who is 'for us' as Father, Son and Spirit must be like this 'in advance' in God's self;[8] there is no other God than one who is open to others in outward-going love, and the God who *makes* communion in the world must already *be* communion.

Putting it in even more technical terms, the 'missions' of God in the world are already 'processions' within God's eternal being. The Gospel story of salvation is of 'sending' (*missio*): the Father sends out the Son into the world, into ministry in Galilee, into the conflict of Jerusalem and on resurrection morning out into Galilee again, into the land bordering the lands of the Gentiles (Mt. 28:10). The Son sends out the Spirit from his Father into the life of his disciples, and so they too are sent with the ministry of reconciliation beyond the borders of Galilee into the whole world (Mt. 28:16–20, Acts 1:8). This story of sending at a particular time and place in history has its roots in an eternal sending within God.[9] As the early theologians tried to express the relationship between Christ and God the Father, they spoke of an 'eternal generation'; from without beginning the Father was sending out or 'begetting' the Son from his very being. Similarly, the Father was sending out or 'breathing' out the Spirit, communicating himself in ecstatic love. The two missions in the world, of the Word and the Spirit, were based in two 'processions' in the inner being of God.

This movement from experience to a doctrine of God is why the church resisted Arius, who wanted to reduce the Son to a semi-divine figure, a perfect created being. Arius had used the logic of Platonist philosophy to argue that the God who was the 'sole unoriginate origin' of all reality could not share his being with others. He must be unique, alone a 'Father and Creator of all'.[10] The church replied that this logic must bow to the experience of salvation in Christ. The story of salvation tells us that God always goes out from God's self in love, sharing the divine being in a communion of life. So, Athanasius replied that while the Father is indeed uniquely 'unbegotten' as the Father, the Son and the Spirit are also 'un-begun', or share the life of the Father which has no beginning.[11] The God of salvation lives eternally in relationship.

Our venture in this book is a pastoral doctrine of the Trinity. I aim to develop an image of God which is appropriate to the demands of experience in pastoral care for others, whether we exercise that care as ordained or lay members of the Christian church, whether as members of the 'caring professions' or as those who have been called, through circumstances, to devote their lives to being unpaid 'carers'. The term 'pastor' in what follows generally refers to all of these, except when I explicitly mention ordained ministers. I intend to explore ways in which this pastoral practice shapes our doctrine of God, and conversely how faith in the triune God shapes our practice. My study thus has an affinity with the discipline that has come to be called 'practical theology' or 'pastoral theology', in which 'religious belief, tradition and practice meets contemporary experiences, questions and actions',[12] and in which there is an imaginative 'interplay between idea and action',[13] although I am more concerned with the creation of doctrine out of this dialogue than is customary. I also want to pursue the more difficult, but potentially even more enriching path, of asking how *participation* in this triune God affects both our images of God and our acts. Yet we should notice that this is no new venture, for the doctrine of the Trinity has been a pastoral theology from its formulation. The Christian idea of a personal God begins historically in pastoral experience, that is, in the experience of the Christian congregation. In the following two chapters in particular I want to show that many of our pastoral concerns about the nature of the person and the building of community are a good place to *talk* about a personal God and to find that all our talk is nothing less than *worship*.

The character of theology as a kind of worship should make clear that my appeal to a journey 'from experience to doctrine' must not be taken as meaning that human experience is a mode of access to God outside God's self-disclosure to us. In terms of a traditional dispute in theology, it is not setting experience or nature *against* revelation.[14] Nor is it taking the view that doctrinal concepts are merely a way of expressing some deep and mysterious dimension in human experience alone.[15] Rather, our experience of ourselves and others must always be understood in the context of a God who is present in the world, offering a self-communication which springs from a boundless love. It is this self-gift of God which already shapes both our experience of being in the world and our language with which we configure our experiences. In taking a path from experience to doctrine we are retracing a journey that God has already taken towards us. Theology is doxology, worship called out from those who have received the self-offering and self-opening of the triune God. We cannot thus do better than close these introductory reflections with the opening words of Augustine from his *Confessions*. In his ensuing spiritual autobiography he is going to search his experience of the world and his own mind and heart, plumbing them to their depths, but first he asks God for mercy to find words:[16]

> This person, this part of what you have created, desires to praise you. Indeed, you so provoke him that he delights to praise you . . . My faith, O Lord, calls upon you, faith which you have given me, which you have breathed into me through the humanity of your Son and the ministry of your preacher.

NOTES

1. *The Guardian* Diary, 'Silent Witness', 14 November 1980.
2. See Wolfhart Pannenberg, 'The Question of God' in *Basic Questions in Theology*, Vol. Two, trans. G. H. Kehm (London: SCM Press, 1971), 228–32.
3. Geoffrey Ahern, 'The Triune God in Hackney and Enfield: 30 Trinitarian Christians and Secularisation'. Unpublished paper presented to The British Council of Churches Study Commission on Trinitarian Doctrine Today (1984), © The C. S. Lewis Centre for the Study of Religion and Modernity, 16.
4. Ibid., 21.
5. Karl Barth, *Church Dogmatics*, trans. and ed. G. W. Bromiley and T. F. Torrance (Edinburgh: T. & T. Clark, 1936–77), I/1, 354–5.
6. Barth, *Church Dogmatics*, I/1, 311, 383f; II/1, 657–60.
7. Eberhard Jüngel, *The Doctrine of the Trinity: God's Being Is in Becoming*, trans. H. Harris (Edinburgh: Scottish Academic Press, 1976), 24–7.
8. Barth, *Church Dogmatics*, I/1, 383. Similarly, Karl Rahner, *The Trinity*, trans. J. Donceel (London: Burns & Oates, 1970), 21–2.
9. This has been emphasised by Jürgen Moltmann, *The Church in the Power of the Spirit*, trans. M. Kohl (London: SCM Press, 1977), 53–6; *The Trinity and the Kingdom of God*, trans. M. Kohl (London: SCM Press, 1981), 65–75.
10. Arius, quoted in Athanasius, *De Synodis* 16; Athanasius, *Contra Arianos* 1.5, 9.

11. Athanasius, *Contra Arianos* 1.31; *De Decretis Nicaenae Synodi* 28–30.

12. Stephen Pattison and James Woodward, 'An Introduction to Pastoral and Practical Theology' in Pattison and Woodward (eds), *The Blackwell Reader in Pastoral and Practical Theology* (Oxford: Blackwell, 2000), 7.

13. Alastair Campbell, 'The Nature of Practical Theology' in Pattison and Woodward (eds), *The Blackwell Reader*, 85.

14. General or universal revelation must therefore not be confused with a purely 'natural theology'. See Karl Rahner's view of 'universal, transcendental revelation', in Rahner, *Foundations of Christian Faith* (London: Darton, Longman & Todd, 1978), 142–61.

15. A recent representative of this way of thinking is Don Cupitt, in e.g. *Only Human* (London: SCM Press, 1985); *Life Lines* (London: SCM Press, 1986).

16. Augustine, *Confessions* 1.1 (my translation).

2

A Personal God
and the Making of Community

Images of the Trinity?

The festival celebrated in the church calendar as Trinity Sunday always poses some problems when there is 'Family Church', and the preacher wants to give a talk to the children on the theme of the day. How is one to communicate simply the ancient formula that God is 'three persons and one essence'? Roman Catholic preachers in Ireland have, from time immemorial, reached for the national emblem and sermonised on the three-in-one of the shamrock, much as early Christian preachers drew attention to the 'root, the shoot and the fruit' of a growing plant, or to the sun, its ray of light, and the point of the ray where it touches the earth.[1]

These illustrations, however, though expressing multiplicity-in-unity, fail to catch the personal and relational nature of trinitarian language to which I drew attention in the introduction to this study. Two attempts to communicate these aspects in talks to children which I have heard in recent years went as follows. In the first the preacher invited the children to raise their hands if they had three names, and asked them to tell him what they were – Fiona Susan Smith', for instance. God, he then informed them, also has three names – Father Son Spirit'. The second talk invited the children to think of the persons of the Trinity as different members of the same football team – the manager (the Father), a player (the Son) and the coach (the Spirit). All too unaware, our preachers had aligned themselves respectively with two historic errors in the development of the doctrine of the Trinity, modalism in the first case and pluralism in the second. The first stresses the one nature or essence of God at the expense of the reality of the persons, and the second emphasises the distinct identity of the persons but fails to articulate the oneness of God. As we shall see, there has been a tendency towards the first in the Western Church, and towards the second in the Eastern.

If we consider these illustrations more seriously – and surely attempts to communicate the Christian faith to children deserve to be treated seriously – we can see that they both fall short in expressing *relations* in God. This is obvious with the first, where persons are only at best roles or aspects of a single God. But it is also true of the second, where the individual persons, though working together in a common task, have only a functional and limited relatedness. They are not defined in their very being as persons through these particular relations, which may be broken off or replaced by others (the frequent sacking of the coach comes to mind immediately). If it be protested that these are only illustrations, educative tools which are necessarily limited, we should note the basic problem about applying such tools at all. The trouble is not that they are 'vestiges' of the Trinity set up to replace revelation, as Barth supposed.[2] Rather, they are attempts to *observe* God, either as an object of our sense perception, or as an object of our mental perception, or as a potential object of perception which *could* be observed if certain restrictions – for example, finitude and sinfulness – were lifted. My aim is to begin to shift our way of thinking away from the purely 'observational' which is characteristic of the split between subject and object in our Western culture, and to introduce the aspect of 'participation' in what is real. This, we shall find, is linked with taking relationships seriously. In this chapter such participation in the triune God will provide a perspective for the pastoral issues that arise from the place of the individual person within human community.

But the defects of our opening examples may have only served to confirm suspicions that the doctrine of the Trinity is a highly speculative topic, detached from everyday experience and best avoided by those whose concerns are largely pastoral. We need then to remind ourselves that the pressures towards formulating this doctrine came from practical areas of experience. To understand where we are now, we need to join the company of the early fathers of the church, to explore the way that they developed their language and thought about 'persons' in God. We can discern three major achievements which we still inherit today.

Three Achievements of the Early Church Theologians

In the first place, the theologians of the third and fourth centuries AD found a language in which to express both the oneness and the diversity of God. They have left us the formula, used in the churches of East and West, that God is 'one essence, three persons'. With the Greek form of this phrase the Eastern theologians developed a conceptual tool for expressing the complexity of the being of God by making a clear distinction between the words *ousia* (one) and *hypostasis* (three). This was a creative move, as for the most part the two words had been used indistinguishably in Greek philosophy, both meaning 'being', although *ousia* could in some contexts carry a more universal meaning for 'being' than *hypostasis*.

Arius hammered away at these terms, claiming that if there is one essence of God there must also be one divine *hypostasis*, one reality without beginning and without end. Consequently he insisted – as did his followers who turned his theology into drinking songs in the taverns of Alexandria – that Christ could not be 'the same in being' as God the Father; as a separate reality (*hypostasis*) he must also be of a different *ousia* (nature), namely created being.[3] So Christ was only 'God' in an honorary way, and was really a creature. If there were three fully divine hypostases there would be three essences and so three gods. Through the dispute with Arius an agreement was gradually reached among Greek Christian thinkers that *hypostasis* should denote the 'otherness' or distinct identity of Father, Son and Spirit, while *ousia* should denote the one divine nature with which each was identified.[4]

Tertullian in the West, speaking Latin, had much earlier proposed the balancing terms one *substantia* and three *personae*,[5] which were now reaffirmed to correspond to the Eastern development of thought. Sweetness and light seemed to break out at the Council of Constantinople in AD 381, meeting in the church of the Holy Peace in Constantinople (modern Istanbul). However, despite this apparent agreement between East and West, the situation persisted that, as Vladimir Lossky puts it neatly,

> In expounding the dogma of the Trinity, Western thought most often took as its starting point the one nature, and thence passed to the consideration of the three persons, while the Greeks followed the opposite course – from the three persons to the one nature.[6]

This is the problem that arises when Christians speak two languages, Greek and Latin. But it also arises from the use of philosophical words taken from a particular culture. What do words like *hypostasis* actually mean? So we move on to a second related achievement of thought.

This insight was first clearly articulated by Athanasius, and it was to find the distinctness of the persons in their relationship of origin to each other. Athanasius could not get very enthusiastic about what the philosophical difference might be between a *hypostasis* and an *ousia*.[7] He was more captivated by the relations of Father, Son and Spirit. To the sceptical Arian question as what the difference could be between the persons if they are one in divine essence (*ousia*), he gave a different kind of answer: the Father is 'other' (*heteros*) in that he alone begets the Son, the Son is 'other' in that he alone is begotten, and the Spirit is 'other' in that he alone proceeds from the Father.[8] They are different in the way that they are related to each other. This doctrine of relations was taken up by the Cappadocians in the East – who spoke of paternity, filiation and spiration – and by Augustine in the West.[9]

Behind this understanding of relations lay a profound challenge to Greek philosophical thought, which has recently been expounded with vigour and perceptiveness by the Orthodox scholar John Zizioulas;[10] that is, the Greek fathers were daring to equate *hypostasis* with 'person' (*prosopon*). Though they usually employ the terminology of 'three hypostases', it is clear they are giving it a personal meaning.[11] In the received tradition of both Plato and Aristotle, to be a 'person', and so to have particular identifying attributes and to be in relation with others, was something additional to the real core of one's being or one's essential nature (*ousia* or *hypostasis*); personalness was thus a passing phenomenon. But the development of the doctrine of the Trinity made the person a matter of 'ontology' (that is, a concept of 'being'). With regard to God, being as a 'person' in relation to others was now acknowledged as inseparable from enduring essence. Inevitably then this ontologising of the person, uniting person with *hypostasis*, would be applied to human persons. For them too, personal relations were not just to be added on to their 'real being' as an extra. The notion of 'being' itself was made relational: as Zizioulas aptly sums this up, 'to be and to be in relation becomes identical'.[12]

This led to a third achievement, which was to make clear the freedom both of a personal God and human persons. In Greek philosophy the universe was bound by necessity of being. As a 'person' one could break free into distinct identity or 'otherness', but there was a conflict between this freedom of the person and the necessity of nature; since to be a person was something transient, added on to the core of what we 'are', the conflict would always be resolved in favour of nature. This was made abundantly clear in the great tragedies where the heroes engaged in a losing struggle with fate – like Prometheus struggling against the edicts of the gods and having his liver eaten eternally by Jove's eagle.

The word *persona* (Latin) or *prosopon* (Greek) actually probably began by meaning the mask worn in the theatre, and so something just fixed on the outside of human beings. But the word was quickly extended to the role played by the actor, and finally then to the role played widely in social relationships. Now the church fathers were rooting *prosopon* in *hypostasis* or being, so what had seemed a futile freedom of the human person was being claimed to have its basis in the ultimate freedom of God. As the modern theologian Karl Barth puts it, a person is 'one who loves in freedom'.[13] God loves like this, and is free to be himself; in Barth's view God is free to do and be whatever he chooses to be in love, not imprisoned by some kind of necessity of divine nature, as if a God is bound to be like this or that. For instance, if God chooses to be humble and even to suffer with his creation, it is not for us to pay God metaphysical compliments by protesting that the divine being will not allow it.

Before the development of Eastern thought, Tertullian in using the term *persona* had already broken through the mere meaning of 'mask'; he defined a person as 'one who speaks and acts', and he found no better expression for the distinction of the persons of the Son and Spirit from the Father than that they are 'other' (*alius*).[14] This makes clear that the 'distinct identity' of a person is inseparable from relationship; to call someone a person means that he or she must be taken account of as 'other' than ourselves when we meet.

Persons in Relation

It has taken many centuries for us to return to these insights of the church fathers. When the fathers used the word 'person' – whether persons in God or human beings – they meant a 'distinct identity', an otherness, which only made sense in relationship. But 'person' soon became a word for an otherness which was an aloneness, a naked individuality of the mind closed in on itself. Boethius defined the person as 'the individual substance of a rational nature',[15] and this was given a new twist by the Enlightenment exaltation of the human being as the only thinking animal. Humans stood out from their environment of nature because they were capable of reflective thought, asserting 'I think, therefore I am' (Descartes). So began the adulation of the absolute subjectivity that controls the world of objects around. Human persons were masters in a world of I–It relationships, dominating the natural world, and God was often conceived as the ultimate Subject validating this human self. Nineteenth-century Romanticism added the idea of the individual consciousness linked to a universal consciousness, and twentieth-century psychology made the person even more of a reflective individual subject, struggling with the conflict between unconscious and conscious desires.

This is a long history in Western culture of the reduction of the person in relationship to the individual subject, so that in the jargon of modern advertising to have a product 'personalised' is to have one's own name stamped on it. In reality, this is not personalising but individualising and privatising. In a doctrine of God this has led to the view of the three divine persons as three individuals, three subjects each with their own mind and consciousness. This has not resulted in tritheism; it has either reduced the doctrine of the Trinity to the mathematical puzzle with which I began, in which God is seen as the supreme individual and three individuals at the same time, or it has fostered the view that while any rational mind can conceive of One God, the *threeness* in God is what is mysterious, a deep secret in the inner being of God. Thus, for all *practical* purposes God is treated as 'a person' or one individual being. Against his intentions, Augustine gave an initial impetus to this trend by insisting that in the outward acts of God towards us the three persons are not only 'indivisible' but indistinguishable.[16] As Karl Rahner has pointed out, Western scholasticism has been subsequently marked by the kind of theological treatises on the doctrine of God which begin with a section on 'the One God', defining God's attributes and essence, and then go on to add a section on the Trinity as a second stage.[17]

In the latter part of this century there has been a determined attempt to regain the idea of person in relation. Martin Buber in his influential book *I and Thou* contrasted the encounter between persons with the 'I–It' manipulation of objects. We are persons because we can say 'Thou' to another, and because our ego is broken open by encounter with the Thou of the other. Through that 'Thou' of other people, Buber added, we meet the transcendent Thou we call God. To be a person is to experience the 'betweenness' that relates Thou's.[18] On the English scene, the Scottish philosopher John Macmurray mounted an attack upon the Enlightenment view of the person in his books *The Self as Agent* and *Persons in Relation*. The heart of the person, he suggested, is not 'I think' but 'I do', and this immediately involves us with others in a social life, in a universe which is structured in terms of relations.[19] In our individuality we think about the way we act in relationship with others, and this reflective process is often driven by motivations of fear (for example, fear for self-preservation), while our orientation to others is characterised by exocentric love.

It was fascinating to find John Macmurray's name cropping up in political commentaries in British newspapers preceding the British general election of May 1997. Macmurray's books were said to have been an inspiration for the soon to be elected Prime Minister Tony Blair in his undergraduate days in Oxford, giving him a vision of a society which was more than a collection of individuals.[20] This was regularly contrasted with the exegesis of the parable of the Good Samaritan once given by the former Conservative Prime Minister, Margaret Thatcher. The whole point of the parable, she was reported to have said, was that the Samaritan 'had money in his pocket' to help the wounded traveller; the lesson was thus that individual competition was the means to become wealthy, enabling those who have riches to do acts of charity to the poor. In an address to the General Assembly of the Church of Scotland in May, 1988, she recalled another person with wealth, adding: 'And remember the woman with the alabaster jar of ointment'.[21] Money in the pocket will in time 'trickle down' to the needy. This is a view of society as individuals making a contract with each other for certain purposes, based in the theories of John Locke and Jean-

Jacques Rousseau, and actualised in the nineteenth-century ethos of laissez-faire liberalism.[22] Macmurray and Buber urge us to take a different perspective on society, to consider that individual persons cannot be made in the first place without the social context of the kind of neighbour-love to others we see in the parable of Jesus. If the universe is relational in nature, then society in some sense pre-exists the individual within it.

All this has become the familiar coin of theological discussion in recent years. But if we accept that persons are what they are in relation, and that this should profoundly affect our view of human society, we are still left with the perplexing problem of the relation of the individual to the community. Unless we completely submerge the person in society, he or she has a core of identity, of particularity, of freedom – in short, 'otherness'. As long as we do not understand 'individual' as an isolated, self-sufficient and autonomous entity ('individualism' as an ideology), then the concept of 'individual' too deserves affirmation, or human rights may be undermined.[23] In her book on the Trinity, Catherine LaCugna offers us this definition of a person: 'A person is an ineffable, concrete, unique, and unrepeatable ecstasis of nature.'[24] This is a helpful, thumbnail sketch. But how shall we integrate the mystery of particularity, expressed in the terms 'ineffable, concrete, unique, unrepeatable', with the relational aspects of being 'ecstatic' – that is, going out from oneself in self-giving love?

This is not just a theological question, but a political one. While the 'Blair vision' of society seemed preferable to the Thatcher one in May 1997, within twelve months voices were being raised from all three major parties about what were detected as the dangers of 'centralisation'. Whatever the vision, the balance in practice is hard to maintain, and this is also the area of several pastoral concerns.

Four Pastoral Concerns about Persons

First there is what the Christian psychotherapist, Paul Tournier, calls the gap between the 'person' and the 'personage'.[25] The 'personage' is Tournier's word, as a doctor, for the mask or the image which we project when we present ourselves to others. I have already mentioned that the word 'person' actually comes from the Latin word for a mask worn by an actor on the stage, and it is in this sense that Carl Jung uses the term 'persona'.[26] It is our interface with society. The essence of what it means to be a person lies deeper than this, beneath the images and appearances, but we have many masks that we wear, according to occasion and our needs for acceptance.

A vivid example of this is given by the biographer of Judy Garland, film star of the 1940s and 50s, writing of his first interview with her in a hotel room in 1968. She had kept him waiting for four hours, and when she finally allowed him to come up, he found she had prepared for the meeting by putting on a circus clown's makeup. He realised immediately that she was coping with a potentially painful meeting by presenting an image of herself as the helpless victim everyone pities, the one more sinned against than sinning, 'seizing on this way out, to hide behind this facade – the wistful, loveable little clown whom no one would dare to hurt'.[27] Less dramatically, we have a personage or a repertoire of personages with which we play the game of life and society. We take on the role, and ask people to see us in a certain way.

But it would be quite wrong to say that these 'personages' are false and artificial and must be stripped away to find the real person underneath. Of course they must not be *confused* with the person, of whom we can suddenly catch a glimpse, or find ourselves meeting at an intuitive level. We can experience communication with the person at his or her core of being in an I–Thou encounter; we know when it happens. But the masks (which belong to the 'it' world) cannot be simply removed like a coat or suit of armour. We are wedded to them and can never be divided from them. When we ask 'who am I?' we ourselves have to search among the personages for the mystery of our person as much as *others* do when they ask who we are. And the images have their part to play. Without them, we would not be social beings but mere individuals.

The sociologist Erving Goffman has reflected here on the relation between 'the face' and the 'the place'.[28] The face (or 'front') is the mask that we ourselves project as what seems to us to be the most effective way of realising our objectives in an interaction with others. But while the face is the role we act, our mask is also shaped by the place in which we are situated and which makes demands on our self-presentation; we are accorded a role by others which is a complex of attributes and behaviours expected of us by society and its institutions, against which our actual behaviour is judged. Goffman's analysis is *reductionist*; the person for him is not much more than the sum of the roles she plays or is accorded. Society is the games people play, or a sacred theatre of ritual; it operates on the basis of rules for interaction worked out between everyone who is busy projecting identities or self-definitions or being given them by others. The rules for the game can be very complicated, depending on the particular set of relationships or interactions: Goffman quotes the case of a typical Southern lady in nineteenth-century America who would edge away from her male neighbour at the table in case they just happened to touch elbows, while being quite happy to lace up her undergarments in the presence of a black male slave.[29]

The perception that any community has a 'grammar' or set of rules for living and finding meaning within it is an illuminating one, especially when linked to the structures and function of language. However, this does not mean that Goffman is correct in reducing the person to nothing more than the wearing of masks and the following of rules; in fact he himself admits that from time to time the actor can be glimpsed behind the mask. But Goffman rightly alerts us to the complex relation between the personage we *project* and the personage *expected* from us.

A Christian pastor, then, will seek to enable someone to live in the interaction between person and personage, to become aware of the way that he or she is using masks, to live in harmony between self and presentation. The problem is not the personage itself, the roles and the rituals, but *discord* between the personage and the person. The pastor will enable people to become aware of when an image is not true to the self, or has become their master, or is an expectation of others which is preventing them growing as persons. They may, for instance, be crippled by trying to live up to the image of being an ideal parent or an ideal child. Pastors themselves will need to be sensitive to the dangers of conforming to expectations – for example of being the ideal spiritual leader whose faith never wavers.

A second pastoral issue is the balance between the integrity of the self and openness to others. We might call it being 'uniquely-centred' without being 'self-centred'. Our discussion so far about the nature of persons in God has envisaged that, whatever we might mean by *hypostases* (and I shall return to this), they are 'ecstatic', that is self-transcending in communication with others, especially in the movement of love. This whole approach contradicts the Enlightenment view of the person in which what matters is the ego reflecting upon itself. Rather, the person lives from openness beyond itself to others; it is a centre in the sense of being a centre of communication. What is primary is not self-reflection, but action in relationships.

The theologian Wolfhart Pannenberg has helpfully developed this concept of the open person, beginning from human experience at birth.[30] Human beings are born into a state of openness to the world in trust, embodied in a relationship of complete openness to the mother. As the mother comes to be seen as a finite object rather than a horizon-filling mediator of life, the trust of the child must be extended to a broader and broader environment, and ultimately beyond the horizon of the world itself to God, who is the only reality capable of sustaining trust without limit. As a matter of fact, however, the self seeks to close itself in defence against others, and attempts to control the world by gathering everything into its centre. Pannenberg thus discerns a struggle between the 'ego' centre, and the true 'self' which is to be received in relationship with others, in community.[31]

This is a vivid analysis of the conflict between openness and closure in the person, but it does tend to see all centring in the self as being selfish, positively sinful. In fact we discover that wholeness requires a certain kind of personal centring, an individual integrity. We may agree that the person is not a ready-made entity, a kind of core of existing identity, but it still develops an identity as a *consequence* of relations with others. Using a geological image, Alistair McFadyen speaks of the person being 'sedimented' from the flow of communication between subjects; individuality is a 'structured, continuous identity sedimented from significant moments' of acts of communication in which there is exchange.[32] McFadyen appears to be using the metaphor of 'sedimentation' in the sense in which a layer of rock is laid down over aeons. David Cunningham, in an exhilarating book on trinitarian theology, suggests that a more appropriate image is the 'sediment' which collects on a river-bed, which is always being composed and re-composed in a dynamic way by the movement of the current.[33] Whether geological or fluvial, the metaphor of sediment does imply that unless there is some centred subject maintaining a spirit of communication, we cannot be there for others at all. In this context, McFadyen even speaks of being 'an independent, centred and autonomous subject'.[34] As he points out, personal relationships may sometimes only be served if the personal subject can *resist* the demands of others which proceed from a distortion of the self in the other. Respect for others, of course, means that we must also be ready to be resisted by *them*.

Pastors need to be aware of this tension within themselves, between integrity of the self and openness to the other. Accordingly, Alastair Campbell urges that in order to care for others, we need a new discovery of the inner self, to understand our own needs and fears. Otherwise we will fail to notice the self-interest in our offers of care, which are really a kind of exploitation.[35] The person who fears the threat of illness and death will often seek out the disabled and the dying and anxiously try to support and comfort them; the person haunted by doubts about belief will demand a religious certainty from others. A desire to help can be a cry for help, and unless this is acknowledged the relationship will actually become depersonalised. Again, Campbell urges the practice of solitude, in order to equip one for being with others.[36] As well as finding God's presence in others, there is a need for a 'return to the still centre' in which the self finds unity by being grounded in God. The exploration of the light and the dark in our own selves will equip us for entering the darkness and the struggle of others.

More politically, the inner experience of conflict with hostile powers, which is typical of the 'desert tradition' of spirituality, prepares us for engagement with oppressive powers in the society around us.[37] Finding the still centre of the turning world in the self is thus not withdrawal from communication; it accompanies, for instance, an openness to others which means really listening to what they are saying, rather than just getting the general sense of it. It means seeing them as they are, noticing the language of their bodies as well as their speech; it means rejecting generalisations that try to fit people into neat and manageable packages. This is the pastoral requirement, to hold together the integrity of the self with an ecstasis beyond the self, but it is more easily stated than practised.

A third way of putting the tension between the individual and the community is the relation between dependence and in-dependence. We know the problem of personalities which are over-dependent upon others: there is, for example, the woman of thirty-six who looks and behaves ten years younger because her mother treats her like a child; there is the businessman who has allowed his life to be ruled by the search of his company for profit, for whom company loyalty is like submission to a dominating parent. Immature dependence shows itself in a desire for magical solutions without having to take responsibility for ourselves; it is letting others always take the decisions. The great complaint against religion is that it produces dependent personalities, and this is a question I want to look at in more detail in the next chapter.

The question of dependence is closely connected with the 'per-sonages' that we present to others, and which we have already explored a little. In his book, *The Pastor as Theologian*, Wesley Carr makes the point that responsibilities attach to the roles that we play in society, and in order to cultivate these responsibilities he suggests that we distinguish between 'relationship' and 'relatedness'.[38] Relationships are about mutuality, reciprocal self-giving, the affecting of each person by the other. In this area there can be mature dependence, in which we recognise what we owe to the other in the making of us what we truly are; but there can also be an immature kind of dependency in which the person demands that another be immediately available, should always be proving his or her dependability, and should offer instant solutions. So relationships between two people can become over-intense, claustro-phobic, breeding an unhealthy dependence. *Relatedness*, on the other hand, describes how people relate to each other through their different social roles, that is through the 'personages' they adopt in their interactions in the community. This kind of relation can be shaped by the taking up of mutual responsibilities, and by an aiming at what people can achieve together. Holding relatedness and relationship together can result in a true sense of interdependence.

The Christian minister, notes Carr, can be deeply uncomfortable at being asked to adopt roles and perform rituals that seem at times to be fostering a kind of folk-religion, encouraging the worst kind of magical dependence. But these can be the context in which people discover their own roles and therefore their responsibilities.[39] Acts of worship can be misused to cultivate a crippling sense of dependence upon hallowed patterns of words, or upon a dominating father figure, embodied in God or priest. But the imaginative play of worship can also become a means in which, for example, a mother can reorientate herself towards the responsibilities of motherhood through a proper sense of dependence upon the com-munity which is the body of Christ. Nevertheless, as Carr rightly observes, 'Pastors working with dependence feel that they are swim-ming in a lake of glue . . . no sooner do you think that you have extricated yourself than you feel you are trapped again.'[40]

A fourth kind of balance we need in community is that between unity and diversity, and this too relates to what we have discovered about the interaction between person and personage. When we meet someone who is quite unlike us, alien to us, our sense of identity is challenged and we become defensive. Because there is a gap between our person and our personage, we are uncertain of our own identity. We are also afraid that the various masks we project will not make us acceptable to others as we deeply crave to be. So we try to overcome this uncertainty by insisting that one particular personage is the standard of normality. We shout: 'This is normal – you must be like me', and in the Western world it seems that those who are white, male, employed and healthy shout louder than those who are black, female, unemployed and disabled. This is a denial of diversity which begins in the playground at school, where teenage children divide themselves into exclusive groups, labelling others as unacceptable by a whole range of names which in the mid-1990s included 'boffins', 'Metallers', 'ravers', 'fashion-victims', 'Sharons', 'Goths' and 'Raggas'.[41]

It is also a rejection of diversity when we attempt to *ignore* the difference of others from us. In the name of equality, we think we can give them respect by pretending that the difference does not exist. So people with a white skin imagine they are being generous to those of different races by pretending they are *really white too*; this often takes the specious and patronising form of claiming to be 'colour-blind'. Until the end of the apartheid era in South Africa, its government could only use the best hotels for accommodating visiting heads of state from Asia, the Caribbean and fellow African countries by granting them the status of 'honorary whites'. Within Britain, many are ready to accept immigrants from the black Commonwealth as long as they adopt traditional English culture, rather than helping to make a new multicultural society. Then there are those with a physical or mental handicap whom (in effect) we pretend to be really able-bodied; it is less embarrassing if we act as if we cannot see their disabilities. The result is to make no effort to provide entrances and exits that the disabled can use easily, or to provide financially for the equipment they need to become employed and make their contribution to society.

To take another example, it is not unusual for men to grant

equality to women as long as they can recognise them as 'honorary men'. In the fourth century AD we find St Augustine taking this approach to women he obviously admired. Preaching homilies on the martyrs' death of Perpetua and Felicitas, who were ravaged by wild beasts in the arena and then beheaded, the greatest compliment he can give them is to say that they faced their death *as if they were men.* 'God allowed these women to die in a manly and faithful fashion' he says, despite their 'womanly weakness'.[42] Perpetua herself, writing down an account of a vision in which she struggles in the arena with the devil in the form of an Egyptian 'horrible in appearance', recounts that in preparation for contest she was stripped and rubbed with oil 'and became a man'.[43] The modern feminist writer and novelist Sara Maitland protests,

> Tell me, tell me why, in your wonderful, powerful dream,
> when you strip naked in the arena and wrestle with the
> giant Egyptian and bestride the air, and smite him with your
> heel and dance upon his fallen head. Why do you have to
> become a man to do it? Why? . . . Why do you have to deny
> your sex, to be strong?[44]

Perpetua has nothing to say to her in this fictional dialogue except, 'That was how the dream was.' That is how it is when people need to win acceptance. When we pretend that others are not different from us, we are justifying ourselves no less than when we insist they must be the same as us. We are still saying, 'You must be like me', but instead of rejecting them outright, or being immediately hostile, we are implicitly saying, 'I will give you a chance to *become acceptable,* to *become* really human.' It is no wonder that these attitudes shape the dreams of the powerless who suffer from them.

Yet, in face of this need to affirm 'alterity',[45] there is also a need for unity in our society, some sense of common purpose and aim, some common values and shared experience. There is a harmful diversity which is simply fragmentation; what is (in the language of ecumenical documents) 'legitimate diversity'? It is desirable, but difficult, to achieve a plurality which is not an ideological pluralism in which all perspectives are as good as each other, but which is a differentiation preserving some sense of a whole to which parts belong. Ironically, the loss of a vision of a cosmic whole may lead to the making of new and false universals which are not in fact comprehensive of relations between people and with the natural world. As Colin Gunton suggests in his analysis of modernity, the quest for diversity and the preferring of the 'many' to the 'one' has only led to oppressive homogeneity; in face of the loss of a sense of God as a focus for unity, new universals such as the market, or a consumer culture, or fashion have rushed in to fill the vacuum.[46]

Personal Language about God

There are, then, what seem to be intractable tensions in the relation between the individual and the community which arise in any building of relations with others. There is a need to create a balance between the person and the personage, between self-integrity and openness to others, between independence and dependence, and between diversity and unity. In the face of these pastoral questions, what is the place of the Christian doctrine of the Trinity, which concerns a personal God who lives in relationships?

One strategy, confronting these problems, is to urge an imitation of God. Our lives should be shaped by a vision of the triune God, and if we are indeed created in the image of God and if God's grace is continually present to transform nature, then making such a rhetorical appeal is not altogether futile. Imitation has a major place in the ethics of the Old Testament writers, who present God as demanding conformity to his own character ('You shall be holy *as I am holy*').[47] Imitation of God is also largely the point of several recent studies on the doctrine of the Trinity. Colin Gunton, for instance, urges that 'a God conceived trinitarianly . . . can surely enable us to conceive the unity in variety of human culture'.[48] In David Cunningham's fine study, he develops an account of trinitarian 'practices' that 'inform and are informed by' the trinitarian 'virtues' of 'polyphony', 'participation' and 'particularity'. If the reader disagrees with the way he has worked these parallels out in such issues as peacemaking, or the place of children in the church, or the nature of sexual partnerships, he generously invites dissent along the lines of saying, 'No, the doctrine of the Trinity doesn't underwrite that practice. Instead it calls us to . . .'[49] One dimension of this present book is to develop a similar trinitarian modelling, to have an image of God in our minds which will be adequate to support pastoral practice, when we are faced by demands upon us for which we need resources of faith. But an imitation of God, a conception of God to be implemented, is not a sufficient pastoral theology. It is not even enough to suggest, with Catherine LaCugna, that a contemplation of the triune God in worship can provoke us into realising our human capacities for fellowship that we share with God, and so to create a renewal of our being in communion.[50] All this modelling can lead to a loss of the sense of the divine mystery and otherness as God is conformed to the human image of community. It can lead to a human effort to conform to God, whatever appeals are made to the grace of God which assists us. It can lead to an over-speculative doctrine of the 'inner Trinity' which becomes detached from experience. It is not enough to plead, 'God is united and yet lives in relations, so we should be like this too.'

As indicated by the title of this book and this section, I am aiming to complement the *imitation* of God with a thoroughgoing attempt to speak of *participation* in God in pastoral experience. On the way to this, we need as a prior question to ask what kind of language we are using about God at all when we stand in the tradition of the church fathers and call God 'personal'. It cannot be the language of observation, describing God from the standpoint of an external watcher or perceiver, as God cannot be an object which we can master in this way. This has led some theologians to propose that talk about God as personal is really only talk about our *experience* of God. Because we are personal beings ourselves we are bound to use personal language, but we can never talk about God directly as God is unique and unclassifiable. We might call this an 'existentialist' approach, and here Martin Buber is rather close to Rudolph Bultmann. Buber affirms that when he calls God 'Thou' it is talk about the encounter rather than about God in God's own self; he is concerned only with the impact of God on human existence and particularly on human relations.[51] Such an approach rules out any development of the doctrine of an immanent Trinity, that is, any account of God's self-related and self-differentiated being.

I do not want my appeal to experience as the starting point of doctrine, with which I began this study, to be taken similarly as meaning that a doctrinal concept such as a 'personal relation' is *only* a way of talking about human experience of God. There is a way forward 'into God', which recognises both the divine mystery and the brokenness of human words in the face of God. If God has taken the initiative in self-disclosure, and we have received the gift of God's self-unveiling in our experience, then we are required to speak both to and about the Giver. The faithfulness and truth with which God has declared God's own self calls out for us to witness faithfully to God. Karl Barth puts this in the form of saying that while human speech in itself is utterly incapable of representing God, in revelation God 'seizes' words to make them capable of meaningful God-talk.[52] While they cannot literally describe God, by God's grace they have been made into analogies which speak truly and reliably about God. While Barth himself tends towards a restricted view of the scope of this commandeering of language (though not as restricted as many 'Barthians' make out),[53] we might build a more general view of the gracing of human language through the self-presencing of God in the world. The question would then be, what analogies are most appropriate for pointing towards the reality of God. Can personal language really bear this weight?

There are influential theological voices who do not believe that it can, and so an alternative to the view that personal language is merely about our *experience* of God is that it is a kind of second-order language about God, subordinate to a more accurate analogy, that God is Being or 'being-itself'. This approach is basic to the theology of Paul Tillich,[54] and has been presented in a more popular form by John Macquarrie. Language of God as 'Being' is thought to be more capacious than language of persons, more capable of expressing both the transcendence of God over the world and the immanence of God in the world, since we cannot think of Being directly but only as that which supports and sustains beings, or which (as John Macquarrie puts it) 'lets beings be'.[55] This in turn leads to a refashioning of trinitarian persons as 'primordial Being, expressive Being and unitive Being'.[56] This approach has the advantage of beginning from experience, while developing an 'ontology' (a concept of being) from it. Macquarrie points to experiences of awe and wonder that we can identify as encounters with 'holy Being'; however, since Being is unique and incomparable, we only come to recognise the presence of 'Being' indirectly through a contrast with another kind of experience, that of 'non-being'. We fall into moods when there seems to be no meaning in life, when we feel we are hanging over an empty void, or when we are brought up against the shock of death when everything seems to cease to be. We have moods of anxiety when the world sinks to nothing, and everything is stripped of significance and value. It is, suggests Macquarrie, when we become aware of the nothingness of ourselves and the world like this that we suddenly notice Being: 'For the first time our eyes are opened to the wonder of Being, and this happens with the force of revelation.'[57]

I do not want to unfold here the trinitarian theology which Macquarrie and Tillich develop from making Being the formative analogy for God, and from regarding 'person' as a symbol for Being (though at times it is not clear whether they remember that 'Being' too must be symbolic and not literal language for our 'ultimate concern').[58] Nor do I want to deny that the analogy of Being has an essential place in theology, whether in its classic form in the thought of Aquinas or in its modern existential–ontological form. The claim I want to resist is simply that one analogy is *superior* to the other, that language about personal relationships in (and with) God is more restrictive than language of Being, and so can only be 'remotely analogous' to the self-disclosure of Being.[59] The nature of this challenge is not that personal language is useless in religion; it is admitted, for instance, to have an indispensable place in public and private prayers, where 'holy Father' seems more appropriate than 'holy Being'. God, after all, is 'not less than personal' because Being lets persons be and so Being has 'the power of personality'.[60] The claim we must meet, however, is that when we set out to think as carefully as we can in theology, 'Being which overcomes non-being' is more adequate.

This theology is right to insist that God is unique and unclassifiable, and therefore cannot be put in a class with other beings by being conceived either as 'a' being or 'three beings', even the most elevated. However, it assumes that speaking of God as 'personal' must reduce God to one or three individual beings, while we have already seen that in our own experience to be personal transcends being an individual. Moreover, there is something mysterious about personalness that makes it an apt image for the otherness of God; we can never get what it is to be personal under our control or objectify it, since it inhabits the space of the 'between' of communication. If we are looking for traces of God as the mystery in our midst, then the area of the personal is most promising. Significantly, Macquarrie himself is not content with speaking of God as 'Being', for philosophers like Sartre who are not religious believers can interpret existence in terms of being and non-being; Macquarrie adds the adjective 'holy', not because in his view it is a personal quality, but because it indicates our attitude of trust in Being.[61] We trust that Being is for us, is graciously on our side. But this surely implies that Being must be trustworthy, inviting trust, and we have not escaped from personal language at all.

If we are to meet the challenge of the theologians of 'Being', we must think the personalness of God in a way that does not reduce God in any way to one individual subject or three; then we might combine analogies and refer to God as 'personal Being', but not '*a* personal being', so that 'Being is communion'. As we shall see shortly, this does not seem to be achievable by drawing a close analogy with individual human persons, although the way that they are formed through relationships certainly points towards the transcending of individual subjectivity. The clue is to think of personal relations in a truly participatory way, and Tillich has in fact already aimed in this direction by declaring that 'the suffering of God . . . is the power which overcomes creaturely self-destruction by participation and transformation'.[62] Personal language for God remains an analogy, but it has the capacity to be a language of participation, pointing to engagement in God and drawing us into such involvement. Unlike the language of Being, this has the advantage of being consistent with the experience and words of worship, and so has a place in the the corporate life of a community.

Barth's insight into the seizing of human language by the self-unveiling of God can be extended here to the nature of communities as a whole. In thinking about the 'personage' we began to see that a person belongs to a community which is shaped by forms of language which embody the rules and practices of the social group. Before any language skills are acquired by the individual person, he or she already participates in a community and its 'language games', so that language itself is not just a vehicle of expression, but *conditions* our perception. We can therefore think of God's self-giving and self-presencing in the world as taking hold of these very structures and shaping these language-games, creating metaphors which are capable of pointing us towards the reality of God and enabling us to participate in it. Alan Torrance aptly sums up this transforming of a community and its language as the creating of both 'doxological and semantic participation' in God.[63]

Talk about personal relations in God is then, I suggest, not an observational form of language ('so that is what God looks like'), but the language of *participation*. The aim of a pastoral doctrine of God should therefore be to ask (a) *conceptually*, what difference it makes to view pastoral issues from the perspective of engagement in God; and (b) *experimentally*, how our experience might be shaped by this engagement.

Engagement in God's Relations

There is in fact a concept of 'person' in God that accords with this theology of participation, and which has a long heritage in Christian thinking. This is the idea of the persons as 'subsistent relations' which has been developed as one strand of the Western tradition of the Trinity. The term, however, is often misunderstood and wrongly used. It does not just mean that the divine *hypostases* can only be *distinguished* by their relations to each other. We remember that Athanasius had been asked how the divine persons are different from each other, and replied that we could identify them because of their different relations. Nor, at a second stage of thought, does 'subsistent relation' just mean that the relations between the persons entirely *make* them what they are. This seems to have been the view of the Cappadocian Fathers of the Eastern Church in at least some of their reflections on the triune God, finding the relations to be those of 'paternity', 'filiation' and 'spiration' (or begetting, begotten and being breathed forth).[64] Similarly, while a number of recent theologians have appealed to the idea of 'subsistent relations', they have then proceeded to a discussion in which the divine persons are effectively *constituted* by their relations to each other, showing similarities (though eminently) with human persons in relation.[65] This is probably also what Gregory of Nazianzus means in saying that the term 'Father' is not a name for being (*ousia*) but for the relation (*schesis*) between the Father and the Son.[66]

The notion of 'subsistent relations', properly understood, is at a third level of meaning. It proposes that relations in God are as real and 'beingful' as anything which is created or uncreated, and that their ground of existence is in themselves. If we use the term *hypostasis* as the early theologians did for a 'distinct reality' which has being, then the relations *are* hypostases. There are no persons 'at each end of a relation', but the 'persons' are simply the relations. Augustine is at least moving towards this meaning when he says, in an experimental (even playful) way, that 'the names, Father and Son, do not refer to the substance but to the relation, and the relation is no accident'.[67] Thomas Aquinas later gave formality to the notion by creating the actual term 'subsistent relation', stating that ' "divine person" signifies relation as something subsisting . . . "person" signifies relation directly and nature indirectly, yet relation is signified, not as relation, but as hypostasis'.[68]

Aquinas helpfully begins his discussion with actions in God, that is with the two processions of 'begetting' and 'breathing forth'. These are not abstract ideas, for – as we have already seen – they correspond to the missions of God in the created world that we have experienced: the sending of the Son and the Spirit, incarnation and inspiration. Then Aquinas shows that two processions imply four kinds of 'real relations' (begetting, being begotten, breathing out, being breathed), which in turn imply three unique relations: begetting (including breathing out), being begotten, and being breathed forth.[69] These are the subsistent relations that we call 'Father, Son and Holy Spirit', and while the result appears at first glance to be similar to the thought of the Cappadocian Fathers, the critical point is that Aquinas has begun with movements or actions within God rather than subjects who act in various ways. Unfortunately the potential here for developing a dynamic concept of being (an ontology) based on action and relationship is spoiled because Aquinas explains the self-existence or subsistence of the relationships by the fact that they are identical with the one essence of God. They subsist because they are *the same* as the one divine substance which itself has self-existence.[70] This gives ample warrant to the suspicion of Eastern theologians that talk of 'subsistent relations' is simply in aid of the typical Western stress on the unity of God's essence; the 'relations' seem to be swallowed up into the one essence with the loss of any real threeness and 'otherness' of persons within God.

For those who are interested in how Aquinas arrived at this point, we may note that he was deeply influenced by the Aristotelian view that the divine essence must be 'simple', or radically unified. If this is so, both the properties and the relations of the essence must be identical with it; so the relations in God will have the same reality as the one essence. This loses the important insight of the early Eastern theologians, that the being of God is communion or fellowship. Augustine has also been accused of losing a grasp on this truth by his use of a psychological analogy for the Trinity, finding a correspondence in aspects of the human mind (memory, understanding, will). His idea that the divine persons are relations is read in the light of this image, and he is thus often reviled as the chief architect of the Western 'modalistic' tendency of stressing the oneness of God at the expense of any real diversity of persons.[71] Admittedly, his concentration on the image of the Trinity within the human soul did leave the impression that he conceived of God as an absolute individual with different faculties. However, we should also notice that his interest in psychological analogies was driven by a deep sense of our participation in God, and he preferred to speak not just of memory, understanding and will, but the actions of our mind's remembering *God*, understanding *God* and loving *God*.[72] Thus he associated the triune persons with our involvement in God.

We can take up this insight, together with Aquinas' strategy of beginning with processions (actions) in God, to put the idea of 'subsistent relations' on quite a different basis from that of one divine essence. Taking a clue from Karl Barth's insistence that 'with regard to the being of God, the word "event" or "act" is final',[73] we may speak of God as an 'event of relationships'. Barth's own definition of the persons as 'modes of being' fails to reflect his own perception of the dynamic nature of the being of God, even though he understood the 'modes' as always being characterised by relationship.[74] It is better, therefore, to speak of 'movements of relationship', or perhaps 'three movements of relationship subsisting in one event'. Of course, it is not possible to visualise, paint, or etch in stone or glass three interweaving relationships, or three movements of being characterised by their relations, without subjects exercising them. But then this ought to be a positive advantage in thinking about God, who cannot be objectified like other objects in the world; the triune God must not, as I have been suggesting, be visualised as three individual subjects who *have* relationships.

Talk about God as 'an event of relationships' is not therefore the language of a spectator, but the language of a participant. It only makes sense in terms of our involvement in the network of relationships in which God happens. While in his later book on the Trinity Jürgen Moltmann portrays the divine persons as three individual subjects,[75] in an earlier book he spoke of God as 'the event of Golgotha' and to the question 'can one pray to an event?' rightly answered that one can 'pray in this event'.[76] We shall later need to counter the criticism that regarding the persons as relationships is to lose any sense of their particular activity, and to subordinate them to one unified activity of God,[77] but for the moment I want to spell out what it means in experience to participate 'in' the event of the divine relations.

The New Testament portrays prayer as being 'to' the Father, 'through' the Son and 'in' the Spirit. This means that when we pray to God as Father, we find our address fitting into a movement like that of speech between a son and father, our response of 'yes' ('Amen') leaning upon a child-like 'yes' of humble obedience that is already there, glorifying the Father.[78] At the same time, we find ourselves involved in a movement of self-giving like that of a father sending forth a son, a movement which the early theologians called 'eternal generation' and which we experience in the mission of God in history. To pray 'in the event of Golgotha' means that these movements of response and mission are undergirded by movements of suffering, like the painful longing of a forsaken son towards a father and of a desolate father towards a lost son. Simultaneously, these two directions of movement are interwoven by a third, as we find that they are continually being opened up to new depths of relationship and to new possibilities of the future by a movement that we can only call 'Spirit'; for this third movement the Scriptures give us a whole series of impressionistic images – a wind blowing, breath stirring, oil trickling, wings beating, water flowing and fire burning – evoking an activity which disturbs, opens, deepens and provokes. The traditional formulation that the Spirit 'proceeds from the Father through the Son' points to movement which renews all relations 'from' and 'to' the Other.

Thus, through our participation, we can identify three distinct movements of speech, emotion and action which are like relationships 'from father to son', 'from son to father' and a movement of 'deepening relations'. They are mutual relationships of ecstatic, outward-going love, giving and receiving. Actively they are such moments as originating, responding, opening; passively they are moments of being glorified, being sent, being breathed. So far in describing them I have followed the form of address that Jesus himself taught his disciples, 'Abba, Father', offering the image 'from son to father' for the movement of response that we lean upon. But these movements of giving and receiving cannot in themselves be restricted to a particular gender, as is quite clear with the images for the movement of Spirit. They can also, in appropriate contexts, give rise to feminine images; for instance, the nature of our participation may require us to say that we are engaging in a flow of relationships like those originating in a mother (cf. Isa. 49:14–15), especially in experiences of being spiritually nurtured and fed,[79] or like those which characterise the response of a daughter. The question of gender and the Trinity is one that I intend to develop further in the next chapter.

Identifying the divine persons as relations brings together a way of understanding the nature of *being* (ontology) with a way of *knowing* (epistemology). The being of God is understood as event and relationship, but only through an epistemology of participation; each only makes sense in the context of the other. We cannot observe, even in our mind's eye, being which is relationship; it can only be known through the mode of participation. Recent studies of God as Trinity have rather surprisingly failed to combine 'being' and 'knowing'. For instance, the study by Alan Torrance has focused on the epistemology of our participation in God. He emphasises helpfully that when God reveals God's self as an event of divine communion this conditions our sociality, 'commandeering our language-games' to create metaphors which enable us to 'participate cognitively' in that communion.[80] Yet he thinks that the term which functions best in achieving this partipation in the triune dynamic is 'person', which he generally treats as an individual subject of communication and relationship. While affirming that there is no 'common essence' between human and divine persons, he thinks there is sufficient 'family resemblance' (Wittgenstein's term) between the associations which the term evokes when used either of human beings or of God for it to be an effective means of enabling us to indwell God.[81] By contrast, the study by David Cunnningham certainly lays stress on the nature of divine persons as subsistent relations, 'relations without remainder'. Yet he deals with 'participation' almost entirely as a *parallel* between the participation that occurs within God's own communion and that within human society; he does not dwell on human participation *in* God.[82]

Only by bringing together being as relation, and knowing as participation, will we begin to overcome the view of the human subject stemming from the Enlightenment, in which observation is the basic paradigm of knowing. This inherited paradigm means that knowledge takes the form of subjecting objects to the control of our consciousness, as things that can either literally be seen with the eyes or 'seen' in the mind. The human mind is thus exalted as master of all it surveys, and correspondingly the task of language has been to represent as accurately as possible what has been perceived, with words as a kind of coin of exchange.[83] A doctrine of the Trinity in which persons are relations makes it clear that it is impossible to know or speak about God in this way. As far as the world around is concerned, we must continue to know it – at least partly – as an object of our investigation; but as we experience a different form of knowing with regard to God, we may be able to open up new dimensions of empathy and 'indwelling' in our knowledge of our world as well.[84]

So far, in developing a participatory doctrine of God, I have been referring to 'movements' of relationship in which we can engage. The analogies I have been using refer to the relationships, as – for example – being 'like a relationship between a father and a son'. Metaphorical language can, as Janet Martin Soskice argues, 'point' to transcendent reality without being directly or exactly descriptive of it,[85] and I have been largely applying this 'critically realistic' view to the relationships which we experience and name as God. They are not merely deeper dimensions of human relationships, but have a self-existent reality which embraces us from beyond us. The modification we need to make to this theological realism is that metaphors give us an entrance into engagement in God, rather than being 'observational' in any sense; they point to the transcendent not as static signposts, but as a movement of pointing, as a flag streams in the wind and shows the direction in which the wind is blowing. We must exercise some caution, then, over Soskice's phrase that metaphors of the transcendent are 'reality-depicting';[86] they certainly provide pictures of the relationships – such as the movement of breath, or the nurturing movements of a mother towards her child, or the patterns of a dance – but the 'depictive' element subverts itself as soon as its task is done of drawing us into the relationship. Metaphor, then, denotes the divine *actions* of giving and receiving in love.

Yet the language of worship, as well as the credal affirmations of the church, move from verbal forms of metaphor ('sending', 'glorifying', 'opening') to noun forms: Father, Son and Spirit – or in some modern reformulations, Creator, Redeemer, Giver of Life, or (more dynamically) Source, Wellspring and Living Water.[87] In what sense then do these nouns indicate 'persons' in God? Can we go on using, in acts of blessing and baptism, a formula such as 'in the name of the Father, Son and Holy Spirit'? I want to offer three answers to this question, all of which are reflected at different times in the language I am using in this book.

First, some names for God, and especially 'Father, Son and Spirit', can properly be used as a kind of shorthand for the movements of relationship. This is in line with the way that Aquinas uses these three names for the three subsistent relations, while keeping verbal forms for the 'real relations'. 'Father', then, can indicate all the relationships which are like those of fatherhood. 'Father' is the name for a fatherly movement in God, and 'Son' for a filial movement. Moreover, we can speak of the Father, Son and Spirit in this sense as 'persons', if by person we mean a 'hypostasis' or distinct reality, rather than a subjective agent. We might call this use of the names of God 'declarative' (following the terminology of Paul Ricoeur).[88] When we say 'I believe in God, the Father, Son and Spirit', or 'The Father is good', we are declaring or announcing God; we are identifying *who* (not what) the God is whom we are talking about or, more fundamentally, whom we are addressing. This is the God who can be spoken of as Father, Son and Spirit. However, this 'declarative' use has the disadvantage that it can distract our attention from the dynamic movement of relationship, as we might relapse into thinking of three individual subjects who are having or exercising the relationship. Praying to God, for instance, is not at all illuminated by this particular use of names, as it is clear that we cannot pray *to* a relation – though of course we can certainly pray *in* relations.

A second use of names for God is *narrative*, in which a story is being told, such as 'the Son is begotten, not made, by the Father' or 'the Spirit is breathed out by the Father through the Son': this is the style of the historic creeds of the church. While this has the grammatical form of 'subject and object', I suggest that it is in fact indicating the direction or orientation of a relationship or communication.[89] To say, for instance, that the Father eternally generates the Son is a way of saying that there is a movement like a father sending forth a son in which we share. There is a distinct direction of movement, like that of a flow of feeling, speech and action from father to son. This is of course a narrative about events *internal* to God; there are also stories in which the object of the action is finite creation, such as 'God, the Father Almighty, maker of heaven and earth and of all things seen and unseen', and we will consider later how these works of God 'externally' in the world can also be understood as particular and distinct movements of relationship.

Third, and fundamentally, there is the *vocative* or appellative use of the names when we address God; we say 'Father, your will be done', or 'Christ have mercy', or 'Come, Holy Spirit'. This is the use of the names of God from which the others (declarative, narrative) derive, and on whose threshold they are trembling. To say 'Father, Son and Spirit' is already implicitly to be calling upon God. The practice of prayer is foundational to the life of individual and community, because address is the normal mode of relationship with God, who has first addressed us. If the narrative use indicates the flow of relationships, with the vocative use we place ourselves into the flow or, rather, in co-operation with God we allow ourselves to be drawn in. As I have already suggested, when we say 'Father' or 'Mother' to God we are being enticed into a movement of speech – responding, obeying, glorifying – that is already there before us.

We notice that, whether prayer is addressed to Father, Son or Spirit, the person praying is always identified with the movement of sonship or daughterhood, that is, with the trustful openness of the child ('for to such belongs the kingdom of heaven' – Mk 10:14). Saying 'Father', the one praying aligns herself *directly* with the active movement of response of the child. Saying 'Christ, only Son of the Father' the one praying identifies *indirectly* with the Christ-movement as she is herself ready to be sent as a servant on the mission of reconciliation. Invoking the Spirit, the one praying is swept up into a movement which is opening up both filial response and filial mission to new dimensions. The filial relation (and the adjective in English is not gender-specific), is the axis of intersection of relations because it is through the particular human sonship of Jesus of Nazareth, expressed in his words, actions and suffering, that we enter the communion of God's being. The relationships in which he lived were perfectly one with the dynamic of God's relations of love in a way that ours are not and never will be; in a phrase of John Hick, he was '*homo-agape*' with God with a numerical identity of love and not simply a generic sameness.[90]

In a later chapter I intend to explore Christology further with the metaphor of the 'body of Christ', but for the moment we must avoid short-circuiting the doctrine of the Trinity by an equation such as: 'Jesus Christ was and is a person: Christ is the eternal Son: therefore a person of the Trinity is a subject of consciousness and action.' The point is, rather, that we can never separate out the response and the mission of this particular person, Jesus the Christ, from the flow of giving and receiving in God. Entering the movement of sonship we find the risen Christ who is the same as the crucified Jesus, and encountering this Christ we are drawn into the movement of relation in which we cry 'Abba, Father'. The truth behind the two-nature Christology of Chalcedon is, as Wolfhart Pannenberg puts it, that 'the personal community of Jesus with the Father shows that he is himself identical with the Son of this Father'.[91]

A page or two ago, I asked what it might mean to baptise or bless in the name of the 'Father, the Son and the Holy Spirit'. To illustrate the way that these nouns draw us into the movements in which God consists, I would like to appeal to two trinitarian practices, one from a Christian tradition other than my own, and one from my Free Church, Baptist heritage. If we make a sign of the cross as we bless ourselves or others with the name of the Father, Son and Spirit, we are of course making a movement with our hand. While the sign recalls the sacrificial self-giving embodied in the cross at the heart of God, it is also a visible demonstration that this is not a static principle but love in movement. It may not be too fanciful to suggest that the vertical sweep portrays the movement of relation from Father to Son as the names are spoken, while the lateral movement cuts across this to recall the Spirit always opening up the relationship to new depths and a new future. Whatever cognitive content we give to the sign, it is surely significant that the names are associated with activities.

The action of baptism is another way that we 'perform' the doctrine of the Trinity, offering an opportunity to enter into the movements of relationship which the names represent. The New Testament phrase 'baptising *in the name* of the Father, the Son and the Holy Spirit' (Mt. 28:19) may be translated '*into the name*', a dynamic sense caught by John Zizioulas when he writes that 'Baptism in the Trinity means entering into a certain way of being which is that of the trinitarian God'.[92] If we baptise believers in Christ by immersion, there is plenty of scope for sacred drama, as the candidate shares in the currents of relationship that interact in God. Being plunged beneath the waters which represent the hostile forces of death and chaos (Ps. 18:15–17), the baptismal candidate shares in the mission of the Son who is sent by the Father to be immersed into the bitterness and alienation of death; emerging from the water, raised with Christ to new life (Rom. 6:4), the believer is taken up into the breath of the Spirit who opens new possibilities even in the waters of death, turning it into life-giving water so that she is born again of water and the spirit. This is baptism *into* the triune name, *into* movements whose direction is shown by the names. The scene of the baptism of Jesus in Matthew's Gospel is full of movement like this: it is as Jesus is 'coming up' from the water that he sees the Spirit 'coming down' from the heavens and hears the voice of the Father speaking to the Son (Mt. 3:16–17).

Using names for God, then, must always lead us into *movements* of divine love, which cannot be reduced to a relationship between a subject and an object. This has some affinity with the witness of the mystical writers of the Middle Ages, who found that they could not in their praying distinguish any difference between the human self and God.[93] For the most part they hasten to assert that this is not because the self *is* God or has *become* God, since the difference between Creator and created remains; but they cannot 'see the diffference' because of the intimate degree of participation of one in the other.[94] It is like, says John of the Cross, the inseparability of the light from the window pane through which it passes.[95] So God is not an *object* of our desire, where we would possess God, and which would only pander to our possessiveness; rather, we desire in God, *with* the desire of God, and especially with the desire of the Word for the Father. John of the Cross expresses this in a poem where he celebrates the sharing of human beings in the extravagant love of Father and Son, which cannot be confined to themselves:

> there to be rapt as God is
> seized by the same delight –
> for even as father and son
> and the third, not less in might,
>
> one in the other endure,
> so with the fond and fair –
> caught into God's great being,
> breathing his very air![96]

The 'negative theologians' such as John make clear that all our speech about God must be a constant oscillation between positive and negative, affirmations and denials, word and silence; talk about God and address to God must be, in technical terms, an interaction between the 'cataphatic' and the 'apophatic'. Speaking of the divine persons as relations precisely shows this double aspect of saying and un-saying. Revelation and experience lead us positively to characterise these relations as, for instance, sending, obeying and glorifying. But since we cannot observe these relations, even in a conceptual way in the mind and imagination, we are immediately plunged into silence.

In his *Romanzas*, John of the Cross depicts the mutual indwelling of Father, Son and Spirit as marked by such an excessive love, overflowing to draw created persons in, that he seems at least to be hinting that the 'names' are best to be understood as pointing to *movements* of relational love. A modern theologian, Rowan Williams, encourages this reading when he comments that in John's trinitarian thought 'the divine subsistents are in no way "objects" to each other as in an interpersonal relation within the world'.[97] Williams suggests that the excessiveness of divine desire, where the delight and joy of the persons in each other becomes the cause of joy in all created beings, means that love within God is 'objectless';

it is an 'endless love' without closure in a determinate object of love. In accord with this reading is the poem which, while not one of the *Romanzas*, stands next to them in the original manuscript. Here John takes up the image (used by the early church fathers) of the Trinity as fount (or spring), river and stream. In the 'dark night' of the soul where God eludes our possession, we can be immersed in this flow of divine life like water:[98]

> The spring that brims and ripples oh I know
> in dark of night . . .

> Bounty of waters flooding from this well
> Invigorates all earth, high heaven, and hell
> in dark of night . . .

> Two merging currents of the living spring –
> from these a third, no less astonishing
> in dark of night . . .

Without the personal aspect that comes from the 'names' of God, this image of 'current' and 'flow' would share the deficiencies of all impersonal images of the Trinity. Using the names in a declarative, narrative and especially vocative way makes clear that the movements in God are relational; they are currents of love.

Engagement and Community

The direct analogy between human community and divine communion lies, then, in the relationships themselves, and not in the 'persons' who are named in the declarative, narrative or vocative usages I have described. Those Christian thinkers who want to affirm that there are three persons in God in some sense of three conscious, acting subjects will of course lay stress on the relational nature of a human person. They will rightly affirm that as persons we are not 'isolated' or 'self-sufficient' individuals, but are constituted by our networks of relationships and our openness to each other. According to this analogy, persons in God differ from human persons in the degree of their mutual openness and involvement in each other; the love of the divine persons for each other is said to be so perfect and their relationships so intimate that they are one God in a way that we can never be one with each other. But however much this 'social doctrine' of the Trinity is based on the relational nature of the human person, it is doubtful whether we can ever get beyond a kind of tritheism in which threeness in God overbalances the oneness.

The strongest case for a relational unity of three divine subjects is based on the idea of *perichoresis* or mutual interpenetration of the persons. We shall be exploring perichoresis in more detail in the next chapter, but here we need to comment on the way that this image is often used to support the claim that three personal subjects can be one God: it is argued that they will indeed be one if each subject *exists in* the other, indwelling each other in a 'mutual interiority'. As Jürgen Moltmann expresses it, 'By virtue of their eternal love they live in one another to such an extent, and dwell in one another to such an extent, that they are one.'[99] But there are consequences here for the dwelling of created beings in God. As Miroslav Volf recognises, this kind of mutual interiority is not possible for *human* persons; however deep our empathy with other people, and however selfless our love, Volf points out that the *subject* in the self cannot be the one who is beloved but only the one who is doing the loving.[100] It follows that, if divine 'persons' are anything like distinct subjects, a human person cannot indwell them in the same way that they are said to indwell each other.

Thus, while Volf himself is a strong advocate (following Moltmann) of a perichoresis of personal subjects in God, he admits that this allows only a limited sense in which we can speak of *our* being 'interior' to God. For example, 'the Spirit indwells human persons, whereas human beings by contrast indwell *the life-giving ambience of the Spirit*, not the person of the Spirit'.[101] Whatever 'ambience' might mean, this one-sidedness hardly takes seriously the prayer of the Christ of the Fourth Gospel, that 'as you, Father, are in me, and I am in you, may they also be in us' (Jn 17:21 *NRSV*). The result of drawing a close analogy between human and divine *persons* in relationship is thus to undermine the participation of created beings in God, and to throw emphasis on the Trinity as a *model* for human relations.

Though Volf and Moltmann dismiss any notion of 'subsistent relations', there seems to be more potential for a mutual indwelling (perichoresis) of created persons and the triune God if the divine 'persons' are conceived as nothing other than relations. But there are equally problems with affirming subsistent relations while continuing to draw a close analogy between human *persons* and God. One way this is done is to take a postmodern view of the self in which the human subject is radically de-centred and viewed as the 'whence' and the 'whereto' of relationships. This is the path taken by David Cunningham, who draws attention to the thought of the philosopher Calvin Schrag about the self as a 'space of subjectivity'.[102] Schrag is critical of the portrait of the human subject developed in the Enlightenment, as a free, self-sufficient and independent centre of consciousness. Yet Schrag also recognises that acts of communication (including speaking and writing) come from somewhere, and we need to answer the questions 'Who is speaking?', 'Who is writing?' and 'Who is acting?' His solution is to restore the idea of a subject as speaker, author and actor, but no longer to understand this subject as being the *foundation* for communicative activities. This would continue the theme of the dominance of the human subject over objects around it. Instead, the subject is *implied* by the network of communication, emerging along with it and with other subjects. For this role of the self Schrag uses the phrase 'space of subjectivity', indicating that the subject is 'not an entity at all, but rather an event or happening that continues the conversation . . .'[103] Cunningham aligns this idea with the image of the person as 'sedimented out' from the processes of communication, as used by McFadyen, and adds to it his own phrase of the person as a 'locutionary space'. That is, we use words to name someone in order to place him or her in their context within the interweaving web of relationships in which we live. Names, asserts Cunningham, do not isolate persons as individuals but connect them to events and other people.

These ideas of Schrag, McFadyen and Cunningham are in my view a helpful contribution towards thinking of the human subject in a more relational way and moderating the Enlightenment arrogance about the human 'I'. But it is not helpful to draw on this view of human persons to illuminate, by analogy, the notion that persons of the Trinity are subsistent relations. Here Cunningham seizes on Schrag's phrase that the subject is 'not an entity', to draw a parallel with persons in God as 'relations without remainder'.[104] Divine persons, he claims, are also 'locutionary spaces'; they are named for their involvement in the communications and relationships of human life, such as God's self-naming as 'Yahweh' in connection with the event of the Exodus (Exod. 3:15). But unfortunate results come from comparing relationships in God with a view of the human subject as the 'whence' of communication. Either we end up by undermining human particularity, or we revert to treating the divine persons as some kind of individual subjects. On the one hand, applying the idea of the divine persons as 'relations without remainder' to *human* subjects means that it is difficult to take seriously the notion that they are 'sedimented out' of relationships, and thus have at least a relative (though not of course isolated) individuality. The human person evaporates into a bundle of relationships and fragmentary experiences, and the identity which Schrag and McFadyen want to retain is lost. On the other hand, to affirm this 'sedimented' identity and to apply it to the *divine* Three means that the latter will be regarded as 'persons constituted by relations' rather than being simply relations.[105]

All this means that, even at its best, the analogy between human and divine 'persons' is a misleading one. While there are echoes and hints which should not be disregarded, a trinitarian theology cannot be built on these. The closest analogy between the triune God and human existence created in the image of this God is not in persons but in the *personal relationships* themselves: 'So God created humankind in his image . . . male and female he created them' (Gen. 1:27 *NRSV*). It is the relations between a mother and the baby in her womb, between children and parents, between wife and husband, and between members of the church community that are analogous to relations in God. The notion of a 'person' will necessarily play a different role in the two kinds of relation with which it is bound up. Because we are created, finite beings there will always be personal subjects with at least a relative individuality who exercise relationships, and 'between' whom the relationships exist. By contrast, because God is uncreated and unique the language of persons will be a way of drawing us into the personal relationships which embrace us and within which God makes room for us to dwell. Volf is right that a human subject could not indwell a divine subject in 'mutual interiority', for this would mean that all divine actions could be attributed to human beings and – perhaps more horrifyingly – all human atrocities become the direct responsibility of the divine agents. But human persons can dwell in the places opened out within the interweaving relationships of God; they dwell, we might say, not in 'spaces of subjectivity' but in 'relational spaces'. It is the relationships in God about which we can be 'theological realists' in our language; they are a kind of first-order metaphor, where images of God such as 'Father, Shepherd, King, Friend' have a second-order but indispensable use in enticing us into sharing in this reality of relationship.

Thus we can never think of the triune God, or name the Father, Son and Holy Spirit, without participation. It is not enough to urge an *imitation* of the triune life, important though this is. I hope that those readers who have not been convinced by my advocacy of 'persons *as* relationships' in God and prefer to adopt a more social doctrine of 'persons *in* relationship' will nevertheless still feel that the rest of this book concerns them, since it encourages a reflection on pastoral issues from this perspective of participation in God. In concluding this chapter, let us then return to the four tensions we identified earlier, associated with the relation of individual persons within community, and ask what difference might be made by placing them in the context of engagement in God.

First, we noticed the problem of living at ease with the roles we assume in relating to others, of achieving a harmony of truth between 'person' and 'personage'. A triune doctrine of God encourages us to *discover* our roles as we participate in a God who is always in the movement of sending. The one who sends out the Son eternally from the womb of his being sends the Son into the world, and Christ after his resurrection from the dead says to his followers: 'as the Father has sent me, so I send you'. The story of this meeting of the disciples with the risen Christ, as told in the Fourth Gospel, probably reflects the experience of early Christians gathered regularly in a house for worship 'on the first day of the week' (Jn 20:19), and it is in this context of the gathering of the church that Christ breathes out the Spirit upon them with an authorisation to pronounce forgiveness of sins (20:22), as Jesus had announced acceptance on behalf of his Father. This scene, like the story of the baptism of Jesus, has a pattern which fits into the later development of the doctrine of the Trinity. It is one characterised by movement, as the narrative is told of a Father sending a Son who breathes out a Spirit, the source of whose activity (forgiveness) lies in the Father. In the language of later trinitarian reflection, the Spirit issues from the Father through the Son.

It is into these interweaving currents of mission that the disciples are drawn. The signs of the ministry of Jesus, represented by the written signs of the Gospel text, are to be reproduced in their own lives in a multiplicity of new ways so that others will believe without seeing the historical Jesus (20:29–31). What is being portrayed here is no mere imitation of the ministry of Christ, not simply a modelling of human community on the relations in God. Participating in the movement of sending, disciples *represent* the actions of Jesus in their acts. There is an identification not of substance but of act and event. It is surely in the light of this open-ended continuation of the reconciling and redemptive activity of Jesus that we should read what commentators have dismissed as over-exaggerated hyperbole at the conclusion of the Gospel, the claim that the world is not large enough to contain the books that could be written about the 'many other things which Jesus did' (21:25).[106] This is the theological context in which the problem of the 'person and the personages' must be set. By being engaged in God's relational life we can discover what roles the community requires, how it needs us to 'represent' the signs of the Christ in order to be a community open to the needs of all. We can also discover how to resist false expectations and type-casting, to reject the masks that others want us to wear for their own satisfaction. That is, we shall find our vocation and true sense of responsibility, not in the flight of the soul as the 'alone to the alone', but in the community gathered in the 'name' of Christ.

The second tension we observed was that between the integrity of the self and openness to others. This calls for a balance between a proper self-centring, which is not a destructive self-centredness, and formation through our social relationships. In correction of the Enlightenment exaltation of the subject, it is now clear that the self is not the centre of all things, and is not even the centre of the language it employs. Even before a person consciously learns to use words, he or she is already shaped through participation in a society with its 'language-games', with its developed 'grammatical rules' for living as a member of the society. How shall we resolve the tension between being formed by language, by the network of communication with others in which we are born and nurtured, and being language-users ourselves? This is also a question of the will: how shall we exercise our own will and resist mere conformity to a corporate will, without a delusionary drawing of all reality into an ego-centre? One answer is that given by postmodern philosophers of the self such as Schrag, that as a subject we are 'co-actors' and 'co-narrators' with others in the human drama.[107] But participation in God opens a new perspective on this practical question.

To participate in God means that there is the ever-present opportunity to be aligned with a movement of communication beyond ourselves which is pure love, and which is also a movement of the will. We can lean upon a movement which is like a willing response of a son to a father, becoming co-actors and co-narrators with his 'Yes, Amen' to the Father's purpose. Openness to others will not mean conformity to the human other, which would be a loss of one's own will, but conformity to the Christ whom we meet in and through the other. The self is properly centred by a conjunction of being directed outwards to others (*ek-stasis*), and having one's will conformed to the relation of Christ to the Father. This ethical conformity of will may then mean resistance to the will of another, or to the mass will of a society, unless this is also conformed to the movement of will which is like the 'yes' of a son to a father in God. The earthly life of Jesus will give us some clues as to how a resistance can be developed which does not succumb to the culture of violence around us.

In this way, there can be what Alistair McFadyen calls a 'mutual will-formation' in society, which leaves space for real choices to be made by the individual person.[108] This translates even into the small-scale setting of pastoral counselling, where the psychotherapist Paul Tournier urges us to remember that 'to live is to choose', and that health at least partly stems from being able to appeal to someone to find their own voice from within the core of their own identity. He relates one incident from his own casebook: ' "Do you think I ought to tell my wife?" I am asked by a husband who has just confessed to me that he has been unfaithful to her.' Tournier replies in the Socratic manner, 'What do you think yourself?'[109]

A third balance for which we registered the need was that between dependence and independence. I have already indicated that in the growth towards maturity there is a place for both, reflected in the dual concepts of 'relationship' (an immediate mutuality) and 'relatedness' (this relation placed in the context of social roles). To this useful distinction Wesley Carr adds a third concept of 'inter-relation', where the fact of relating between two or more people has a wider effect; it creates a new context of inter-relation which affects not only those directly involved but others as well.[110] Particular relationships are always part of a wider sphere, a network of relationships whose edges we can never calculate. A similar insight is offered by Francis Jacques, reflecting on the nature of communication as a 'joint discourse-creating activity' in which the keynote is 'we say'. He points out that in addition to the interplay of speaker and listener ('we'), there are always the 'third persons', the 'he/she/they' who do not appear and yet are implicated in the discourse. In all meaning and communication, he affirms, there is a mutual dependency between 'I', 'You' and 'They'.[111]

A maturity of interdependence comes therefore from a recognition of these wider relations, opening up what can be an oppressive situation of over-dependency between an 'I' and a 'Thou'. For this, participation in the triune God provides an all-embracing dimension; the Trinity is a movement of relations which is as wide as the universe, as God, in an act of self-limitation, opens the divine communion of life to enable all created beings to dwell within it. The Trinity is – in the phrase of Pannenberg, re-using a scientific image – a 'field of force'.[112] Moreover, this wider force-field of relationships is not just spatial but temporal; the Spirit is continually opening it up towards the future, giving our relations a place in the movement of God's purposeful journey towards new creation. One practical implication for engaging in this wider web of dependencies is the practice of intercessory prayer, and I devote a chapter to this later on.

The final tension we noticed was between diversity and unity, between recognising the distinctiveness of identity of another and sharing a common purpose. Engagement in the life of God means an experience of otherness, and not only the otherness of God from humanity, the otherness of the Creator from the created; it is to participate in the otherness of the personal relations in God, which are united at the same moment in a communion of love, will and purpose. Since there is a difference between begetting, being begotten and proceeding – or between sending and being sent – there must be differences within God which are greater than anything we know in the world where senders are also sent and begetters are also begotten.[113] We may envisage this otherness between the three movements of relation as taking on tragic depth in the cross, where a forsakenness and alienation opens up between the Father and the Son (Mark 15:34). Indeed, as Hans Urs von Balthasar has perceived, this separation and brokenness in communion is only possible because there is already, eternally, a 'self-destitution' of love which constitutes the Father, Son and Spirit in their self-gifting to each other, a 'gulf' between them which is 'founded on the infinite distinction between the hypostases'.[114]

While it is meaningful to urge an imitation of the unity and diversity within God, to work out what practices of plurality in the church community are 'informed' by this doctrine, talk of absolute otherness in God only makes sense in the context of a theology of participation. In the first place, the kind of otherness to which the self-disclosure of God in the cross points us cannot be known by observation or description. Nothing in the world can prepare us for this gulf of otherness in a God who abides in the unity of love. In the second place, because it is an otherness which arises in participation within God, it can only be known *through* participation. To engage in the relationships in God means that we are brought up against the challenge of the alien, the radically different, the unlike; but at the same time we have the security of experiencing a fellowship more intimate than anything we can otherwise know.

In these four ways we can begin to see what the difference might be between the Trinity as a model for human practices, and the Trinity as place of engagement with divine activity. We not only begin to explore the *relevance* of a personal God to pastoral concerns; we can explore the personal God who is *known* in pastoral experience. Any other God can be left to the philosophers. To return finally to the illustrations with which we began this chapter, preaching to children and adults about the Trinity should seek to provide illustrations of places and situations in which we can participate in the triune life of God, where talk of God as Father, Son and Spirit comes alive.

NOTES

1. Tertullian, *Adversus Praxean* 8, lists these and adds the spring, river and channel drawn off the river.
2. Karl Barth, *Church Dogmatics*, trans. and ed. G. W. Bromiley and T. F. Torrance (Edinburgh: T. & T. Clark, 1936–77), I/1, 334–44.
3. Arius, *Epistola ad Alexandrinum* (Athanasius, *De Synodis* 16); also in Athanasius, *Contra Arianos* 1.6.
4. E.g. Basil, *Epistolae* 236.6; Gregory Nazianzen, *Orationes* 42.15; Epiphanius, *Ancoratus* 81. The formula 'one ousia, three hypostases' was perhaps first used by Didymus of Alexandria, *De Trinitate* 1.16–36; 2.16ff.
5. E.g. Tertullian, *Adversus Praxean* 12.
6. Vladimir Lossky, *The Mystical Theology of the Eastern Church* (Cambridge: James Clarke & Co., 1957), 56.
7. In fact, for some while he treated them as identical; see *Contra Arianos* 1.11; *De Decretis* 27; *De Synodis* 41.
8. Athanasius, *Contra Arianos* 3.4–6, cf. 1.9, 39, 58.
9. See e.g. Gregory Nazianzen, *Orationes* 29.16; Augustine, *De Trinitate* 5.6–13.
10. John D. Zizioulas, *Being as Communion: Studies in Personhood and the Church* (London: Darton, Longman & Todd, 1985), 27–41.
11. The terms *prosopon* and *hypostasis* are clearly identified in e.g. Basil, *Epistolae* 210.5, 236.6; Gregory Nazianzen, *Orationes* 43.13.
12. Zizioulas, *Being as Communion*, 88.
13. Barth, *Church Dogmatics* II/1, 301–5; cf. IV/1, 186–8.
14. Tertullian, *Adversus Praxean* 5, 25.
15. Boethius, *Contra Eutychen et Nestorium* 3; followed by Aquinas, *Summa Theologiae* 1a.29.1.
16. Augustine, *De Trinitate* 2.8, 13, 35; 3.3; 5.15; *Enchiridion* 38.
17. Karl Rahner, *The Trinity*, trans. J. Donceel (London: Burns & Oates, 1970), 15–21.
18. Martin Buber, *I and Thou*, trans. R. Gregor Smith (Edinburgh: T. & T. Clark, 1937), 28–34; *Between Man and Man*, trans. R. Gregor Smith (London: Collins/Fontana, 1961), 126, 244f.
19. John Macmurray, *The Self as Agent* (London: Faber & Faber, 1957), 89–94; *Persons in Relation* (London: Faber & Faber, 1961), 64–76.
20. See Tony Blair, speaking to Matthew D'Ancona, *The Sunday Telegraph*, 7 April 1996; Stuart Wavell, article, *Sunday Times*, 9 May 1996; cf. Roy

McCloughry, *Belief in Politics* (London: Hodder & Stoughton, 1996), 49–51.

21. 'Text of Mrs Thatcher's Address to the General Assembly of the Church of Scotland, 21 May 1988'; reprinted in *The Guardian*, 23 May 1988.

22. This kind of view has been most strongly represented in recent years by Friedrich A. von Hayek, regarding the market as an exchange between individuals for their own interest, and so calling for deregulation and 'spontaneous order' : see *Law, Legislation and Liberty* (London: Routledge, 1998).

23. See Miroslav Volf, *After Our Likeness: The Church as the Image of the Trinity* (Grand Rapids, MI: Eerdmans, 1998), 220.

24. Catherine M. LaCugna, *God for Us: The Trinity and Christian Life* (San Francisco, CA: HarperCollins, 1991), 289.

25. Paul Tournier, *The Meaning of Persons* (London: SCM Press, 1957), 71–83.

26. Carl G. Jung, *Collected Works*, 17 volumes (London: Routledge & Kegan Paul, 1953–), 9.ii, 8–10; 12.38.

27. Gerald Frank, interviewed in *The Guardian*, 10 September 1975.

28. Erving Goffman, *The Presentation of the Self in Everyday Life* (London: Allen Lane/Penguin, 1969), 19–25; *Interaction Ritual: Essays on Face-to-Face Behaviour* (London: Allen Lane, 1972), 5–8, 42–4, 82–4.

29. Goffman, *The Presentation of Self*, 132–3.

30. Wolfhart Pannenberg, *What is Man?* trans. D. Priebe (Philadelphia: Fortress Press, 1972), 7–13, 30–8; *Anthropology in Theological Perspective*, trans. M. O'Connell (Edinburgh: T. & T. Clark, 1985), 71–9.

31. Pannenberg, *Anthropology*, 87–103.

32. Alistair I. McFadyen, *The Call to Personhood: A Christian Theory of the Individual in Social Relationships* (Cambridge: Cambridge University Press, 1990), 7–8, 72–3.

33. David S. Cunningham, *These Three Are One: The Practice of Trinitarian Theology* (Oxford: Blackwell, 1998), 199.

34. McFadyen, *The Call to Personhood*, 162.

35. Alastair Campbell, *Rediscovering Pastoral Care*, new edn (London: Darton, Longman & Todd, 1986), 99–100.

36. Ibid., 106.

37. See Kenneth Leech, *Spirituality and Pastoral Care* (London: Sheldon Press, 1986), 36–8.

38. Wesley Carr, *The Pastor as Theologian* (London: SPCK, 1989), 176–8.

39. Ibid., 213ff.

40. Ibid., 180.

41. Article, 'The happiest days of my life?', *The Guardian*, 24 May 1993.

42. Augustine, *Sermones de Sanctis* 280: 'In Natali martyrum Perpetuae et Felicitatis'.

43. *The Passion of the Holy Martyrs Perpetua and Felicitas* 3.2, in A. Roberts and J. Donaldson (eds), *The Ante-Nicene Fathers*, Vol. III (Grand Rapids,

MI: Eerdmans, 1973), 702. The account, presented as the diary of Perpetua, is probably authentic and is preserved in a text perhaps edited by Tertullian.

44. Sara Maitland, *Women Fly When Men Aren't Watching: Short Stories* (London: Virago Press, 1993), 83.
45. See Elaine Graham, *Transforming Practice: Pastoral Theology in an Age of Uncertainty* (London: Mowbray, 1996), 143–62.
46. Colin Gunton, *The One, the Three and the Many: God, Creation and the Culture of Modernity* (Cambridge: Cambridge University Press, 1993), 31–4.
47. Leviticus 11:44–5; cf. Deuteronomy 5:14–15; Isaiah 3:8–15, 5:11–16; Hosea 3:1.
48. Gunton, *The One, the Three and the Many*, 177.
49. Cunningham, *These Three Are One*, 236.
50. LaCugna, *God for Us*, 366–8.
51. Buber, *I and Thou*, 75–81.
52. Barth, *Church Dogmatics*, I/1, 430.
53. See Barth's reflections on 'true words spoken in the secular world', *Church Dogmatics* IV/3, 116ff.
54. Paul Tillich, *Systematic Theology*, combined volume (London: Nisbet & Co., 1968), Vol. 1, 261–71.
55. John Macquarrie, *Principles of Christian Theology*, revised edn (London: SCM Press, 1977), 115–22, 142–5.
56. Ibid., 200–2.
57. Ibid., 87.
58. See Paul Tillich, *The Courage to Be* (London: Collins/Fontana, 1962); *Systematic Theology*, Vol. 2, 9–12; Macquarrie, *Principles of Christian Theology*, 140–3.
59. Macquarrie, *Principles of Christian Theology*, 93–4.
60. Tillich, *Systematic Theology*, Vol. 1, 271; Macquarrie, *Principles of Christian Theology*, 204.
61. Macquarrie, *Principles of Christian Theology*, 121.
62. Tillich, *Systematic Theology*, Vol. 2, 203.
63. Alan Torrance, *Persons in Communion: Trinitarian Description and Human Participation* (Edinburgh: T. & T. Clark, 1996), 356–62.
64. Gregory Nazianzen, *Orationes* 23.8, 11; 29.2, 16; 30.11; 31.9–16; Basil, *Contra Eunomium* 2.9–10, 22, 29; Gregory of Nyssa, *Contra Eunomium* 2.2.
65. E.g. E. L. Mascall, *The Triune God: An Ecumenical Study* (Worthing: Churchman Publishing, 1986), 11–23; T. F. Torrance, *Trinitarian Perspectives* (Edinburgh: T. & T. Clark, 1994), 27–8, 134–9, cf. T. F. Torrance, *The Trinitarian Faith* (Edinburgh: T. & T. Clark, 1988), 321–6; Leonardo Boff, *Trinity and Society* trans. P. Burns (London: Burns & Oates, 1988), 88–90; Thomas Weinandy, *The Father's Spirit of Sonship: Reconceiving the*

Trinity (Edinburgh: T. & T. Clark, 1995), 82–3; Robert W. Jenson, *Systematic Theology, Volume 1, The Triune God* (New York: Oxford University Press, 1997), 108–114.

66. Gregory Nazianzen, *Orationes* 23.8.

67. Augustine, *De Trinitate* 5.6; translation from *The Trinity*, trans. S. McKenna, *The Fathers of the Church* (Washington: Catholic University of America Press, 1963), 180.

68. Thomas Aquinas, *Summa Theologiae* 1a.29.4: translation in Blackfriars Edition (London: Eyre & Spottiswoode, 1965), Vol. 6, 61.

69. Aquinas, *Summa Theologiae* 1a.27.1; 28.4.

70. Aquinas, *Summa Theologiae* 1a.2y.4; cf. 1a.3.6; 1a.27.4.

71. E.g. Colin Gunton, *The Promise of Trinitarian Theology* (Edinburgh: T. & T. Clark, 1991), 38–41.

72. Augustine, *De Trinitate* 14.15–20.

73. Barth, *Church Dogmatics*, II/1, 263.

74. Barth, *Church Dogmatics*, I/1, 348.

75. Jürgen Moltmann, *The Trinity and the Kingdom of God*, trans. M. Kohl (London: SCM Press, 1981), 171.

76. Jürgen Moltmann, *The Crucified God*, trans. R. A. Wilson and J. Bowden (London: SCM Press, 1974), 247.

77. See Ch. 3, pp. 83–9.

78. 2 Corinthians 1:20; cf. Romans 8:34, Hebrews 7:25.

79. See Michael Jacobs, *Living Illusions: A Psychology of Belief* (London: SPCK, 1993), 68–71.

80. Torrance, *Persons in Communion*, 341–2.

81. Ibid., 335; cf. 256.

82. Cunningham, *These Three Are One*, 166–90. There is a brief section, 172–4, on participation in God, which is restricted to participation in the Body of Christ.

83. See Nicholas Lash, *The Beginning and the End of 'Religion'* (Cambridge: Cambridge University Press, 1996), 77–88.

84. Cf. Michael Polanyi, *Personal Knowledge: Towards a Post-Critical Philosophy* (London: Routledge & Kegan Paul, 1958), 270ff.

85. Janet Martin Soskice, *Metaphor and Religious Language* (Oxford: Clarendon Press, 1987), 133–41.

86. Ibid., 137.

87. Cunningham, *These Three Are One*, 73–4.

88. Paul Ricoeur, 'Fatherhood: from Phantasm to Symbol', trans. R. Sweeney in Ricoeur, *The Conflict of Interpretations* (Evanston, IL: Northwestern University Press, 1974), 477–8; however, Ricoeur is not referring to trinitarian language.

89. Similarly Cunningham, *These Three Are One*, 213, suggests that 'particularising the Trinity by naming them is an attempt to specify the orientation of activity within a relational whole'; but he does not link

the 'flow' of relationship with human participation in God. Cf. Jenson, *Systematic Theology*, Vol. 1, 108, on the 'narrative' of the Trinity.

90. John Hick, *God and the Universe of Faiths* (London: Collins/Fount, 1977), 156–9, 164. I differ from Hick in believing that this function of identical loving has ontological consequences.

91. Wolfhart Pannenberg, *Jesus – God and Man*, trans. L. Wilkins and D. Priebe (London: SCM Press, 1968), 335.

92. Zizioulas, *Being as Communion*, 18.

93. See Denys Turner, *The Darkness of God: Negativity in Christian Mysticism* (Cambridge: Cambridge University Press, 1995), 160–3.

94. E.g. Julian of Norwich, *Revelations of Divine Love*, trans. E. Spearing (Harmondsworth: Penguin Books, 1998), ch. 54, 130.

95. St John of the Cross, *Ascent of Mount Carmel* 2.5.7; in *The Complete Works of St John of the Cross*, trans. E. Allison Peers (London: Burns & Oates, 1964), 78.

96. *The Poems of St John of the Cross*, trans. John Frederick Nims, third edn (Chicago: University of Chicago Press, 1979), Ballad 4, 61.

97. I am much indebted to Archbishop Rowan Williams for pointing this out to me, and allowing me to quote here from an unpublished paper presented to a consultation on 'Apophasis and Incarnation', University of Birmingham, March 1999.

98. *The Poems of St John of the Cross*, 'Song of the Soul', 43–5.

99. Moltmann, *The Trinity and the Kingdom of God*, 175.

100. Volf, *After Our Likeness*, 211.

101. Ibid.

102. Calvin O. Schrag, *Communicative Praxis and the Space of Subjectivity* (Bloomington: Indiana University Press, 1986), 137–8; cited in Cunningham, *These Three Are One*, 220ff.

103. Schrag, *Communicative Praxis*, 121.

104. Cunningham, *These Three Are One*, 65, 221–5; cf. 208–9.

105. In my view, Cunningham shows the latter tendency, applying the trinitarian virtues of polyphony, participation and particularity to human persons in relation.

106. See e.g. Rudolph Schnackenburg, *The Gospel According to St John*, Vol. 3, trans. D. Smith and G. Kon (New York: Crossroad, 1990), 374.

107. Schrag, *Communicative Praxis*, 137.

108. McFadyen, *The Call to Personhood*, 183–7.

109. Tournier, *The Meaning of Persons*, 204.

110. Carr, *The Pastor as Theologian*, 177–8.

111. Francis Jacques, *Difference and Subjectivity: Dialogue and Personal Identity*, trans. A. Rothwell (New Haven, CT: Yale University Press, 1991), 31–5.

112. Wolfhart Pannenberg, *Systematic Theology*, Vol. 1, trans. G. W. Bromiley (Grand Rapids, MI: Eerdmans, 1991), 382–3.

113. See Heribert Mühlen, *Die Veränderlichkeit Gottes as Horizont einer Zukünftigen Christologie* (Münster: Aschendorf, 1969), 26–32.
114. Hans Urs von Balthasar, *Mysterium Paschale*, trans. A. Nichols (Edinburgh: T. & T. Clark, 1990), ix; *Theo-Drama: Theological Dramatic Theory*, Vol. IV, *The Action*, trans. G. Harrison (San Francisco, CA: Ignatius Press, 1994), 323–5.

3

The Triune God and Questions of Power and Authority

Images of Domination

Let us consider two images of power, one from the beginning of 'Christendom' and another from the period when Christianity was being consolidated as the religion of the state in Europe. The first comes from the fourth-century Christian church and is the emblem adopted by Constantine, shortly before he became the first Roman Emperor to establish the Christian faith as the official religion of the Empire. This sign, often called the 'Chi-Rho', was what he claimed to have been shown by God in a vision before the battle of Milvian Bridge in AD 312, and to have been instructed in a subsequent dream to take into battle. According to one version – by Lactantius[1]- he placed the emblem on the shields of his soldiers; according to another – by Eusebius[2] – he carried it as a military standard. Against the odds, Constantine was victorious over his rival and brother-in-law Maxentius, becoming sole Emperor of the Western section of the Empire; later he was to add the Eastern provinces as well.

The account by Lactantius of the famous dream implies that the 'heavenly sign' was simply a diagonal cross, combined with the first two letters of the name of Christ in Greek – X or C(h), and R –

that is, a monogram of *chi* and *rho*. But even in this basic form, it also appears to incorporate the crossed double axes that were already a military and imperial symbol. This adaptation of an imperial standard is even clearer in the more elaborate version of the image described by Eusebius, which Constantine ordered to  be carried at the head of his army throughout his reign; an upright cross was made from a spear, the Chi-Rho was placed at the top and surrounded by a golden sun-burst, a portrait of the emperor and of his children was fixed below the transverse bar of the cross, and the whole was adorned by a jewelled and golden banner.[3] Later this standard was called the 'Labarum', although in Constantine's lifetime it was simply called 'the sign' or 'the saving sign' or 'the life-giving sign' or 'the victory-bringing sign'.[4]

There is a fierce debate among historians and theologians as to whether, and if so when, Constantine became a true Christian believer.[5] There is much to be said for Alistair Kee's view that in adopting this emblem Constantine was bearing public witness to an alliance that he believed he had made between his royal house, which was under the patronage of the (monotheistic) sun-god, and the God of the Christians.[6] The sun-burst around the Chi-Rho, and Constantine's report that he had seen the sign in the sky 'above the sun', tends to support this theory, at least with regard to that early period in Constantine's career. But our interest here is in what the sign tells us about the nature of political religion. It is a kind of cross, but Constantine's personal version of it, based on a symbol of human power – the imperial axes – and carrying the image of the human ruler.

We know what Constantine's theology was. As expressed by his favourite apologist (and 'spin-doctor'), Bishop Eusebius of Caesarea, it was a strong doctrine of the One God, an absolute monotheism. According to this imperial theology there is one transcendent God who is the 'Supreme Sovereign'; there is one divine Logos or Word of God who governs the universe, and who is indistinguishable in essence from the one God; and there is one human monarch who governs the earth as God's representative. The last in this succession, of course, is Constantine, who regards himself as the image on earth of the Logos, 'deriving his imperial authority from above'.[7] The Logos rules over the universe and fights spiritual battles against demons and the hosts of darkness; Constantine rules over the earth and fights with the sword against the enemies of truth.[8] So there is one Almighty King, one Logos in the heavens, and one Emperor to represent him on earth. God – Word – Emperor, all exalting a powerful unity. Constantine was constantly perplexed about how to keep the two very different sides of his Empire together, East and West; it seemed to him that Christianity could provide him with the unifying force, a kind of cosmic glue.

Human ideas of power and authority are clearly being applied to God. People were already accustomed to the idea of a sole emperor with absolute powers who dominated his empire as a dictator – though sometimes a benevolent one. Power was understood as overcoming one's enemies, making people do what one wanted, making other people suffer, and *avoiding* suffering oneself. The truly powerful monarch did not not need to suffer at all. It is all too easy to take these worldly ideas of power and project them on to God. While the Apostle Paul writes to the Corinthian church that the cross of Jesus reveals the 'weakness' of God (1 Cor. 1:25), in these early days of the church political ideas of power merged with the Platonist philosophy of a higher spiritual world; the result was to produce a picture of a God who is invulnerable and coercive, a supreme ruler who cannot really feel with us in our weakness. Then, if we hold this picture of God, the reverse happens; it validates the power of the earthly dictator. If God is the heavenly Emperor, ruling through the Logos, he guarantees the reign of the earthly emperor. He supports the earthly king as his deputy, who 'directs in imitation of God himself the administration of this world's affairs' (Eusebius).[9] This is what came to be called in the Middle Ages 'the divine right of kings'. Constantine wields the sword in

God's name, and his policies show what this implied. While he did not exactly force people to become Christians, he only tolerated other religions as long as they were monotheist and so able to be identified with the worship of the one God who sanctioned him; he persecuted those who practised polytheism. He was also not above favouring Christians with his laws; for example, if a Jew attacked a Christian, he could be put to death.

Whenever Constantine refers to 'the saving sign' or the 'life-giving sign' he thus means his own imperial symbol, the Labarum, not the cross of Calvary. The cross has been assumed into an imperial symbol. In his theological reflections, Constantine shows no interest in the incarnation of the Logos as the man Jesus Christ, and his humble and suffering servanthood. He is only interested in the Logos who rules the heavens and whom he represents.[10] That is, his concern is a theology of success and prosperity. As Alistair Kee sums up Constantine's piety, 'he who prays, wins'.[11]

The second symbol of power I want to mention is less well known, but is the logical continuation of this theology. It is the royal crown of Hungary ('The Holy Crown'), dating from the twelfth century, which can be seen today in the National Museum in Budapest.[12] On the upper front of the crown facing outwards is a portrait, Christ Pantocrator, Christ the world-ruling Logos. As his subjects approach the king, they see above his human face the divine face of Christ. The heavenly King sanctions the rule of the king on earth, who thus wears the face of Christ and has become one with him. Political theology is incarnate in gold.

We may think that these ancient ideas of monarchy are no longer relevant to us; if we in Britain do not have the often-cited 'monarch on a bicycle' of Holland, at least we have one who is subject to Parliament (on most matters). But what persists beyond the age of the absolute monarchs is the character of power itself as the desire to unify, to place oneness and universality above diversity and difference. Whereas the divine right of kings is past, and belief in a heavenly king is no longer a constant factor in human society, there is still a drive towards the One as a source of power. The critique of theological absolutism in modernity has led to a void which has been filled with secular universals. In democratic capitalism, there is an exaltation of the one market, the one economic system of supply and demand. Individuals compete with each other to gain the approval of the 'invisible hand' of the market, which is increasingly being linked through electronic networks into a global market. There is still a domination by one class or group of people, those who own the capital, property and the means of communication; increasingly these are multinational corporations. Socialism by contrast ought to express a sense of community and the worth of all within it, but often there has been the attempt to impose a social order from above, ending in the uniformity of the collective and obliterating differences. Matching the one dominant class in a capitalist system, the 'Party' has ruled as the one centre of allegiance and has claimed to be the one interpreter of history and the one maker of the revolution.

The Christian idea of the Trinity has the potential for challenging and undermining this domination of the One. It forbids us from conceiving of God as the absolute individual, the solitary Father, the supreme Judge who provides support to a powerful human individual in his image. There is, to be sure, no straight line between the notion of 'three persons' in God and a truly democratic society, as if the Trinity simply provides a model for pluralism in government. As we have already seen, the point of trinitarian language is not to provide an example to copy, but to draw us into participation in God, out of which human life can be transformed. But the language of Trinity certainly encourages the values of relationship, community and mutuality between persons. It is about interdependence and not domination.

Indeed, with regard to theology, the church fathers resisted a heresy they called *monarchianism* – that is, the emphasis of the *monarche* or the sole rule of God at the expense of the diversity of the triune persons. Many (especially in the East) were for this reason at first suspicious of the Nicene Creed with its description of the Son as *homoousios* (of one substance) with the Father because it seemed monarchian, making no difference between Father and Son except names. Rightly understood, this term can express the depth of communion between Son and Father and their possession of one equal nature in being God, but perhaps some Eastern bishops had a legitimate suspicion when it was so strongly advocated by Constantine. It seems he wanted to affirm the *homoousion* of the Logos with the Father because he saw himself as the earthly image of the Logos. He had a built-in interest in this theology of unity.

The church fathers thus resisted theological monarchianism, keeping alive the vision of the Trinity. But they were unfortunately not so sensitive to *political* monarchianism that could foster a worldly concept of God as supreme king. Nor did they always notice *ecclesiastical* monarchianism. The picture of a bishop developed by Cyprian in the early third century lays great stress upon a unitary form of leadership. He repeats the insight of the earlier fathers (such as Ignatius) that the bishop is the focus of unity of the church, but now he gives it a stronger meaning: because God is one, each Christian community must have one leader living in unity with fellow leaders.[13] The bishop thus *guarantees* unity because whoever separates himself from the bishop separates himself from the church. Later we are going to look at modern forms of this argument in greater detail: Joseph Cardinal Ratzinger, for instance, affirms that 'the one bishop at a single locale stands for the church being one for all, since God is one for all'.[14] At this point I simply wish to register that there is a danger here that the one may come to oppress the many. For example, Cyprian's argument that the church is united because of personal attachment to the bishop leads him to the view that to separate oneself from the bishop is to separate oneself from salvation in Christ, even if the dissenter is a martyr.[15]

Those who are in favour of a less episcopal, more charismatic kind of church leadership ought not, however, to compliment themselves on supposing that the danger of ecclesiastical monarchy does not apply to them. There is, for instance, a kind of 'theology of subordination' that prevails in some free evangelical churches and house-church movements. There is a hierarchy of submission that runs 'from the bottom upwards': children submit to parents; wives submit to husbands; husbands submit to elders or 'shepherds'; elders submit to an apostle; the apostle submits to God. This kind of hierarchy is sometimes supported by an appeal to the ideal of a shepherd-king. David in the Old Testament is portrayed as a shepherd who rules his people, and Jesus, it is said, is the true successor of David, bearing the titles of both the Good Shepherd and the King of kings. So, as David had elders to whom he delegated authority in the nation, and Jesus had disciples to whom he delegated authority, the argument runs that Christ now delegates his authority to under-shepherds who also have the responsibility of ruling.[16] This is nothing less than a succession of unitary power. Submission to a 'shepherd' may mean accepting guidance on questions of career, marriage, finance and family. One woman, trying to explain the benefits of this system to her vicar said, 'It is such a relief not to have the responsibility of making decisions yourself.'[17]

Implicit in some of the models of authority I have described is a sexism in which women suffer the domination of a patriarchal society. This is sometimes unhappily sanctioned by an appeal to the concept of God as Trinity. In its crudest form this builds on the gender language of traditional trinitarian doctrine, in which a Father begets a Son; both the unoriginate origin and the eternal issue from this origin are understood literally to be male, and so only male human persons are claimed to be in the direct image of God. A more subtle, but no less dangerous kind of theology builds on the unity and distinction within the Trinity. Taking up the language of the obedience of the Son to the Father, it is pointed out that while the Son obeys the Father in all things he is no less divine in nature. Thus the conclusion is drawn that women are no less equal as human beings because their role is to follow the leadership of men. It is urged that women are 'equal in nature, but different in function', and their function is to obey. They are equal in honour but subordinate.

Both these arguments, we shall see, are based on a misunderstanding of the doctrine of the Trinity. But before we explore further the image of the Trinity which shatters all human images of domination, we ought to notice that people may themselves submit to domination because of a false sense of dependence. This is the other side of domination, which prevents people protesting against oppression.

Domination and the Search for Security

Here we re-enter the area of pastoral experience that I opened up in the previous chapter, the tension between dependence and autonomy. It was Sigmund Freud who criticised all religion as a 'collective obsessional neurosis' in which people regress to the ambivalent feelings they had as a child about authority figures. Especially, he suggested, they regress to their feelings about their father, which they project on to a transcendent God.[18]

In the first place, according to Freud's influential account, the child regards the father as the protective figure, the one with magical power to make everything come right. This dominating father may be internalised within the psyche as a despotic superego, always criticising what the child does. At the same time, however, the child is anxious because of the father's superiority and wants to kill him. The father is resented for his apparent omnipotence, which the infant feels is depriving him of his own nascent power, frustrating his own dream of immortality. In Freud's view, the desire to kill the father and seize his privileges is also related to the desire to possess the mother sexually, as expressed in the Oedipus myth, but for our present concerns we need not pursue this interesting angle further. Freud's diagnosis of the unhappy human state is thus a mixed longing for *security* in a father figure and a desire for *liberation* from his domination. In his fantasy life, deep within the self, the child does kill the father but then finds the victim has become immortal, resulting in feelings of remorse and a never-ending search for propitiation. The religious person develops rituals, or obsessional repetitions, in order to repress the sense of guilt and to appease the almighty and offended father. Hence religion is a collective obsessional neurosis.

We do not have to follow Freud's conclusion about the nature of religion to learn from his insight that we have a mixture of feelings surging within us; there is a conflict between the longing for security and the desire for freedom. While strict Freudians frown on making a transference from depth psychology to social behaviour, illuminating links have been made by analysts such as Eric Berne.[19] In observing 'the games people play', he notes that people swing between playing the role of the parent and the child. They may take up a paternal attitude towards others, asserting their own freedom by either lording it over them or appearing to care for their interests; but in order to win an advantage they can equally well shrink suddenly into an attitude of childish dependence, playing the helpless infant in the hope of being looked after by some powerful authority. The analyst hopes to free someone from this oscillating behaviour by getting them to recognise both the parent and the child within the self. Similarly, others have pointed to the way that people take up the alternating roles of persecutor and victim, according to the advantage this brings.[20]

Authority figures other than the father can thus be invested with magical power to release us from anxiety. Using religious language, we can create 'idols' that seem to promise us security – whether these be a political party, an economic system, or an ideology. With a previous British Prime Minister, Margaret Thatcher, we can fall into the habit of declaring that 'there is no alternative' to a particular policy. As Paul Tillich puts it, we can give 'ultimate significance' to what is only penultimate,[21] to things that are only finite and will disappoint in the end. All these searches for security, in which we allow ourselves to be dominated, will only make us more anxious. Nor can we escape anxiety by swinging to the opposite extreme of asserting our own control over persons and events, by making the self the ultimate idol, since this is the final disappointment.

So a Christian pastor is faced by a multiple problem. The prophetic voice of protest must be raised against all domination and absolute power, but there is also the need to release people from the wish *to be dominated* by what seems to promise protection and security. As I have proposed in the last chapter, we need more than a model of the triune God to copy. We need to become aware of the way that we are actually engaging in the triune life of God, sharing in the currents of the personal relationships of God. Language of Trinity, I have been stressing, is not that of observation but participation. Perhaps no concept better expresses this than that of *perichoresis*.

Perichoresis and Participation

By the end of the fourth century, it was agreed among the church fathers of both East and West that the nature of God – that is, God's *ousia* or *substantia* – should be thought of as a *communion* of persons. To explain this further and to account for the unity of *ousia* in God, the verb *choreo* was sometimes used to express the way that each person 'penetrated', 'filled' or was 'contained' in the others.[22] Somewhat later this was expressed in a noun, *perichoresis* (first used, it seems, in a trinitarian context by Pseudo-Cyril in the sixth century, followed by John of Damascus in the eighth),[23] which had the advantage of emphasising reciprocity and exchange in the mutual indwelling and penetration of the persons.

The term 'perichoresis' thus expresses the permeation of each person by the other, their coinherence without confusion. It takes up and develops the words of Jesus in the Fourth Gospel: 'believe me that I am in the Father and the Father is in me' (Jn 14:11). Two Latin translations were used which together bring out quite well the sense of the Greek term. First, *circuminsessio* means that one person is contained in another – literally 'seated' in another, filling the space of the other, present in the other. This stresses a state of being, and was preferred by Thomas Aquinas.[24] Second, *circumincessio* is a more active word, evoking a state of doing, the interpenetrating of one person in another; it captures the sense of a moving in and through the other, and was preferred by Bonaventure among other theologians in the West.[25]

This second aspect is expressed in a metaphor that occasionally came to be applied in the Middle Ages to describe the perichoresis, the image of a divine dance. The word *perichoresis* is not actually derived from the root of the verb 'to dance around', *perichoreuo* (related to *choreia*, 'dance', with which we are familiar in the English word 'choreography'), but the play on words does illustrate well the dynamic sense of perichoresis. In *this* dance the partners not only encircle each other and weave in and out between each other as in human dancing; in the divine dance, so intimate is the communion that they move in and through each other so that the pattern is all-inclusive. In fact, I suggest that the image of the dance makes most sense when we understand the divine persons as movements of relationship, rather than as individual subjects who *have* relationships. In the last chapter I argued that when we talk about the Trinity we are not trying to observe personal agents on the 'ends' of relationships, but that we are sharing, in speech and worship, in the flow of relationships themselves. We do not, for instance, attempt to visualise a Son praying to a Father, but we take part in a movement of speech like that of a son responding to a father.

So the image of the divine dance is not so much about dancers as about the patterns of the dance itself, an interweaving of ecstatic movements. When we speak of parts played by divine persons in perichoresis – for example, the Son 'indwells' the Father, the Father 'contains' the Son, the Spirit 'fills' the Father – we are telling a story which enables us to enter the personal currents of love within God, but the closest analogy is with perichoretic *movements* in human life, not with the *movers*. The *actions* of love of two human lovers, or of members of a Christian congregation, can interpenetrate and occupy the same social space simultaneously in a way that the personal *subjects* cannot, even though they can put themselves 'in each other's place' through empathy and imagination. As I argued in the previous chapter, the first-order personal analogies between created and Creator are those between *relationships*. The patterns of a dance overlap and intersect in perichoresis where the human dancers can only circle *round* each other.

It is perhaps significant that the earliest theological use of the verb *perichoreo* was in discussion of the humanity and divinity of Christ, by Gregory of Nazianzus and Maximus,[26] and that here it was used to portray the reciprocity and exchange of the divine and human *actions* in the one person of Christ; some of the illustrations they used for this perichoresis were the simultaneity of the actions of cutting and burning performed by a red-hot knife, or the interchange of the uttering of a word with the conceiving of a thought in the mind.[27] When transferred to the concept of Trinity, we should not, of course, think of a perichoresis of actions exercised by one subject, but simply the perichoresis of actions themselves. The point is that it makes perfectly good grammatical sense to speak of a perichoresis of *movements*, though the theological tradition has referred to a perichoresis of divine subjects.

It seems that the picture of the dance did not take hold on the Christian imagination as a metaphor for the inner participation or perichoresis of the Triune God. Dance was, however, a widespread image for the participation of all created beings in God. Plotinus (following Plato) had envisaged the cosmic dance as holding the many created intelligences in harmony with the One source of mind and being.[28] In the Christian version, there is a 'never-ending dance' of the angels around the throne of God, in which Christians may aspire to participate in eternity; according to Basil the Great, their ring-dance (*choreia*) may be imitated here and now in prayers and hymns to the Creator.[29] Denys the Areopagite, deeply influenced by Neoplatonism, envisages a threefold hierarchy of dancing celestial choirs, moving in distinct patterns around God, providing a spiritual ladder of ascent for the soul to approach God.[30] Françoise Carter comments on the cosmic dance generally, that 'the never-ending circling dance, whether it be of stars and planets or of angels in heaven, reassures man that in the midst of flux there is permanence; in the midst of mutability there is everlasting life'.[31]

However, we notice that in these accounts, the dance is an image of harmony and stability because God is envisaged in a Platonic way as the still, unmoving centre of the dance, beyond the categories of either motion or rest. So, as early as the third century, Clement of Alexandria describes the way that the Christians he knew accompanied their prayers with dancing: 'We raise the head and lift the hands to heaven and set the feet in motion at the closing utterance of the prayer, following the eagerness of the spirit directed towards the intellectual essence.'[32] While dance is an image for participation in God, in the Neoplatonist vision the aim of the dance is to reach a point of stillness, in the likeness of God as pure intellect. This surely explains why dance, though an attractive metaphor for perichoresis, was rarely used in this way. Dance implies a God in movement, even in the process of change, rather than a God whose intellectual love simply moves other things and people through their contemplation of it.[33] This is, however, exactly the dynamic image of God that I am commending for a pastoral theology. It is also the triune image of God that the music scholar Wilfrid Mellers finds reflected in the cello suites of J. S. Bach. This is music that is shaped by the rhythms of the secular dance of Bach's time, but also (Mellers argues) from Reformation faith in the incarnation of God in the material world. In his study, *Bach and the Dance of God*, Mellers finds theological symbolism throughout Bach's work, for instance a reference to the Trinity in the E flat major triads (= key of three flats) of the Fourth Cello Suite. Mellers comments that 'the music springs from the dance and from the corporeal act of playing the cello . . . as a human being *dances* and *sings* through the physicality of the cello, he becomes a dancing god'.[34]

While theological metaphysics affirmed the essential immutability of God as 'beyond Being', the idea of perichoresis in the Trinity kept alive, within the theological system itself, a challenge to the image of a dominating God whose power lies in immobility and in being secure from being affected by the changing world. The challenge was especially acute where perichoresis was understood in the sense of mutual movement (circumin*cessio*). Perichoresis was, however, envisaged somewhat differently in East and West, and in looking briefly at their respective accounts we can see how in different ways this vision of the Trinity enables resistance to the authority of the absolute individual, as well as ways in which it might be misused to sanction it. Even before the technical term 'perichoresis' appeared, the idea that the persons were mutually 'in' each other[35] and receptive and permeative of one another (*choretikos*)[36] was there, and so it is quite appropriate to discuss divine communion in terms of perichoresis. The metaphor of the dance is admittedly anachronistic for these early years, but I intend to use it as an interpretative tool.

Among Eastern theologians of the fourth and fifth centuries God the Father was celebrated as the origin (*arche*) or the fountainhead of the communion of persons in God. The Father first sends forth the Son and then the Spirit through the Son, so that the Father is the cause both of the other persons and their communion. The persons are 'in' each other and permeate each other, but the source of this mutual penetration is the Father's ecstatic love. If we use the image of a dance, then there is a kind of 'progressive' dance in which participants move outside the inner circle of dancers to make contact with others, and then come back in again, bringing other dancers with them. So the dance goes out from the Father and back in again to the Father. The Father sends out the Son through whom the Spirit proceeds as the life-giver in creation, and in the Spirit created persons return in worship through the Son to the Father. In modern times Jürgen Moltmann has expressed this as being a 'Trinity of sending' and a 'Trinity in glorification', with the Father as the origin of the sending and the goal of the glorifying.[37] The 'story' of the dancers ('the Father sends out the Son') draws us in to participate in the movements of mission and worship within the dance.

There are advantages with this way of envisaging communion in God. There appears to be no gap between the 'immanent' and the 'economic' Trinity, that is, between God in God's own self and

God for us, since there can be no other communion of persons than the one in which we are included; the dance returns to the Father carrying us with it. As Jesus prays in the Fourth Gospel: 'As you, Father, are in me and I am in you, may they also be in us' (Jn 17:21 *NRSV*). Salvation is conceived essentially as divinisation (*theosis*), which means not becoming God, but being incorporated into the fellowship of the divine life. Through their order of emergence the persons have a distinct identity within the internal and external life of God, and divine personalness has a priority over divine nature: a person, i.e. the Father, and not some abstract essence is the origin of the Trinity.

But there are also problems with this Eastern picture of communion, its version of the divine dance. In the first place, there is the danger that the Father will be seen as a dominating figure, subordinating the other persons to him as their cause, despite the balancing features of perichoresis; this perception might consequently have an effect downwards into the world, sanctioning the kinds of hierarchies of power to which I drew attention at the beginning of this chapter. An associated point is that, if the distinction between the persons is portrayed as an ordering or sequence of processions, there will be a tendency to present a highest level of divinity which is mysterious and ineffable, a hidden dimension of God like the hidden side of the moon. The Father then might be presented as absolutely transcendent and not involved in the world; alternatively, the one *ousia* (as the communion itself) might be conceived as an incomprehensible and utterly remote factor. Though Orthodox theologians deny that there is any 'mysticism of the divine essence' in the thought of the Cappadocian Fathers or in later Orthodoxy, Gregory of Nyssa seems occasionally to hint at the idea.[38]

In the Western picture of communion, the dance is more like a circle dance. The origin of the Trinity is not in one Person, the Father, but in the one nature of God. While the mistake might then be made of treating the divine essence as if it were a kind of fourth or ultimate factor behind the three persons, the best Western theologians understand the one nature as nothing other than the perichoresis of persons.[39] The interweaving relationships of Father, Son and Spirit are themselves the divine essence which is the source (*arche*) of the persons, in the sense that the persons are constituted by relations with each other. This vision of God lays stress upon the equality, mutuality and reciprocity of the three persons. The whole of God indwells each person; each person wholly indwells the other. Using the image of a dance, each person moves out in the direction of the other. This picture of a symmetrical fellowship, an ever-circling movement, has been traditionally capped in the West by the idea that the Spirit is the bond of love between the other two persons. Thus, while the Eastern thinkers affirmed that the Spirit proceeds *from* the Father alone, but *through* the Son, Western theologians stated that the Spirit proceeds from the Father *and* the Son (*filioque*), completing the circle.

There is something attractive about this stress upon a fellowship of equality among the persons, so very unlike our own inequalities in human society. Rather than persons being derived from each other as in the Eastern model, there is reciprocity, three persons simultaneous in origin. It is no wonder that, in the present day, theologians concerned with the liberation of people from oppressive governments, or with the liberation of women from inequality and discrimination in society, have turned to this Western model of the Trinity in preference to one based on the monarchy of the Father.[40] In fact, modern trinitarian thinking in the Western church has taken mutuality in God further than the church fathers did. For Leonardo Boff, for instance, a Latin American liberation theologian, it is not just a question of the Spirit's coming forth from the Father *and the Son* (*filioque*); the Son is to be confessed as begotten from the Father *and the Spirit* (*spirituque*), so that 'the Father begets the Son in the maternal-virginal womb of the Holy Spirit'.[41] Similarly, the Father does not only send forth the Son and the Spirit; in so far as he receives his fatherhood through this act of sending,[42] he receives himself 'from the Son' and 'from the Spirit'. So Boff concludes that the co-ordinate conjunction 'and' applies to all three persons: ' "and" is always and everywhere' in God. Everything is triadic in God, so that 'each Person receives everything from the others and at the same time gives everything to the others'.[43] A similar view is taken by Thomas Weinandy, who devotes a whole book to the thesis that 'the Father begets the Son in the spiration of the Spirit, and so it is the Spirit that makes the Father to be the Father of the Son and makes the Son to be the Son of the Father'.[44]

There is, however, a problem with this way of thinking of peri-choresis: it is possible to think of the circle of God's inner triune life as a closed circle, a self-sufficient dance, as if God were content to find dancing partners within the divine communion alone. Of course we can insist that God *does* open up the circle to others, that the Creator invites the created to join the eternal festivities. But the stress upon the one substance – even as communion – means there is the danger of emphasising the oneness and so the self-enclosure of God at the expense of the generous threefold richness. The Eastern image of the 'progressive dance' suggests that there cannot be a dance without human partners to be brought in, but it runs the risk of making the one *ousia* and even the com-munion a mystery; the Western 'circle-dance', on the other hand, can make the *distinction* of the triune relations a mystery within God's inner life, a matter of speculation rather than a practical experience. As we have seen, Augustine unfortunately veers in this direction when he re-mints the Cappadocian insistence on the *inseparability* of the persons in their actions externally as an *indistin-guishability*.[45] In effect, the God who works among us in the world is then conceived as one person, and this can lead to the concept of God as a dominating subject no less than the Eastern view of the supreme Person of the Father.

As I suggested in my last chapter, a stress upon our *engagement* in God helps us to see the best in the insights of East and West. The Western theology of mutuality and reciprocity tells us how the relations in God interact and shape each other. Moreover, while this picture *can* be understood in terms of three subjects who live in intimate relationship, it makes most sense as a communion of subsistent relationships, that is as an interweaving of relational movements and actions in which we can become involved. We do not try to observe the persons on the 'ends' of the relationships, but are drawn to share in the movements of the divine dance. At the same time, however, the Eastern insight that the Father is alone the *arche* of the Son and the Spirit makes clear that the dance in which we are involved is not a swirling vortex of arbitrary currents. There is a direction to its flow, a pattern which is like the movement to and from one ultimate source. Though the dance is a complex one, it does not strain the imagination to conceive of a greater mutuality than in a purely 'progressive' movement, integrated with a greater directionality than a purely circular movement. There is no need (with Moltmann and Volf, for instance) to envisage two levels of divine life, one for the constitution or procession of the persons, and the other for their existing relations, or 'how they exist as God'.[46] We may agree with Pannenberg, however, that the relations are not *confined* to relations associated with the origin of the persons.[47]

In the subtle patterns of this dance, there will be some boundaries to the symmetry of relations, though not to their reciprocity. That is, the movement of sending (mission) in which we find ourselves involved is always like that from a father to a son, not from a son to a father. There is mutuality in so far as we only know this movement to be orientated 'from a father' because it is directed to a son; that is, there can be no 'fatherhood' without there being a generating of a son and without there being a movement like that of spirit breathed out. Nevertheless there is no movement of the dance that we could say is 'like a son sending forth a father' or 'like a breath breathing out a father' (though we can certainly speak of breath 'filling' both the Father and the Son). There seems no point in describing this asymmetry as a difference between the Father's 'constituting' the other persons and their only 'conditioning' him, as Zizioulas proposes from an Eastern perspective.[48] If the Son and Spirit in any way make the Father what he is through their self-surrendering love, this must be a mutual 'constituting'. The point in reserving the term 'source' (*arche*) to the Father is to affirm that woven in and through these to-and-fro movements that form the relationships there is a movement of 'sending out' that always flows one way, ultimately 'from the Father'.

This is a strong reason for siding with the Eastern rejection of the *filioque* clause which the West added to the Nicene Creed, making it read that the Spirit proceeds from the Father 'and from the Son'.[49] It is true that the community of the church within history finds that it receives the Spirit in a movement of love like that of a breathing from a father and a son; in narrative terms, the Son shares with the Father in sending the Spirit into the lives of his followers. But to say that the Spirit proceeds eternally 'from the Father and the Son' makes the Son the same kind of source as the Father, obscuring the unique direction of 'sending' within the communion of God. As Pannenberg points out, it makes it difficult to affirm that the Son himself receives the Spirit from the Father, not only in his human nature but in his being as God.[50] The direction of the dance, we might say, is indicated by there being no movement like that of a father receiving a spirit from the son, even though he receives *fatherhood* from the spirit and the son. As Boff points out, the reciprocal fellowship of God comes 'from' all three persons, so that the conjunction 'and' is everywhere (including *spirituque*); but this does not mean that either the 'from' or the 'and' is of the same kind.

The combination of reciprocity with a basic uni-directionality is well illustrated by a mingling of a circle-dance with a progressive dance. But two issues about the dangers of domination still arise. First, it may be objected that to understand the persons as pure relations ('subsistent relations') only fosters a theology of domination. If they are not particular subjects with their own centres of consciousness and action, the argument goes, they must be absorbed into the one nature of God which then becomes a model for the tyranny of the 'one' in church and society. Second, protest may arise about the continuing affirmation of the *arche* of the Father. Does not this entrench the language of patriarchal domination in the Trinity? We might agree that the picture of the Trinity as a dance in which we share is a criticism of the absolute power of any sole rulers in our world. But is it all spoilt by the emphasis on the Father as the source from which processions and missions flow, so that to address the Father provides an entrance into the dance? Is Freud right that this is a father-religion which promotes an infantile regresssion? We shall explore these objections in turn, though they can be seen to be linked.

Relations Which Are Not Absorbed

The image of the perichoresis of the Trinity as movements of a dance – not as a group of dancers – accords well with the identification of the divine persons as relations. The 'participatory' rather than 'observational' character of this language was explored in the previous chapter, but here we need to face the criticism that unless the divine persons are conceived as subjects and agents they will lose all distinct identity (*hypostasis*). The objection runs that this loss means not only lack of diversity within God, but the submerging of the persons into an 'all embracing dominance of oneness of substance',[51] and this will encourage totalitarianism in church and society.

We can discern two main strands to this critique, concerning *identity* and *activity*, which together point to an effect on human structures of power and authority. The first objection is that 'relations' in God can have no particular identity of their own. Colin Gunton, for example, laments the general loss of particularity in our age, stressing that true particularity or the 'this-ness'[52] of objects and persons does not mean an isolated individuality, but identity within networks of relations. He blames the Western tradition of 'subsistent relations', beginning from Augustine, for the loss of a sense of particularity in God, and consequently in the world. Instead of a vision of creation diversified into a myriad things and persons of unique substantial reality, springing from the creative will of God for 'otherness', there is a depressing homogeneity in our present culture. Despite lip-service to 'pluralism', this turns out to be a submission to the dominant philosophy of the market place and an 'assumption that deep down everything is really the same'.[53] He traces the root of the problem to a lack of grasp upon persons in God as 'concrete particulars';[54] the persons have vanished into the relations that constitute them, and thence into the one substance of God.

Miroslav Volf similarly argues for the complementarity rather than sameness of persons and relations in God, with the concern that when human persons are conceived on the analogy of 'pure trinitarian relations' they have no 'rights of persons' to defend them against human hierarchies and the abuse of unitary power.[55] His particular interest here is in structures of authority in the church, and the ecclesial model he is reacting against is that of Joseph Cardinal Ratzinger, who draws a straight line between a doctrine of subsistent relations in God and individual Christians who ideally 'lose themselves' in being 'from and to others' within the one corporate Christ, who is the church universal.[56] In Ratzinger's thought, just as divine relations exist selflessly in the one divine substance, so believers abandon their claim to being 'self-contained subjects' and are inserted into a new social subjectivity, which is the church existing as 'one subject with Christ'. This single subjectivity is mediated sacramentally to the local church community through the one person of the bishop, representing the whole Christ and ensuring the unity of the church. Volf is writing from the perspective of a Free Church ecclesiology, which does not regard a bishop as being necessary to constitute a local congregation as a church of Christ; the presence of Christ through the Spirit and the confession of faith by believers are sufficient. However, his point here is also relevant for episcopal churches. Personal rights, he argues, cannot be derived from the idea of a person as a pure relation, and so when this view of the person is held there is a danger that the bishop's authority, vicarial though it is, 'can easily degenerate into oppressive ideology'.[57]

In reply to this objection we must, in the first place, affirm that understanding the persons in God as relationships precisely recognises their 'concrete particularity'. There can be nothing more distinct from each other than a movement of relationship like that from a father to a son ('Father'), a movement like that from a son to a father ('Son'), and an opening up of these relationships to new depths and new possibilities ('Spirit'). Because this particularity is known through participation, it will also give rise to other concrete ways of talking about it. Moreover, criticism of Ratzinger's model of a trinitarian ecclesiology does not undermine the whole idea of subsistent relationships. A perichoresis of relationships does not in itself imply a single subjectivity to which they are subordinate;[58] as we have seen, it is just as meaningful to apply the words perichoresis and communion to relationships as to persons. Perhaps most significantly, there is no question of transferring the 'pure relationships' in God to the nature of human persons, as Ratzinger does. Our whole argument has been that the analogy is between divine and human *relations*, so that the idea of a 'person' will function differently in God and in human life. Finite persons do indeed have a 'centring' through which they can resist oppression, and we may affirm that they have human rights to be respected just because they are called to live in the image of God, that is, to participate in the dynamic relations within God. It is because someone shares as a daughter of God in the movement from Son to Father that she has rights to life, liberty and equal opportunities. It is also because she shares in this relational life, interacting with other persons in society, that she has duties to fulfil as well as rights to be defended.

The second main objection to 'persons as relations' in God is closely associated with the first. It may be said that 'subsistent relations' not only have no particular identity, but no ability to *act* in a particular way. How, it may be protested, can we think of a relationship as doing anything?[59] Surely, action can only be ascribed to an agent who *has* relationships. Again, then, it seems that if the persons are 'pure relations' they must be absorbed into one substance which is the single acting subject, and it is this one divine subject – or even one divine person – who acts in an undifferentiated way within the world. A supreme individual subject acting in the world has then all the potential for dominance and for sanctioning the power of a human 'sole ruler' which we saw evident in the ideology of Constantine.

It is because Pannenberg wants to ascribe particular activity to the three persons that he is compelled to 'cling to the idea of subject[s]' in God, which he also describes as 'living realizations of separate centres of action'.[60] He begins with the concrete, historic happening of Jesus of Nazareth, who shows his identity in the act of bearing witness to God his Father. In pointing away from himself to the Father – 'Why do you call me good? No one is good but God alone' (Mk 10:18) – he thus distinguishes himself from the Father, and Pannenberg concludes that the Son is eternally a separate person because he actively distinguishes himself from the Father who begets him; his identity is not just established by being passively begotten. This in turn leads Pannenberg to the insight that all three persons have real identity (*hypostasis*) because of active self-distinction from each other.[61] For instance, the Father hands over the Kingdom to the Son for the course of history, and the Son hands back the Kingdom to the Father at the end of time; the Spirit glorifies the Son, and the Kingdom of the Father in him, by raising Jesus from the dead. Yet because this self-distinction is mutual, the Son and Spirit in different ways manifest the monarchy of the Father, and there is one God.

If there are no distinct actions in God, and all are submerged in one subject, then there is also the danger of fostering a hierarchy of ruling subjects in the world. Volf again sees this happening in the kind of ecclesiology espoused by Cardinal Ratzinger, in which Christ's salvific work, submerged into the action of the one divine substance, is embodied in the activity of the entire church and represented by one bishop (or the priest who stands in for the bishop). The congregation assembled for eucharistic worship becomes the subject of Christ's action, since it is one subject with 'the whole Christ' who is identical with the church universal.[62] Yet this singleness of action has to proceed through 'the instrumental acts of the visible hierarchy' because the congregation can act as whole only through the one who makes it into a unity and joins it to the church universal, that is, the bishop. The local church needs the bishop as one human person in order to be able to act as a single subject. The conclusion is that, although the members of the local church are co-participants in the liturgical action, lay persons cannot lead the church in worship or create their own liturgy. All this Volf traces to the identification of person in the Trinity with 'pure relationship'.

What can we say in response to this challenge about affirming a diversity of divine actions? Instead of Pannenberg's vision of three 'living realizations of separate centres of action', I have been speaking of something like three living realisations of movements or directions of action, but these can equally be conceived as distinguishing themselves from each other. We have already identi-fied the active aspects of these movements (sending, responding, filling) in which Pannenberg finds the self-distinction of the persons, alongside passive ones (becoming a father, being begotten, being breathed out). We become engaged in movements of love and pain which are like a handing over the Kingdom, a returning it to its giver, and a raising from the dead, though we can never be as completely identified with them as was Jesus. In these active move-ments the *hypostases* distinguish themselves from each other.

All this has implications for liturgical and diaconal acts within the church. The multiple actions of God within the triune com-munion are expressed outwardly in a diversity of action in the world, which is manifested in turn in the multiplicity of spiritual gifts – *charismata* – in the local assembly of believers, and in the diversity of local congregations among themselves. Through the generous distribution of the Spirit, all members of the church are empowered to participate in the leading of worship as well as in the 'liturgy after the liturgy' in service to the world. There is thus no necessary link between a concept of 'subsistent relations' in God and the kind of unification of divine action which ends with the universal church as a single subject sustaining the life of the many churches through the ministry of the one bishop. Ratzinger develops this pattern because of his understanding of the priority of the one divine essence, and because of the close analogy he draws between divine and human persons. But there is no basis for supposing that the idea of 'pure relations' in God in itself increases the tendency to reserve certain actions to the bishop, or that it increases the danger that this will lead to 'a partially coerced subordination of the many to the dominant one' (Volf's critique).[63]

There is, by contrast, a natural association between the being of God as a *communion* of relationships, and the universal church as a communion (not a single subject) which is reflected in the life of the local church. If the person of Jesus Christ is deeply immersed into the flow of relationships within God, and is the point of access where human persons can participate in the dance of these relations, then Christ himself is 'many in one' (as Origen expressed it)[64] or a supremely corporate personality. The insight of both Catholic and Orthodox traditions that the universal church is the 'whole Christ', body and head, does not have to lead to the view that this church is a 'single subject' exerting domination through the medium of other single subjects. Rather we can stress its perichoretic nature, as a point of intersection of many relationships, a vast confluence of relations between all individual believers and also those between the churches in which they assemble. In reaction against the dangers of coercive action, Volf, however, refuses to accept that there is at present such a universal church which is a total 'communion of saints'; he discounts it as a 'theological abstraction' this side of the new creation, since he believes the true universal church to be the eschatological gathering of the whole people of God. Until the new creation, he asserts, the church 'exists concretely only in the individual local churches' which *anticipate* this eschatological communion.[65] Relations between individual members of a local church and relations between individual churches can and should mirror the perichoresis in the Trinity, but there is no universal ecclesial reality which is a perichoresis. The Trinity indwells local churches, he asserts, 'in no other way than through its presence within the persons constituting those churches';[66] the churches are related to one another in so far as the Spirit indwells the hearts of those of whom the church consists.[67] He can find no meaning in saying that the universal church is present or manifest in the local assembly of believers.

It appears that Volf is fearful that not only conceiving the universal church as a unified subject, but even envisaging it as a communion in the image of the Trinity, will lead to the oppressive action of one person. That is, a bishop will be made the necessary 'contact' point between the local and universal dimensions of the Body of Christ. So Volf is critical of John Zizioulas' Orthodox ecclesiology, even though Zizioulas identifies every local church with the universal church since it is a eucharistic assembly, so denying that there is any subservience of the local church to any wider ecclesial structures.[68] Volf objects that to conceive the church universal as an already existing communion in which the local church participates will inevitably be to elevate the importance of the representative figure, the bishop; he sees this demonstrated in the restriction of the charismatic action of the congregation in the eucharist to 'receiving the action of the bishop' and speaking the 'Amen' to it.[69]

In claiming that his approach is a 'Free Church' and specifically a 'Baptist' ecclesiology stemming from the thought of John Smyth, Volf, however, ignores the English Baptist tradition which attributes much more importance to the universal church and its identity with the one body of Christ than he allows. According to this perspective, a local congregation cannot be imposed upon or coerced by wider ecclesiastical authorities, because it stands under the direct rule of Christ in the congregation, as discerned in the Church Meeting. This is not a view of autonomy based in an Enlightenment concept of individual rights, but is a freedom from human rule stemming from the presence of Christ who lays his own demands upon the community. The covenant-rule of Christ endows the local assembly with the 'seals of the covenant', or the freedom to call its own minister and celebrate the sacraments.[70] At the same time, however (and this is what Volf misses), this rule which grants liberation from all external human authority gathers the local church together in fellowship with other churches who also live under the rule of the same Christ. So an association of Baptist congregations in London in 1644 could speak of themselves as 'all one in communion, holding Jesus Christ to be our head and Lord', and could describe their 'particular congregations' as being 'members of one body in the common faith under Christ their only head'.[71] The freedom of the local congregation to exercise a variety of spiritual gifts and ministries is therefore linked theologically to the whole body of Christ as a reality transcending the local scene.

While the immediate 'trans-local' dimension is fellowship between congregations in any one region, the principle of the 'one body' of Christ opens up a universal scope. The 'bishop' (*episkopos* or 'overseer') is understood in Free Church tradition as the minister or presiding elder (*presbuteros*) of the local congregation, rather than a further order of ministry, and is called by the members to serve it. But he or she still has the responsibility of linking the particular congregation, as a manifestation of the body of Christ, to the gospel and mission of the whole body, opening its horizons beyond its own local concerns. It is in this larger context of the worldwide church that members can better understand and better exercise their own spiritual gifts. In the words of P. T. Forsyth, a Free Church theologian in the Congregationalist tradition, the minister is 'the most effective agent of the one Church', with a ministry that is 'sacramental of the new creation'.[72]

If we regard the communion of the universal church as an entity to be 'observed', then it might indeed appear to be a 'theological abstraction', as Volf regards it. He is also right to deny that it is a fixed group of the elect, and to affirm that it is open to the future and to the ingathering of peoples at the *eschaton* when all things are renewed. However, if communion in the body of Christ is not just a *model* of the Trinity, but a means of *entering* the relational movements of the triune God, this has the reality of participation, which is just as 'concrete' as the immediate communion within and between local churches. As I have been arguing, we need to think in a participatory rather than an objectifying way, and the idea of 'persons as relations' in God enables us to do so. The result is not to absorb the relations into one identity and into one activity, but to prompt us to share in God rather than attempting to observe God. Far from resulting in the unifying of the divine substance and creating a chain of command and action through single church officers, to understand divine persons as relations is to foster a participative model of the church. While John Zizioulas envisages the universal church as communion, reflecting the being of God, he does not follow the path of identifying the divine persons with relations. To do so, I suggest, is to be drawn into a communion where the saying of 'Amen' by every member becomes a sharing in the Amen of the Son to the Father; so the 'Amen' of the congregation to the liturgy of the eucharist is not simply a passive reception, but an entering into a divine activity which will be expressed as the exercising of a charismatic gift.

Fatherhood Which Does Not Oppress

So far I have been speaking of participating in movements in God which are like a relationship 'between a son and a father'. I have also suggested that the dance of the divine perichoresis is marked by a foundational pattern which is like a sending out by a father. The question to be faced, hinted at several times before, is whether this does not entrench patriarchy and male domination at the heart of trinitarian theology.

The argument I wish to set out is that the language of 'Father, Son and Spirit' is central and indispensable, but not exclusive or exhaustive for a pastoral theology of the Trinity. I also hope to make clear that this is not an oppressive language, especially when set in the context of complementary images. It is, however, essential for Christians to identify the movement of relationship by which we enter the divine dance as being 'like that between a son and a father', because we are dependent on a particular relationship in history, that between Jesus of Nazareth and his Father in heaven. When we enter the dance, we lean on this particular cry of 'Yes, Amen', and as Robert Jenson has put it, 'That Jesus called on God with "father" rather than with "mother" is a fact about the historic person Jesus that we can no more change by decree than we can decree that he was not Jewish, or a wandering rabbi, or unpopular with the Sanhedrin.'[73] Jenson adds that the church's address of God is authorised only as a 'repetition' of Jesus' address, but we must add that it is more than a repetition. If Christians find the nature of God finally and fully disclosed in the speech and acts of Jesus, then we can never separate the address of Jesus to his Father from the movements of relationship within God, and it provides the key for us to enter the divine communion here and now. When we say, 'Abba, Father', we are using the pathway into God opened up by Jesus, a pathway which, as the risen Christ, he continues to tread. This is the meaning of the traditional image of the 'heavenly inter-cession' of Jesus as High Priest, entering the inner sanctuary (Heb. 4:14–16, 7:25); it not a picture of Jesus as a successful lawyer in court pleading our case before the Judge of heaven and earth, but a picture of Jesus making a prayer for our prayers to ride upon.

Through the self-unveiling of God in Jesus, we have thus been given words of prayer which enable us to enter the divine peri-choresis. This historical particularity means that we cannot follow the argument that since all words for God are metaphors, we are therefore completely free to dispose of past metaphors shaped by the culture of their time, and to select new ones for new cultural settings. It sometimes urged, for instance, that if the word 'Father' is offensive to women or anyone who has had a bad experience of human fathers, it can be entirely *replaced* by 'Creator' or by 'Mother'. This would be to suppose that God was an object that we already have in mind, for which we are looking for appropriate means of representation. Rather, addressing God as 'Father' – or, indeed, 'Mother' – is the means by which we enter the communion of a God whom we cannot represent.

However, we must also take issue with those who take the totally opposite view: namely, that only 'Father', together with 'Son' and 'Holy Spirit' are the proper *names* of God, whereas terms such as 'mother' or 'friend' or 'lover' are merely metaphors.[74] The same sort of distinction is made by those who propose that 'Father, Son and Spirit' are a kind of speech that comes much closer to literal description than to a metaphor, in accord with the way in which Aquinas used the term 'analogy'.[75] Similarly, others claim that God 'is' a Father, where God is only 'like' a mother. Behind these proposals may be the belief that if the name 'Father' has come by way of revelation, it cannot be a metaphor. It is salutory here to pay attention to the theologian of the twentieth century who has laid most stress upon the self-revelation of God, Karl Barth, who still recognises the broken nature of talk about God:

> If these three names [Father, Son and Spirit] are really in their threeness the one name of the one God, then it follows that in this one God there is primarily at least − *let us put it cautiously* − *something like* fatherhood and sonship, and therefore *something like* begetting and being begotten . . .[76]

Those who point out that the primary use of 'Father' by Jesus is in addressing God, and so 'Father' is a proper name which identifies the God whom we are worshipping, are certainly on to something.[77] I have already urged that the normative use of the word 'Father' is in prayer, enabling us to enter the divine communion of life. But this does not in itself refute the fact that the name 'Father' is *also* a metaphor for God, and nor does it exclude the possibility that the self-unveiling of God has so seized hold of our networks of language that other words can function appropriately as proper names in prayer. Ancient Israel, for instance, thought that 'Yahweh' was God's name, though they hesitated to actually speak it out loud in prayer, replacing it by euphemisms such as 'Lord'.

The reason why the word 'Father' is indispensable is thus not any unique linguistic status it has, and certainly not because there is any gender in God, but simply the givenness of the fact that Jesus used it in prayer: 'Our Father in heaven, your *name* be hallowed.'

Since the persons in God are nothing other than relations, the names are used in order to draw the one who employs them into movements of communion. The movements and their direction are what are being identified; the analogy with human fatherhood, as I have argued, applies to the relationship itself – 'something like begetting and being begotten', as Barth puts it. Since we are completely dependent on the relationship of Jesus with his Father, we must always say that this relation is 'something like' a relation between a son and a father. But we can certainly use other metaphors alongside this primary one, as they arise out of situations in which God discloses God's own self and seizes hold of human language. Israel, for instance, feeling deserted by God in exile, finds herself held in a relationship like that between a mother and a child who is never forgotten (Isa. 49:14–16); hoping for the flourishing of the nation after exile, she finds herself nourished in a relationship like that between a mother and a child being nursed and suckled (Isa. 66:12–13); confronted with her unfaithfulness to Yahweh, she finds herself in an uncomfortable relationship like that between a child and a mother (*or* father) whose nurture she has spurned (Hos. 11:1–4). To be sure, the prophets who use these images of human relationship with God do not use the direct address 'Our Mother', but there are obvious cultural reasons for this inhibition, given the prevalence of mother-goddesses in neighbouring religions, and anyway God is directly designated as 'Father' only eleven times in the entire Old Testament and never invoked in prayer as 'Our Father'. If we accept the identification of person with relationship that I have been urging, then it is fully appropriate to use the invocation 'our Mother' (without *replacing* the 'our Father') if we are participating in a movement of emotion, speech and action like that between a mother and a child, or if we wish to do so.

The rarity of Old Testament references to God as Father and the extraordinary frequency with which Jesus invokes God as Father should lead us to perceive something non-oppressive about the fatherhood of God when it is evoked in the context of Jesus' own prayer. The philosopher Paul Ricoeur suggests that the primary revelation of the 'name' of God as the non-name 'I am who I am' in ancient Israel (Exod. 3:14) abolishes all ideas of a biological-father God such as were common in surrounding religions.[78] The cleansing of names and the death of the supreme biological father thus creates a space where God may be called 'Father' in a new way, from tentative declarations in the Old Testament, to the invocations of Jesus. It is as if the term 'Father' is an empty concept waiting to be filled, and the content given to it by Jesus (as well as in the few Old Testament declarations[79]) is not a patriarchal oppressiveness but tenderness, pity, nurturing and compassion. This is the father who delights to be addressed by the intimate term 'Abba',[80] who is compassionate (Lk. 6:36), who waits out anxiously on the road for the return of a prodigal son, and who searches for his children like a woman searching for lost coins (Lk. 15). There are qualities that we associate with both fathers and mothers in these pictures, so that we can appropriately speak, with Moltmann, of a 'motherly father',[81] adding also (as does Boff)[82] 'a fatherly mother'. This need not imply that certain characteristics would normally belong exclusively to *each* gender (compassion to mothers, for example) and are now being integrated, but simply that we can recognise in this Gospel portrait of the Father aspects of both motherly and fatherly behaviour. I intend to return to this point again later.

The development of the doctrine of the Trinity in the work of the church fathers continues an implicit critique of patriarchal religion. The affirmation that the Son is 'eternally generated' from the Father, poured out from his very being, appeals to an image of *birthing* as well as begetting. It is only in birth from a mother that one identity emerges from the being of another. Hilary, Eusebius and Basil all refer the phrase of Psalm 110:3 (LXX and Vulgate), 'I bore you from the womb before the morning star', to the Father's generation of the Son, defending the image 'from the womb' as a means of stressing the reality of the begetting, 'from the being' of the Father.[83] Later, the Council of Toledo (AD 675) appears to lean on this tradition when it affirms that 'the Son was not made out of nothing, nor out of some substance or other, but from the womb of the Father, that is . . . he was begotten or born from the Father's own being'.[84] The language of a 'father's womb' startles us, and forces us to question the attribution of male gender to a 'Father' in this instance. There is thus an undermining of gender in God at the heart of trinitarian formulations.

However, on their own, these surprising uses of the name 'Father' in Gospel and patristic writing might not be a substantial enough critique of patriarchy, but could be understood as an imperialistic absorbing of the mother into the father. The critique only becomes convincing, I suggest, when 'Mother' becomes a name to be invoked in prayer as well as (but not replacing) 'Father'. Such complementarity does not mean a mechanical political correctness of adding 'and Mother' to the term 'Father' in every text of scripture, in the manner of one modern attempt at an 'inclusive-language lectionary'. There, for example, the Jesus of the Fourth Gospel is represented as saying that 'true worshippers will worship [God] the [Mother and] Father in spirit and truth'.[85] The point is not just, as Roland Frye protests, that this 'violates the integrity of a text';[86] if divine persons are relations, as I have been arguing, we use mother-language specifically on those occasions when we are involved in relationships in God that make it apt for us to call on God as mother. In this book I therefore do not avoid using the pronoun 'he' where 'Father' or 'Son' occurs in relation to God, since the *image* – though not the reality of the relationship into which it draws us – is male in gender, even if the father is 'motherly'; a feminine pronoun is appropriate where the imagery is female, even if the mother is 'fatherly'. I do not myself, however, use either 'he' or 'she' in reference to the word 'God', since this identifier must refer to the triune God who, as a perichoresis of relationships, is neither singular nor plural, let alone male or female.

Re-imaging God as father in a non-oppressive way is not only a matter of gender. There is a critical issue over the relation of 'father' to the notion of 'creator', as indicated in the first clause of the Nicene Creed, 'God the Father Almighty, maker of heaven and earth'. We tend to understand the 'fatherhood of God' in the light of ideas we already have of God as Creator. This is the sense in which Plato spoke of the creative principle (*demiourgos*) as the 'Father and Maker of the universe',[87] and it leads naturally to the idea of total transcendence, an awe-inspiring authority of the uncreated to which we simply submit as creatures. The gap then is absolute between Creator and created, infinite and finite.

In the Christian story, by contrast, the Father means the one to whom Jesus bears witness and upon whom he calls. 'Father' means in the first place not Creator, but Father of *this* Son. This in turn takes us into the story of the Trinity, to which the relation of Jesus with his Father gives us access. When we speak of the Trinity in narrative terms,[88] we envisage the Father sending forth the Son in an ecstasy of love, and the Son responding to the Father in reciprocal love; this love is so intense and overflowing that God desires that other sons and daughters should share in the same relationship. The divine longing is for the movements of the dance between Father and Son to be opened up to include a myriad of other partners. God is not content to be self-sufficient, and in this divine discontent we can see the work of the Spirit, the provoker, the innovator, the opener of the future, the divine joker in the pack. All human creatures are held within the divine intention for fellowship, at the eternal moment of the begetting of the Son. As Karl Barth expresses it, it is as the Father makes covenant with the Son from all eternity that he also makes covenant with the man Jesus of Nazareth, and through him with all men and women.[89] By God's free choice, not because God is forced to do so, the begetting of the Son and the adopting of many sons and daughters is an indivisible act. The perichoresis of the divine persons with each other cannot be torn apart from the perichoresis of God with creation. So the fatherhood of God (sending forth the Son) is *prior* to God's work as Creator (making many sons and daughters). Creation does not determine the meaning of fatherhood; the truth is quite the opposite.

There is a major implication here for our theme of power. If

God desires to include created persons within the communion of divine life, the dance will not be complete until this has been achieved. The moment of begetting and creating is thus one of humility, and an opening of the divine life to pain and suffering. This Father opens himself to a patient waiting upon his creation, a frustration at being rejected, and a reconciliation that will cost nothing less than a confrontation with death and nothingness. What this openness will mean we see in history in the cross of Jesus, when we find a son forsaken by a father, a father losing a son and the spirit of self-surrender uniting them. This Father cannot be invoked to sanction human structures of authority that show their power in inflicting suffering upon others and avoiding it themselves. This God is on the side of the victims, not the oppressors. A suffering God protests against suffering and does not cause it. We shall see shortly how this image of God not only undermines political patterns of domination, but can help to resolve patterns of domination deep within the psyche.

So far we have been exploring the way that the image of the triune God is a critique of human power structures, but we need to get beyond a model of thought to participation. The question is, how can we find ourselves *engaging* in the threefold relationships of God as we encounter situations of human domination and dependence? Let us then return to the areas of power – in the state, the church, gender-relations and the psyche – that I outlined at the beginning.

Areas of Domination

Oppressiveness in the state

Many people have the political experience of confronting authorities which want to limit freedom, or which want to impose legislation which is everything to do with the survival of the powers themselves, and little to do with making life better for members of society. It often takes the form, as I have suggested, of a drive for uniformity in the name of efficiency. While this experience is most acute in countries which have not yet developed a fully participative form of democracy, even in those which have there can be aspects of oppressiveness in the machinery of the state. Here I suggest that experience of participation in the relational life of the triune God will bring at least two distinctive perspectives.

First, through engagement in God there comes the discovery of the power of suffering to change events. This does not mean mere *passiveness*, putting up with the situation in the hope of being rewarded in heaven later on. It means *passion* – that is, resistance, disturbance and protest, with a willingness to suffer the painful consequences in ourselves. For many Christian people, especially in the Western world, there will be channels available within the law for the expression of resistance, but even here, in the last resort, there may need to be forms of civil disobedience such as Martin Luther King employed to great effect in the struggle for racial equality. Christians will be committed to the basic pattern of non-violent resistance and protest which was characteristic of Jesus himself, though we should not confuse 'non-violent' with 'non-forceful'.[90] All such passionate actions, at every level, share in the movements within God which are always making space within the divine dance for new participants. While these are characteristic of all three 'persons', there is a special alignment with the actions that are like those of a Father to whom belongs the Kingdom of peace and justice. In the parables of Jesus the image of the 'rule' of God is merged with the image of a compassionate father, so that the Kingdom of the Father is not an area held by a controlling power; the 'kingdom' is rather a kind of 'space' in which persons have the freedom to grow and develop.

But the making of this space in the world is a painful process, involving hurt and sacrifice as God the Father meets resistance to his liberating rule. We can share in this divine suffering which has the power to win space in the world, corresponding to the space God makes in himself. Worldly authorities who repress this suffering witness will in the end hasten their own downfall; passion does make revolution. As Leonardo Boff points out from his experience in South America, those who act unjustly to suppress the witness of the martyrs lose their ability to control people, to win hearts and minds, and they will fall in due time.[91] This is the story of the triune God in history. At the same time, involvement in the movements within God that 'make space' will help us to perceive where our actions of protest and resistance are truly making space for others, and so enable us to perceive at what level of forcefulness to pitch them.

Engagement in the triune God also means the experience of *participation* in the making of freedom. As we participate in the liberating movements within the communion of God's life, we discover that those who are bound and oppressed must share in the action of their own liberation.[92] Freedom cannot be handed over in a patronising way; this is only another form of domination, another form of imperialism. This should make us cautious, for instance, about recent groups – both Christian and Muslim – that have urged the *men* in society to be the leaders in the making of freedom for women and children as well as themselves. One example of this kind of movement was the recent 'march of a million men' in Washington, organised by the black Islamic leader Louis Farrakan. Unlike the earlier marches of Martin Luther King, black women were excluded, and the men were urged to take the responsibility for liberating themselves and their families. There is a true insight here, that men have often shuffled off responsibility on to the shoulders of their wives and partners in the past; but men cannot now hand freedom to women as a present. One woman who grew up in Farrakan's 'Nation of Islam' movement recently wrote about her experience, pointing out that the theory of a 'totally responsible' husband does not work when he dies, goes to prison or leaves home. Then, she affirms, 'black women have to take on the dominant role, yet women are condemned for that . . .'[93]

Engaging in God we discover that freedom needs the participation of the oppressed or it becomes another form of domination, and this will guide our actions as pastors as well as political prophets.

An example from my own personal experience was the well-meaning effort of a denomination of Christian churches in South Africa to achieve a greater integration of the training of black and white candidates for Christian ministry following the ending of the restrictions of the apartheid era. During the long years of apartheid there had been separate colleges for black and white ministers, while the property rights for both had, according to the law, been held by the administrative church body whose members were white South Africans. When apartheid came to an end, this body sold off the college for black ministers, and used the money to fund scholarships to enable black ministerial candidates to study at what had formerly been the white-only theological college. It was astonished at the hostile reaction to these actions, and the breakdown in relations that ensued. The white church officers protested that they were following the mandates of the gospel to break down barriers between races and to liberate the oppressed. But, despite the best motives, they had in fact been acting in a dominating way. Before selling off the college they had not consulted with the black churches in the townships, poor congregations who had regarded the college for black ministers as their own and had given generously to it from very low incomes. Nor had they involved the black congregations in deciding how to spend the money released, and above all they had not talked with black churches and their ministers about the way that a totally new kind of college might be created for all of them in this new situation. They presumed that *they* could free the oppressed. The result was alienation: black students could not afford to move their families into the affluent white-resident area in which the college was situated, and anyway many did not want the charity of being special scholarship students in a college that they did not feel to be their own.

Authority in the church

This story of mistaken good intentions leads us to the danger of *domination in the church*, or clerical monarchianism. I have already suggested that a trinitarian theology of 'persons as relations' does not lead to a unified ecclesial structure, where the many are subordinated to the one spiritual leader, but instead fosters the exercise of many spiritual gifts. I have also maintained that there is a place within this multiple ministry of the people of God for a pastoral overseer (*episkopos*) who links the local congregation with the universal communion of the Body of Christ, although this office will take different forms in the various traditions of the Christian church. Now I want to add that involvement in the triune God will lead us to shape this office in a way that reflects the character of participation.

Pastoral overseers in the church, no less than political leaders, must involve people in their own spiritual and social liberation. Participating in the triune God we find actions which open up 'space', and interwoven with the kingdom-movement of the Father we discover the movement of the Spirit, opening up closed systems; the Spirit opens new horizons, breaks with taboos, sets new frames of reference, innovates and removes blockages of tradition. We may say that the Spirit is the power of unmasking, showing up theories for the concealed ideologies they are, even the best theories of charity and help for others. Engaged in this movement, we discover the need to take risks in involving people in both the tasks and structures of the church, which means trusting them.

Correspondingly, as we share in the self-giving movement of Father and Son in the power of the Spirit, we see that the only authority lies in being trusted. In the Christian congregation, in whatever way the nature of the pastoral overseer or bishop (*episkopos*) is conceived, authority cannot be imposed but only won through humble service. This was the truth about authority embodied in Jesus himself (Mk 10:42–5). It is when pastors have won trust through their serving that people will allow them to lead them in initiating new things or putting an end to the old. No other authority is of any worth.

Pastors naturally want to build trust in themselves, or to gain the confidence of those whom they want to help. They may think they can do this by exhibiting strength and efficiency, to show how professional they are. For instance, pastors sometimes suppose that by presenting an appearance of knowing the answers to life's intractable problems they will gain the trust of others. They may even say 'I know what's wrong with you', supposing that people will trust them if they have magical skills in diagnosis. But this kind of strength only intimidates, and drives people further into dependence. Pastors cannot lead others without risking themselves, without showing that the healer too has wounds.

Subordination and sexuality

A third area of domination, mentioned several times already in various parts of this chapter, is male oppression of women. A theology of engagement in movements of relationship in the Trinity can once again add a distinctive perspective. I have already suggested that a concept of 'person as relation' makes clear that there can be nothing male about the *arche* of God the Father, that this maternal-father has a 'womb' from which the Word is born. But here I want to tackle the misuse of trinitarian language about submission.

In traditional concepts of the Trinity, the Son and Spirit have different functions from the Father and yet are still equal in nature; they are sent forth from the sending Father, but are no less God. As Karl Barth puts it, the Son is fully divine precisely in his obedience and submission to the Father; it is only our idolatrous idea of God that regards humility as something less than God. There is thus a relation of 'above and below', a 'superiority and a subordination' in God, and divine unity and glory consists in exactly this.[94] The conclusion, however, is then drawn by theologians of both East[95] and West (including Barth),[96] that similarly women are no less equal when their function is to follow and be subordinate rather than to lead and command; they are equally and fully human, it is urged, but their God-given function is different. They are 'submissive, but equal'.

The immediate response to this argument is to observe that the *arche* of the maternal-Father forbids any human pretensions to take up this role; human creatures are invited to join the dance of the Trinity as adopted sons and daughters, not as replacement fathers. Catherine LaCugna rightly labels the attempt to be the *arche* of another as the 'ultimate male fantasy' of self-possession and self-sufficiency:[97] fantasy, because all men owe their origin to women. They are not unoriginate origins. Moreover, if we identify the 'persons' with relationships then no transfer can be made between the Father who commands and men on the one hand, and between the Son who obeys and women on the other. To be made in the image of God does not mean to be a copy of an individual divine person, but to be called into a relationship with God which is like that between a son (or daughter) and a father (or mother). All, regardless of gender, whether sons or daughters, can equally participate in that relational movement, in the openness of the Spirit.

Nevertheless, the question about different functions in God is worth looking at again with regard to human gender, in the light of participation in the divine perichoresis. In this communion we find that functions are not absolutely reserved to any one person, or personal movement: not only the Father, for example, is Creator; the Word is also active in creation as the pattern of all reality, and the breath of the Spirit is (in the words of the Creed of Nicaea-Constantinople) 'the Lord and giver of life'. All three movements of relationship engage in reconciliation, not only the Son; and all three redeem or renew life, not only the Spirit. Because the relations indwell each other in perichoresis, they are all identified with all the functions of God's work in the world. If human beings, male and female, reflect in their mutual relationships the relations in God, there is thus no model for excluding women from certain functions in society and church, as 'an unsuitable job for a woman'.

But at the same time we find real distinctions in the 'persons' of the Trinity. Otherwise the Trinity would simply be a hidden secret of God's inner being, and not perceived in God's *oikonomia* in the world. I have already rejected the idea that the three 'persons as relation' are submerged into one undifferentiated divine activity in the world. The distinctions, however, are not in function, but *in the way* that the persons express the function. There is a way of creating which we identify as particular to fatherhood, sonship and spiritness, that is, to actions like those initiated by a Father, Son and Breath of life. There is, for instance, a way of reconciling that is particular to Sonship which alone becomes incarnate in human flesh. As Moltmann puts it, both Father and Son suffer in the cross, 'but not in the same way'.[98] Moreover, we associate some functions in a particular, but non-exclusive way with particular persons (which earlier theologians called 'appropriation') because we find one movement in God takes the 'leading edge' in a particular context.

There may be a clue here to what the feminist theologian Rosemary Radford Ruether calls the 'male and female way'. As Ruether maintains, it is an elusive enterprise to label some characteristics of personality as male and others as female: for example, to regard aggression as male and supportiveness as female, or the power of analytical argument as male and intuition as female. These are futile as well as patronising attempts at identifying gender differences.[99] In support of Ruether's contention a recent survey has shown that one of the parameters of marital satisfaction in clergy couples is having high levels of both 'so-called masculine' and 'so-called feminine' characteristics evident in both partners.[100] But this does not necessarily invalidate the idea of gender differences altogether. Ruether suggests that 'some women are right when they instinctively feel that they have a specifically female way of developing their persons that is different from men's';[101] she goes on to suggest that there is a specifically female way of *integrating* the different elements of the personality, though the elements themselves are shared by men and women.

Rather than dividing up functions between men and women, if we live in engagement with the persons of the Trinity we shall seek to foster *different ways of expressing the same function*. I would urge, for example, the exploring of a 'male and female way' of priestliness. But we are now only on the way to discovering what this male and female way of integrating characteristics is, and we shall only really be able to talk about it when women participate in all areas of work in society and church, and when men participate fully in what has been traditionally regarded as women's work. As long as there is no equality of opportunity, social stereotypes will block the path to finding the real distinctiveness between male and female that reflects the distinction in unity within God. It may be that on the other side of equality and liberation we shall even find in what contexts particular women or men can take, temporarily and for a specific purpose, the leading edge.

Dependence and Domination

Finally, we can return to aspects of domination and dependence in the psyche that we considered earlier in this chapter. Freud may be right that our infantile experience of our parents, and especially our fathers, can lead to neuroses in adult life. He is probably right that we project the image of a powerful father figure beyond ourselves to try and quieten our sense of guilt and insecurity. But, as Jürgen Moltmann puts it, 'certainly the fathers and parricides still dream in us. But if one can laugh at them, one need no longer repress them. They are still there, but they have lost their power.'[102] Christianity, he affirms, is not a father-religion, that is, a religion of the fearful appeasement of a powerful father; Moltmann describes it as a son-religion (and we can add, a daughter-religion) in which earthly fathers and sons alike can be made sons of God.

In fact, Freud also described Christianity as a 'religion of the son', within his own scheme of guilt and repression. That is, Christ as the representative Son expiates for us in his penal death all the guilt of having killed the Father (God); but then, having taken over the guilt he becomes God at the side of the Father and effectively replaces the Father as a figure of power.[103] We have, as it were, simply come under new ownership. It is not possible to make this reading of the Christian story, however, if we think of *participation* in the triune God; we are not engaged in a power-play between two supreme individuals (the Father, the Son), but sharing as sons and daughters in a movement of relationship like that between a son and a father. Moreover, the movement from Father to Son is characterised by pain and humiliation, as the triune God is fully identified with the self-giving sacrifice of the particular son, Christ, in a shameful death; in the story of the Trinity, the Father suffers with the Son, making space within the divine communion for all who are humiliated and oppressed.

Paul Ricoeur, in his reflections on God's name of Father, suggests that in this suffering and 'weakness' of God there is a parallel with Freud's insight into the way that the Oedipus complex can be demolished in the growing child. Freud thought that the harmful effects of the complex could be overcome through a restructuring of the psyche, to be achieved by a recognition of what it really means to be a father and a son. That is, the father must be recognised as who he is in himself, beyond the biological necessity of the blood tie with the child. The father must be accepted as mortal and vulnerable to death, just as the child must renounce his own desire for immortality and accept his own death. Immortality is only a fantastic projection of the desire for omnipotence in the childish psyche. Now, Ricoeur suggests that the Christian faith encourages this kind of healthy recognition of God as Father. As we have already seen, the patriarchal concept of God as the 'biological' father of the nation was assaulted in the faith of Israel, and in Jesus' own renewing of the image of Father; this process, Ricoeur proposes, is brought to fulfilment in the Christian story that the Father himself has freely endured death in the cross of the Son.[104] Here is the acceptance of the death of both the father *and* the son, and so an end to all power-struggles in the psyche. The death of the Son is not then to be understood as a satisfying of the Father through punishment but rather, declares Ricoeur, 'here is completed the conversion of death as murder into death as offering'. We may add that this conversion of symbols within the fantasy of the psyche can surely not be accomplished by conceptual understanding alone.

We have to be immersed into movements of relationship in which such a self-offering is actualised.

Through participation in the divine communion of relations we are thus freed from the vicious cycle of alternatively rebelling against and appeasing a supreme Father. But what of the longing for security that, as we observed earlier, is part of the mixture of feelings within us? Here we need to distinguish, as I suggested in the last chapter, between unhealthy and healthy dependence. Regression to a childlike feeling of dependence is not in fact always a bad thing. In the adult culture in which Freud lived at the end of the nine-teenth century, it was assumed that a return to the phases of childhood was always reprehensible. Today, as Moltmann remarks,[105] we regard such temporary periods of regression as being enriching. They enable us to relive various aspects of life with which otherwise we would lose contact. They open up the present to the past and so prepare us for hope in the future. Wesley Carr makes a similar point when he says, 'When we deny the significance of regression, we cease to develop towards maturity.'[106] What is needed, he urges, is structured or managed regression to help us integrate our past and present and to help us acknowledge our necessary dependencies.

Towards the end of the previous chapter I suggested that a healthy sense of dependence was rooted in being part of a network of interdependencies, in which we discover our responsibilities. Engaging in the relationships of the Trinity, we saw, is the context in which that discovery can happen. Now we can add that a true sense of dependence, as created beings, includes an awareness that we have an ultimate origin for our existence that lies outside and beyond us. Children in their relative helplessness have something like this sense of dependence upon their parents and other adults, though as we have seen, it can result in some corruptions of the self; it can either lead to a desire for 'magical' solutions, meeting the child's every demand, or it can come into conflict with her own growing sense of power, and be resented. That is, it can either become a desire to be dominated or a rebellion against what is perceived to be domination. These distortions are bound to happen because the dependence is of one finite being on other finite beings. If we can recapture that early childlike sense of dependence and trustfulness, however, it can be set in a very different context.[107] Participating in the relationships in God, we experience a sense of dependence upon an uncreated origin as we lean upon a son-like movement of being sent forth from a father. We take our experience of being a child into the communion of God's life, and discover a motherly-fatherhood which is not oppressive.

A Christian minister should, therefore, not be afraid of offering ritual actions which awaken a sense of childlike dependence on the mystery of God as our ultimate origin. These are not simply to be rejected as folk religion, or obsessional acts of neurosis. I mean, for example, words of blessing spoken at childbirth or on entering a new home, words of Scripture and committal spoken in the moments of dying, and anointing with oil at times of sickness. Movements in worship like standing, kneeling or processing can also invite the participants to rest on a reality beyond themselves and their immediate control; such movements are a kind of play or dance reflecting the dance of all creation in the perichoresis of God.

Giving children a place in our worship, rather than excluding them, may assist this recovery of dependence. To take just one example, at least occasionally we might not feel disturbed (or even irritated) when young children interrupt a period of prayer by loud talking and crying. Instead of trying to ignore them, we might use that time to listen to children's voices and internalise them as part of our own petition and intercession. We might take into God the cries of helpless frustration at a lack of power to influence what is going on around; we might hold before God the cries of desire for security and comfort; we might rest upon God the questions that are asked with the trustfulness that parents will have an answer. Making these voices our own, we can recapture the dependence of a child with all its ambiguities and confusions, and let it be assumed into the pure dependence of Son upon Father, child upon mother, within the triune communion.

Dependence is not the same thing as being dominated. We should not of course encourage a retreat to an infantile submission to a powerful father; it is not childishness but *childlikeness* we are aiming for, that is, a recovery of the way that our being rests upon the God who is the origin of all life. From this recovery, this relaxation from the demands of our daily roles, we can be reorientated to our responsibilities. In this dependence we make an amazing discovery: that God who does not need dependence freely desires to be dependent on us for the completeness of fellowship, for the joy of the dance.

NOTES

1. Lactantius, *De Mortibus* 44.4–5.
2. Eusebius, *De Vita Constantini* 1.29–31.
3. Eusebius, *De Vita Constantini* 1.31.
4. See Eusebius, *De Vita Constantini* 1.40.
5. Alistair Kee, *Constantine Versus Christ: The Triumph of Ideology* (London: SCM Press, 1982), argues that the values of Constantine were not Christian ones (28–34, 141–7). Timothy D. Barnes, *Constantine and Eusebius* (Cambridge, MA: Harvard University Press, 1981) judges that Constantine was a sincere and intelligent Christian (48–53, 272–5).
6. Kee, *Constantine Versus Christ*, 14–17.
7. Eusebius, *Oratio de Laudibus Constantini* 2.
8. See Kee, *Constantine Versus Christ*, 125–7.
9. Eusebius, *Oratio de Laudibus Constantini* 1.
10. Kee, *Constantine Versus Christ*, 37–46, argues that Constantine sees himself as a Messiah, and the new incarnation of the Logos. Thus he is converted to the God of the Christians, but not to (the incarnate) Christ, having a pre-Christian, Old Testament personal covenant religion.
11. See Kee, *Constantine Versus Christ*, 85.
12. From the fourteenth century, only kings crowned with the 'Holy Crown' were regarded as legitimate rulers of Hungary. The lower band of the crown is actually the sole surviving example of a Byzantine woman's crown; the upper part was possibly part of a reliquary and was probably added in the twelfth century.
13. Cyprian, *De Ecclesiae Unitate* 23; cf. 5–6.
14. Joseph Cardinal Ratzinger, *Zur Gemeinschaft Gerufen: Kirche Heute Verstehen* (Freiburg: Herder, 1991), 73; trans. in Miroslav Volf, *After Our Likeness: The Church as the Image of the Trinity* (Grand Rapids, MI: Eerdmans, 1998), 56.
15. Cyprian, *Epistolae* 73.21.

16. E.g. Ronald Trudinger, *Built to Last* (Eastbourne: Kingsway Publications, 1982).

17. Cited in David Watson, *Discipleship* (London: Hodder & Stoughton, 1981), 71.

18. For the following analysis, see Freud's *Moses and Monotheism*, trans. K. Jones (London: Hogarth Press, 1939), Part III.

19. Eric Berne, *Games People Play: The Psychology of Human Relationships* (New York: Grove Press, 1964). Berne represents what is often called 'transactional analysis'.

20. See David Miller, *Three Faces of God: Traces of the Trinity in Literature and Life* (Philadelphia: Fortress Press, 1986), 139, who criticises this application of Freudian depth psychology.

21. Paul Tillich, *Systematic Theology*, Vol. 1 (London: Nisbet & Co., 1968), 14–17.

22. So Hilary (*De Trinitate* 9.69); Cyril of Alexandria (*Dial. de Trinitate* 3.467C).

23. Pseudo-Cyril, *De Sacrosancta Trinitate* 24; John of Damascus, *De Fide Orthodoxa* 1.14.

24. Aquinas, *Summa Theologiae* 1a.42.5.

25. Bonaventura, *Liber Sententiarum* I, Dist.19, 1.1.4, concl.

26. Gregory of Nazianzus, *Epistolae* 101; Maximus, *Scholia in Dionysium*, in *Epistolae* 4:8; *Ambig.* 112b. D. See G. L. Prestige, *God in Patristic Thought* (London: SPCK, 1959), 290–6.

27. Maximus, *Disp. Pyrrh.* 187A; *Opuscula* 102B.

28. Plotinus, *Enneads* 4.4.33.

29. Basil, *Hom. in Hexaemeron* 4.

30. Denys the Areopagite, *Celestial Hierarchies* 7.4 (209D–212B); cf. 7.1 (205B–C).

31. Françoise Carter, 'Celestial dance: a search for perfection', *Dance Research* 5/2 (1987), 15.

32. Clement of Alexandria, *Stromata* 7.7; trans. in *Nicene and Post-Nicene Fathers*, 534.

33. The three dancing Graces could be used as an image for the divine triad by Marsilio Ficino in the Renaissance, because the Trinity to which they pointed was the Neoplatonist version in which the unmoving One is diversified through subordinate principles of Mind and Soul.

34. Wilfrid Mellers, *Bach and the Dance of God* (London: Faber & Faber, 1980), 18–19; cf. 26–30.

35. E.g. Athanasius, *Ad Serapion* 3.4, appealing to John 14:11.

36. Pseudo-Gregory, *Adversus Arianos* 12; see also above, note 24.

37. Jürgen Moltmann, *The Church in the Power of the Spirit*, trans. M. Kohl (London: SCM Press, 1977), 54, 59–60.

38. E.g. Gregory of Nyssa, *Contra Eunomium* 2.3.

39. This is stressed by T. F. Torrance, *The Trinitarian Faith* (Edinburgh: T. & T. Clark, 1988), 236–40, 310–13.

40. So Leonardo Boff, *Trinity and Society*, trans. P. Burns (London: Burns & Oates, 1988), 120, 147–58; Patricia Wilson-Kastner, *Faith, Feminism and the Christ* (Philadelphia: Fortress Press, 1983), 127–9 (implicitly).

41. Boff, *Trinity and Society*, 147.

42. Ibid., 141.

43. Ibid., 146–7.

44. Thomas Weinandy, *The Father's Spirit of Sonship: Reconceiving the Trinity* (Edinburgh: T. & T. Clark, 1995), 79.

45. See Ch. 2, note 16.

46. Jürgen Moltmann, *The Trinity and the Kingdom of God*, trans. M. Kohl (London: SCM Press, 1981), 165f., 175f.; Volf, *After Our Likeness*, 216–17. Wolfhart Pannenberg offers a critique of this approach in *Systematic Theology*, Vol. 1, trans. G. W. Bromiley (Grand Rapids, MI: Eerdmans, 1991), 325.

47. Pannenberg, *Systematic Theology*, Vol. 1, 317.

48. John Zizioulas, 'La mystère de L'Église dans la tradition orthodoxe', *Irénikon* 60 (1987), 330; cf. *Being as Communion: Studies in Personhood and the Church* (London: Darton, Longman & Todd, 1985), 40–7.

49. The *filioque* clause seems to have been first added to the Creed of Nicaea-Constantinople at the Council of Toledo in AD 589.

50. Pannenberg, *Systematic Theology*, Vol. 1, 317.

51. Volf, *After Our Likeness*, 70–1, 204ff.; similarly, Colin E. Gunton, *The Promise of Trinitarian Theology* (Edinburgh, T. & T. Clark, 1991), 42.

52. Notably, Duns Scotus wrote of '*haecceitas*' ('thisness') in his *Opus Oxoniense* (Oxford Commentary on the *Sentences* of Peter Lombard), 2.3.q.1, q.6. In our age, see Iris Murdoch on the 'thinginess' of art: 'The sublime and the beautiful revisited', *Yale Review* 49 (1960), 249–50.

53. Colin Gunton, *The One, The Three and the Many: God, Creation and the Culture of Modernity*, (Cambridge, Cambridge University Press, 1993), 204.

54. Ibid., 191–2.

55. Volf, *After Our Likeness*, 72, 214.

56. Joseph Cardinal Ratzinger, *Dogma and Preaching* (Chicago: Franciscan Herald, 1984), 212–20; Volf, *After Our Likeness*, 67–72.

57. Volf, *After Our Likeness*, 214.

58. If participation in these relations makes talk of consciousness appropriate, then this can be a corporate consciousness corresponding to communion.

59. Volf, *After Our Likeness*, 71, 205–6; cf. Moltmann, *The Trinity and the Kingdom of God*, 171–4.

60. Pannenberg, *Systematic Theology*, Vol. 1, 319.

61. Ibid., 309–14.

62. Volf, *After Our Likeness*, 58–66, 214, 223–4; cf. Joseph Cardinal Ratzinger, *Introduction to Christianity* (London: Burns & Oates, 1969), 132–40.
63. Volf, *After Our Likeness*, 236.
64. Origen, *In Lib. Iesu Nave (On the Book of Joshua)* Homily VII.7.
65. Volf, *After Our Likeness*, 250.
66. Ibid., 203.
67. Ibid., 213.
68. Zizioulas, *Being as Communion*, 149–54.
69. Volf, *After Our Likeness*, 224.
70. See Paul S. Fiddes, ' "Walking Together: The Place of Covenant Theology in Baptist Life Yesterday and Today' in W. H. Brackney, P. S. Fiddes and J. H. Y. Briggs (eds), *Pilgrim Pathways: Essays in Baptist History in Honour of B. R. White* (Macon, GA: Mercer University Press, 1999), 47–74.
71. *The London Confession, 1644*, Art. 47, in William Lumpkin (ed.), *Baptist Confessions of Faith* (Valley Forge, PA: Judson Press, 1959), 168–9. In modern times the Congregationalist P. T. Forsyth similarly wrote of the local church as an 'outcrop' of the universal, because Christ is 'a corporate personality . . . with all the Church latent in him': *The Church and the Sacraments*, 2nd edn (London: Independent Press, 1947), 66.
72. Forsyth, *The Church and the Sacraments*, 144.
73. Robert Jenson, ' "The Father, He . . ." ' in Alvin F. Kimel (ed.), *Speaking the Christian God: The Holy Trinity and the Challenge of Feminism* (Grand Rapids, MI: Eerdmans, 1992), 104.
74. E.g. Alvin Kimel, 'The God Who Likes His Name: Holy Trinity, Feminism and the Language of Faith' in Kimel (ed.), *Speaking the Christian God*, 191–5.
75. E.g. J. A. DiNoia, 'Knowing and Naming the Triune God: The Grammar of Trinitarian Confession' in Kimel (ed.), *Speaking the Christian God*, 178–86.
76. Karl Barth, *Church Dogmatics*, trans. and ed. G. W. Bromiley and T. F. Torrance (Edinburgh: T. & T. Clark, 1936–77), I/1, 363. My italics.
77. See Robert Jenson, *The Triune Identity* (Philadelphia, PA: Fortress Press, 1982), 1–20.
78. Paul Ricoeur, 'Fatherhood: From Phantasm to Symbol', trans. R. Sweeney in *The Conflict of Interpretations* (Evanston, IL.: Northwestern University Press, 1974), 482–90.
79. See for example Deuteronomy 32:6; Jeremiah 3:4, 19–20; Isaiah 64:8.
80. The sheer frequency of Jesus' use of 'Father' for God is impressive, although Jeremias' claim that this use is 'unique' cannot be sustained in the light of recent research: see Joachim Jeremias, *New Testament Theology*, Vol. 1, trans. J. Bowden (London: SCM Press, 1971), 73–6.
81. Jürgen Moltmann, 'The Motherly Father: Is Trinitarian Patripassianism

Replacing Trinitarian Patriarchalism?' in J.-B. Metz and E. Schillebeeckx (eds), *God as Father? Concilium* (Edinburgh: T. & T. Clark, 1981), 53.

82. Boff, *Trinity and Society*, 166.

83. Hilary, *De Trinitate* 6.16; 12.8, 10; Eusebius, *Historia Ecclesiastica* 1.3; Basil, *Adversus Eunomium*.

84. Translation in Moltmann, 'The Motherly Father', 53.

85. *An Inclusive-Language Lectionary: Year A*, revised edn (Atlanta, GA: John Knox Press, 1986), 88.

86. Roland M. Frye, 'Language for God and Feminist Language' in Kimel (ed.), *Speaking the Christian God*, 23.

87. Plato, *Timaeus* 28C.

88. See above, Ch. 2, p. 41.

89. Barth, *Church Dogmatics*, II/2, 161–5.

90. See Walter Wink, *Engaging the Powers: Discernment and Resistance in a World of Domination* (Minneapolis, MN: Fortress Press, 1992), 175–93.

91. Leonardo Boff, *Passion of Christ, Passion of the World*, trans. R. Barr (Maryknoll, NY: Orbis, 1987), 123.

92. See Stephen Pattison, *Pastoral Care and Liberation Theology* (London: SPCK, 1997), 254–7, 263.

93. Emma Lindsey, 'Secrets of the sisters', *The Guardian*, 23 October 1997, interviewing Sonsyreta Tate.

94. Barth, *Church Dogmatics*, IV/1, 201–2.

95. E.g. Vigen Guroian, *Incarnate Love: Essays in Orthodox Ethics* (Notre Dame, IN.: University of Notre Dame Press, 1987), 132–3.

96. Barth, *Church Dogmatics*, IV/1, 202; III/2, 311–12.

97. Catherine M. LaCugna, *God For Us: The Trinity and Christian Life* (San Francisco, CA: HarperCollins, 1991), 398.

98. Jürgen Moltmann, *The Way of Jesus Christ*, trans. M. Kohl (London: SCM Press, 1990), 173; cf. *The Crucified God*, trans. R. A. Wilson and John Bowden (London: SCM Press, 1974), 243.

99. Rosemary Radford Ruether, *Sexism and God-Talk: Towards a Feminist Theology* (London: SCM Press, 1983), 111–12.

100. Sue Walrond-Skinner, *Double Blessing: Clergy Marriage Since the Ordination of Women as Priests* (London: Cassell, 1999), 66–8, 206–8, 219–22.

101. Ruether, *Sexism and God-Talk*, 113.

102. Moltmann, *The Crucified God*, 307.

103. Sigmund Freud, *Totem and Taboo*, trans. J. Strachey (London: Routledge & Kegan Paul, 1960), 154.

104. Ricoeur, 'Fatherhood: From Phantasm to Symbol', 492–3.

105. Moltmann, *The Crucified God*, 310.

106. Wesley Carr, *The Pastor as Theologian* (London: SPCK, 1989), 213; similarly, Michael Jacobs, *Living Illusions: A Psychology of Belief* (London: SPCK, 1993), 70–5.

107. See E. Erikson, *Young Man Luther* (London: Faber & Faber, 1959), 257–8.

PART II

Further into God and the World

4

The God who Acts and the Point of Intercessory Prayer

'Give peace in our time, O Lord'; 'Let your priests be clothed with righteousness'; 'O Lord, save the Queen'. Whatever prayer book – or none – we use, what are we expecting to happen when we make requests like this? When we pray for the peacemakers in the world (the United Nations, for example), or for Christian ministers and missionaries, or for rulers and politicians – what are we really expecting God to do about it? Whether prayers of petition work, especially the prayers of petition for others that we usually call 'intercession', is a question bound up with *another* question: how does God act in the world at all? How does God *give* peace, or righteousness, or health and salvation? Whether our prayers change anything depends first on how we think *God* changes anything.

All Christians are called to be intercessors; this is a large part of their ministry in the 'priesthood of all believers', to bear the world before God in prayer. Christian ministers focus this priestly act, often by making representative prayers in the liturgy; but beyond this specific function it is part of their whole way of being. The interlaced questions of intercession and God's way of acting are thus at the heart of any pastoral theology.

Our reflections so far on a doctrine of God have laid stress upon a God whose life consists in relationships. Moreover, these relationships are not static links between individuals, but are love in movement, making an interweaving dance of 'perichoresis' in which we are summoned to be involved. God happens, moves and comes. We have begun to speak, however hesitatingly, about distinct activities within the communion of God's own life; if the divine persons are 'subsisting relations', then they do not act like individual agents, operating as subjects upon objects, but act by being *in action*. I have also claimed that this multiplicity of action in God ('processions') is expressed outwardly in a diversity of God's actions in the world ('missions'). So now it is time for us to move on to the question, *how* does God act in the world? Scientists trace the causes of events in the natural world; sociologists and psychologists examine the causes of events in the human world (even though they rarely agree, or even understand each other's jargon). How does the action of God fit in to these worldly causes? If rain is caused by condensation of water vapour, in what sense is God the creator of rain? If an illness is cured by antibiotics, then in what sense is God the healer? How does God act in a world, which we can explain (at least to a large degree) by other causes?

I intend to review various answers offered in Christian thought to the question of how God acts in the world, and to test them against the challenge of intercessory prayer. At the same time, since prayer is participation in the relationships of the triune God, we can begin to answer the question 'how can a divine relationship act in the world?'

The 'Two-Cause' Theory

One traditional answer to the question of how God acts in the world has been to say that every event has two causes – its immediate cause as supplied by the world, and an ultimate cause which is God. Thomas Aquinas called these 'secondary' and 'primary' causes. So, the secondary cause of rain would be the condensation of water vapour (now portrayed in glowing computer graphics on our television weather reports). But the primary cause would be God who creates the water, the clouds and the winds and sustains them in being. Straightaway, however, another question arises: how are these two causes related to each other?

One influential Christian answer to this further question has been that in the end, for God to be sovereign, the primary cause must be the overwhelming one. The secondary causes are to be taken seriously, since (as Aquinas put it), 'God governs the lower through the higher . . . from the abundance of his goodness imparting to creatures also the dignity of causing.'[1] But since God is finally the Maker and Mover of all things, in working through 'lower' causes God always has God's will and way.[2] We might take the illustration of an author writing a play. From the perspective of the characters in the play, they are themselves causing things to happen; Hamlet is avenging his murdered father, or the characters in *EastEnders* are getting married, divorced or sent to prison. But in fact, though the characters act as if they are the cause of these events, it is all in the script. The author is the primary cause.

Indeed, this point of view goes on to say, when God wishes God can bypass the secondary causes altogether and act directly in a primary way. The result has usually been called a 'miracle', and has often been understood as God's breaking of the laws of nature to intervene in the fabric of the world as its sovereign Lord. Aquinas himself is more subtle than this: when God acts outside the normal processes of nature, he is not violating the order of nature but simply doing without it. Whether using secondary causes or not, he is the same Creator who is always present to his world.[3]

Although Karl Barth refuses to name God's action as a 'cause' since it is of a totally different order of reality from causes in the world, he essentially has the same view of double agency. Instead of primary and secondary causes he discerns the two aspects of the 'rule of God' and creaturely causes; but like Aquinas he believes that all causality in the world is subordinate to God's irresistible rule, so that while the creature goes its own way, 'it always finds itself in a very definite sense on God's way'.[4] Like Aquinas also, he does not regard miracles as a breaking of natural laws, but this is because he regards all such 'laws' as only laws in our order of knowing, our observation of regularities in the world.[5] There is, for instance, no immutable law that 'makes' water vapour condense when it meets colder air, but we observe that this is what always happens. Only God *ordains* things to happen, and so is free to act in ways that do not appear lawful to us.

But if God is sovereign in this way, if – as Isaac Watts says in one hymn –

> clouds arise and tempests blow
> by order from Thy throne,[6]

then we have a double problem. First, the world does not seem to have any real freedom; second, God appears to be responsible for everything that happens in the world, including evil and suffering.

Some Christian thinkers have thus proposed a second, revised form of the 'two-cause' theory, separating the two causes out into a remote primary cause and more immediate secondary causes. The rather complicated idea that the primary cause is always at work within and through secondary causes ('double agency') is abandoned, in favour of a picture of creation in which God sets up the universe in the beginning and lets it run with its own freedom. In order to make this view (often called 'deism') more concordant with the Christian story, it can be combined with the proposal that God nevertheless acts here and now in a limited number of deeds of intervention (a kind of 'theism').[7] Thus, the characters in the world's drama do cause their own revenges and divorces, but from time to time God steps in to put things back on course, or to wake us up to the divine will and purpose. Then the 'primary cause' would normally be very distant indeed, way back in the mists of time, not a continual activity; but God would still be free to act directly in place of secondary causes from time to time, making, for example, a special wind to drive back the waters of the Red Sea.

Some variation or other on this view is held among many (even perhaps most) Christian people who are not theologians, and so it is aptly expressed by the writer who prided himself on being a straightforward, common-sense kind of Christian, namely G. K. Chesterton. In the first act of a play called *The Surprise*, Chesterton portrays an author writing and performing a puppet play in which the characters naturally do exactly what he wants: a wandering poet marries a princess, in the style of good romances. In the second act, however, the puppets turn into real people with minds and hearts of their own; they quarrel and fight, and just as the poet is about to kill the Princess's father, the author bursts in through the scenery, shouting, 'And in the devil's name, what do you think you are doing with my play? Drop it! Stop! I am coming down.'[8] Chesterton is, of course, affirming that the world is more than a puppet-play and that God is not one who simply pulls the strings like the author depicted in Act One. In fact he retires behind the scenes, and lets us be actors who 'ad-lib' our lines spontaneously rather than following a script. But when the play drifts too far from the Author's intention, God will 'come down' in person to put things right.

At first sight this version of the relation between the 'two causes' may seem to resolve the problems of freedom and evil more efficiently than the first approach, but on further thought it seems even more problematic. God appears to be absent from the world except on special occasions; having once created, this God is not the continuous creator of a developing creation. So the divine sovereignty appears to be put into question. Then, although God is not responsible for evil in the first place, the question still arises why God does not intervene more often to stop it, if God can and does at times. Why, for instance, did God not take up the divine prerogative to intervene, to 'come down', when things got out of hand in Auschwitz or Rwanda? Moreover, in the events where God is said to act here and now, the human and natural freedom which was earlier granted seems to be set entirely on one side. Where God does intervene, coming out from behind the scenery, nothing can hinder the divine will. And we notice that these are usually selected as the really important events in history; in those events which are central to the life of the world, the ones which make a decisive difference, the world is not free to go its own way. It is allowed to make its own little storms in nature or human life, but the decisive ones are made by God.

Thus, in the face of these problems, other Christian thinkers have suggested a third version of relating the two causes, that we should simply place the sovereign acts of God alongside the world's activities as a sheer paradox. God acts continually and the world acts continually, and that is all we can say. The two affirmations are complementary, and we should not ask how they relate to each other.[9] There is, of course, already a mystery within the classical form of the 'two-cause' theory, as the 'causal joint' between primary and secondary causes remains ineffable. But the mystery can be made more absolute by refusing even to advance the limited explanation that the idea of primary and secondary causes provides. The two causes, it might also be said, are not related in the 'two-storey' way proposed by Aquinas ('higher' and 'lower' causes), but are 'two stories', two completely different kinds of language about reality which should not be confused. Talk about what God does, and what the world and its inhabitants do, are two quite separate language-games.

This way of thinking is widespread today, and seems to be a modest and moderate way for Christian believers to proceed. But I suggest that it is profoundly unsatisfactory. We are left with no connections between the world-view of faith and the world-view of science. The two worlds fail to meet as faith and science are allotted to two totally separate compartments. Significantly, it is those theologians who have also been professional scientists who are the most emphatic that we cannot give up the quest for 'one world'.[10] Perhaps it is the failure of Christian theology to hold a holistic view of spiritual and physical realities that has led to the emergence of new cults which lay claim to do so, and notably the advance of the New-Age movement.

Causes and Prayers

So far, I have been identifying some conceptual problems with a two-cause view of God's action in the world, centring on the issues of evil and freedom. But our experience of intercessory prayer also raises difficulties with it.

In the first place, why should we make any requests to God at all if God is the final irresistible cause of events? If the divine will is fixed upon a certain action, it seems that our prayers of intercession cannot make any difference. This objection applies to all three versions of the 'two-cause' theory outlined above, though it emerges with particular force in the most sophisticated form as propounded by Aquinas. He urges that 'our motive in praying is . . . that we might obtain that which God has decreed will be obtained by prayer'.[11] That is, as Brian Davies comments, 'God may will from eternity that things should come about as things prayed for by us.'[12] Prayer is itself a kind of 'secondary cause'; if we do not pray, this does not affect the outworking of the eternal will of God, and so we cannot regard events that happen as caused in a decisive way by our praying. Aquinas thinks that God wills to bring certain things about through our asking rather than without it, because 'in this way we gain confidence in God and acknowledge him as the source of all our blessings'.[13] All this, however, is hardly likely to encourage us to pray.

Some have suggested that this problem is solved if in prayer we leave time behind. God, it is proposed, lives in a timeless state in which past, present and future are one simultaneous moment, in an eternal now. So, in acting as a primary cause, God has already taken our freely offered intercessions into account, even when we have not yet prayed in terms of the world's timescale. Our prayers do make a difference to God's forming of an eternal plan; as C. S. Lewis once wrote, 'He has all eternity in which to listen to the split second of prayer put up by a pilot as his plane crashes in flames.'[14] The logical extension of this argument, some suggest, is that we can pray for things that have happened in the past as if they have not yet happened. We can pray for Jesus as he enters the garden of Gethsemane; we can pray for the martyr facing the lion; we can pray for an exhausted child labouring twelve hours a day in a nineteenth-century English factory; we can pray for a black man about to be lynched by the Ku Klux Klan in the American South of the 1930s; we can pray for the terrified inhabitants of Pompeii as the lava flow drowns them . . . and so on. I have, by the way, not invented these examples but taken them from a book on 'the psychology of prayer' by Ann and Barry Ulanov.[15]

But this, I think, raises more problems than it solves. If time means *nothing* to God, it is hard to see how God can really be involved in *our* time and history. Philosophers of religion have questioned whether God can know the world as it really is – in passing time – without any experience of time,[16] leading to such interesting questions as 'does God know what time of day it is?' It seems doubtful whether we can speak of God's 'acting' at all unless there is some temporality in God, some movement from one state of being to another.[17] Moreover, a timeless God cannot receive any influence from the world, since this too requires an inner movement, and so the idea that God is affected by our prayers in a timeless eternity is self-contradictory. It has become clear, in much recent discussion, that the notion of an absolutely timeless God is a concept of Greek philosophy, replacing the biblical picture of the 'everlasting God'[18] for whom time has meaning, but who is not trapped within it as we are. To affirm that God is temporal does not require God to have exactly the *same* relation to time as do beings who are creatures of history, and I am going to explore this difference further in thinking about the pastoral issues of facing death in a later chapter. For the moment, we may recall that a triune God is in eternal movement, subsisting in an interweaving of relationships; this means that God has a 'story', some kind of successiveness in which one thing comes after another, and so time is in God rather than God in time; we may conclude that this is the basis for God's creation of our time, in which (in Barth's phrase) 'God has time for us'.[19]

So there is the first problem: if God acts as the final overwhelming cause, why ask at all? A second objection to a 'two-cause' view of God's action arises from a further aspect of experience of intercessory prayer. In praying for others we find that we are being pulled into a zone of interconnection. Prayer is supremely social. We are swept into a current in which nothing is separated from anything else, no one from anyone else. We find we are being urged by the Spirit to pray for those far away in the world, some of whom we have never met; we find that we can enter with empathy into the experience of the hungry and needy of the world, and that this opens up an awareness of the hungry and needy parts of ourselves. We who pray for others find that we too are being prayed for as we enter the community of prayer. When we pray for others we find that we are also dependent upon them, and on a great storehouse of past prayers, some preserved in the church's tradition in great images and phrases on which we rely.

Intercessory prayer is an experience of connectedness and mutuality, because it is praying 'in God' who lives in relationships. In intercession we meet others in the perichoresis, the divine dance of Father, Son and Spirit. As the letter to the Hebrews puts it, Christ 'always lives to make intercession' for us (Heb. 7:25), echoing the words of the Apostle Paul that 'Christ . . . who is at the right hand of God . . . intercedes for us' (Rom. 8:34); this Son communicates eternally with the Father, not in order to plead a case for us as a kind of lawyer in heaven, but so that we can lean upon the prayers he makes and make this movement of prayer our own. We enter into the life of prayer already going on within the communion of God's being; we pray to the Father, through the Son and in the Spirit. This is why the everlasting God 'has time for us'.

Now, if this is the experience of intercessory prayer, no theory of God's action can be non-relational and non-mutual. We notice that the 'two-cause' theory operates with the concept of God as a single acting subject. All discussions of it within philosophy of religion, from Aquinas onwards, simply refer to the primary or sovereign cause as 'God'. In this case, the persons of the Trinity appear to be not only inseparable in their operations outwardly in the world, but indistinguishable from each other, since 'primary causation' can hardly be appropriated or assigned as a characteristic to any particular person.[20] Reflection on the Trinity with regard to the 'causative power' of God seems to be at best an unnecessary complication, and at worst irrelevant. But prayer tells us that any concept of divine action must be relational, trinitarian, and participatory. If a theory can be established without this, it is is defective.

For all the problems in the 'two-cause' view that make it finally unsatisfactory, we must, however, acknowledge that it is on to something important, especially in the classical formulation by Aquinas. That is, it wants to affirm that in some way God and the world act together, that there is a cause in nature and a cause in grace. Aquinas is anxious to make clear that God respects the secondary causes God uses, in ways appropriate to their nature; he wants to say that God uses rather than violates human freedom, which is itself sustained by God's primary activity.[21] Grace comes through nature, rather than abolishing it; the supernatural is in the natural. This is what Aquinas wishes to say, but I suggest it cannot be held within the framework of 'higher and lower causes'. I am going to propose that it should be envisaged more radically as a co-operation, a process of mutual contribution.

The 'Inner Transformation' Theory

The theory we have just reviewed is an ancient one in origin. A theory with its roots in the modern age tries to meet some of the problems of evil and human freedom by taking God's action off the stage of the physical and historical world altogether. This world is abandoned to scientific theories of causation, whether they are those of the physical sciences or the social sciences. God's action is confined to the inner world of the human consciousness, to the world of human 'existence' in the sense of what we find to have meaning and significance in our life, what makes us 'stand out' (*ex-ist*) in authentic living. God's action thus transforms our knowledge of ourselves, creates faith and trust, and gives hope for the future.

This kind of approach is usually dubbed 'existential' and has been most associated with the thought of Rudolf Bultmann. All talk of God's taking part in physical or historical causation is defined as 'mythological', or a way of speaking about the action of God in the sphere of our faith.[22] So, for example, to say that God raised Jesus from the dead is not to make an objective statement about what happened to the body of Jesus, but is to say that God revived and re-created the faith of the disciples in what Jesus had revealed about human existence. Or, to speak of God as Creator is not talking about any act of God in the origin of the universe, any involvement in the 'Big-Bang' beginning, but is witnessing to our feelings of absolute dependence upon God. The bang God causes is in our consciousness, in our hopes, our fears, our need to be challenged to live fully.

If we think of God's activity in the world like this, then our view of intercessory prayer will be that it changes not the world but us. We who pray are transformed through our own prayers, brought more into line with God's purposes, brought to a deeper knowledge of ourselves. Of course, there is a profound truth in this. When we pray for our enemies, we discover the parts in ourselves that are enemies to life; when we pray for those who hate us, we explore and release the hateful parts of ourselves. When we pray for those whom we love, we learn to love them less possessively as we place them in God's hands; we learn much about the nature of our love. If we pray for the dead, we discover how much we are living in gratitude for life and how much we are accepting the fact of our own deaths.

It is certainly true, then, that praying for others changes our selves and brings us more deeply into God. But if we *are* immersed more deeply into the interconnectedness of all things in God, and are more engaged in God's interrelational life, it would seem odd if we did not also have an effect upon other people and other things through our prayers. If *we* are being transformed by being drawn more deeply into community, it seems that the community in the world which God embraces should be changed by our involvement.

The experience of intercession therefore contradicts the dualism between the self and the world that this existential view of God's activity promotes. The dualism is also challenged by any holistic view of self and the body. How can we deny the action of God in the physical world and yet affirm the action of God in human consciousness? Consciousness is more than the brain, but it has a physical basis in the brain, which is implicated in the whole physical world around us. To declare that God does not act in nature but only in the human will is a very curious insulation of the self from its environment.

This restriction to inner transformation also assumes that the world and history are a closed web of cause and effect that can be reduced to immutable scientific laws, and into which it is not possible to draw God. But this Newtonian, mechanical view of the universe as a closed system has been overtaken by new insights of science. The relativity of space and time, the indeterminate nature of quantum systems on the smallest scale, and the unpredictable sensitivity of 'chaotic' systems on the large scale all point to an openness in nature.[23] This makes it possible to think of the physical universe as being in some way open to God. In our age the witness of science and the experience of prayer may be speaking with one voice.

The 'General Purpose' Theory

If a purely existential view of divine action is unsatisfactory, a third approach makes God's action as general as possible. The idea goes that God is present in creation, giving purpose to the whole of it in a universal way, but not giving special purpose to special events. God is not, as in deism, a remote primary cause, absent from daily contact with the world since it depends on God continually; but neither does God act in particular purposeful ways.

The divine action, then, is everywhere in general, but nowhere in particular. God holds out, for example, the possibility of living a full human life to all in an impartial way, but only some cash their options and take up the offer. Where we notice an event in human life which seems to be a 'special act' of God, it is not actually a special operation from God's side, but the person herself taking up a universal possibility for fulfilment. Or it is the circumstances in which it happens which draw our attention to the general purpose of God; this event stands out because of the context which makes it shine brightly. Finally, it stands out because we happen to interpret it in this way ourselves. As explained by a notable exponent of this approach, Maurice Wiles:

> . . . particular events by virtue of their intrinsic character or the results to which they give rise give (like the beauty of the lilies) particular expression to some aspect of God's creative purpose for the world as a whole. They are occasions which arouse in us, either at the time or in retrospect, a sense of divine purpose. But that sense does not necessarily entail any special divine activity in those particular events.[24]

Let us, for example, consider Cyrus, whom Wiles mentions briefly in this context.[25] In the mid-sixth century BC the prophet Isaiah of Babylon calls Cyrus, King of Persia, the 'shepherd' and 'anointed' of the Lord. He speaks of God as having raised him up, called him by name, and commissioned him to send back God's people Israel from exile to their homeland. '[The Lord] says of Cyrus, "He is my shepherd, and he shall carry out all my purpose . . . whose right hand I have grasped, to subdue nations before him . . ." ' (Isa. 44:28, 45:1 *NRSV*). But then, we might ask, what of Cyrus' own freedom? Was it just an illusion that he was formulating his own foreign policy? The theory of divine action we are considering therefore dismisses the idea that God was taking any special initiative with Cyrus; it suggests that Cyrus was simply responding to the general aims that God offers to all human life to act with justice and compassion. The circumstances of Israel in exile

made Cyrus' actions stand out, and the prophet was there to interpret them as a special act of God. The event brought home to the
prophet the general purpose of God for all peoples and all times;
the particular event was a kind of window into this overall general
purpose and activity of God.

To clarify this theory of divine action we might take (as Wiles
does not) the illustration of waves beating against a cliff. The waves
beat continuously and without partiality; they do not choose to hit
one part of the cliff rather than another. But some stone is less
resistant to the pressure of the waves than others, and shows the
impact more. In fact, an observer, wandering by, might say 'The
waves have made the shape of a man's head in these rocks', and
ever afterwards the cliff is called 'The Old Man's Head'. But the
waves did not choose to make this sculpture; it was the nature of
the rock, and the interpretation of the observer – the effect made
upon the one who saw it.

The theory proposes similarly that God acts everywhere in
general and nowhere in particular. Wiles refers to God's giving
a 'general purpose to the whole', while Gordon Kaufman speaks
of God's 'master act', whose purpose is disclosed by 'subordinate
acts'.[26] This is an attempt to ease the problem of evil and to preserve
the reality of creaturely freedom; both seem to become more problematic the more particular God's actions are, and so the ascribing
of a general purposefulness to God claims to avoid the worst of the
problems.

But in criticism we must question whether this kind of view
does justice to the notion of God's having a purpose at all. Talk of
'purpose' surely implies that the holder will have specific intentions
as well as general ones; living in particular circumstances, it is
impossible to detach the one from the other. This indeed is the
point of the image of 'election' in Scripture; it is about God's
choosing particular people, a particular nation, a particular time, to
do something new. The particular is not exclusive since it is meant
to have an effect which spreads to all, so that Israel is called by
God to be a blessing and a light to the nations (Gen. 12:3, Isa.

49:6). Christians have wanted to apply this elective intent above all to Jesus Christ; he is the 'beloved Son', the 'chosen' and 'anointed' one, so that God's promise can be universalised through him. A 'general purpose' view is left with saying the same kind of thing about Jesus as Cyrus, that in his circumstances he cashed the options held out to all people in general; it was the totality of his response, and his circumstances at the confluence of Jewish tradition and Roman civilisation, that made him stand out as disclosing the truth about our existence.[27] Talk of election is 'a retrospective way of expressing' the total commitment of Jesus to the divine purpose.[28] But the Christian faith has wanted to tell a story about God's 'sending' of the Son, that is intentionally giving Jesus of Nazareth a particular aim and mission, so that the universal effect of reconciliation is created by the particular event of the cross.

A further critique of this 'general purpose' view emerges, moreover, from the experience of intercessory prayer. Through intercession we enter a great ocean of interconnectedness, a community in which God does indeed give purpose to 'the whole'. Our sense of wholeness is enhanced as we make connections we never made before, and see how our particular request takes on a new aspect in the light of the wholeness of the world's needs. But we enter this zone through particular instances of intercession, praying for those who concretely come across our path: we name them individually; we have a mental picture of their circumstances; we enter the community of all who pray and are prayed for by particular doors of particular daily events. We feel instinctively that a general prayer like 'God bless all the children of the world' does not engage us and bring us into God's relational life as does holding before God the image of a particular child in hospital. If we were to say that this was simply an aid, a tool to bring us to a sense of God's general purpose, it would be to deny the love that we know is concrete and incarnate in the particular as we pray.

What we want to affirm about prayer, as well as about the biblical notion of divine intention, cannot be sustained by the 'general purpose' theory. We might add, as does John Polkinghorne, that this view has not commended itself to theologians skilled in science, who 'do not suppose that modern science condemns God to so passive a role'.[29] Nevertheless, I suggest that it is valuable as a *partial* explanation of God's activity. We might well agree that *some* – but not all – happenings that stand out as special acts of God might be of the kind proposed. Because of the way they happen, they draw our attention to the overall purpose of God for our lives and the life of the world. They alert us to God's overall care and love, without being special acts themselves.

People who talk constantly about what 'the Lord does' in a way that implies special intention and even intervention in every detail of the day's events are denying the freedom of the world and its inhabitants to be themselves. Those who pray that God will find them a parking space, or give them a fine day for a church outing, provoke the question as to why a God who can manage such trivial matters was less successful in preventing a Holocaust. Those who believe God has stepped in to prevent them from getting on a plane that crashed raise acute moral problems about those who have apparently not been so guarded and guided. Yet confronted with such events, small and great, we cannot help feeling thankful, and wanting to express thanks. Might we not say that *some* events that stand out, that strike us as special acts of God, are actually *reminders* of God's overall purpose for our lives rather than a particular providence? Their circumstances, the shape of the events, awaken us to realise that God has an overall purpose for the world, despite all the evidence to the contrary. Such disclosures will always, of course, be ambiguous; others involved in the event, perhaps damaged by it, do not find any disclosure there at all.

But agreeing thus far with the 'general purpose' view does not exclude the possibility that it is not the entire explanation. Affirming a general providence does not prevent there being special acts of God, events to which God gives a particular intensity of purpose. We can say this, I suggest, if we take the fourth line of approach I want to consider.

Divine Action as Persuasion

The views we have looked at so far assume that when God acts, God cannot be resisted. The only questions are *whether, where* and *when* God acts. But our critique of domination in the last chapter should have alerted us to the thought that God never acts in a coercive way. We might say that God does not *make* us do certain things, but that God influences and persuades us, or lures us with love, to co-operate with the divine mission. There is no mechanical causality here, no inevitable link between cause and effect. God knows what will make for the utmost satisfaction in our lives, but is humble enough to want to entice us towards it rather than force us to accept it. As H. H. Farmer put it, God as supremely personal does not seek to manipulate our wills, but persuades by 'haunting the soul with the pressure of an unconditional value'.[30] God's action, in summary, is never unilateral.

If God's action is persuasive, however, how do we receive this persuasion? How do we come into the sphere of its attraction? One way of thinking of this would be a kind of 'apprehension', in which we would be influenced by our grasping hold of God and thus actively absorbing various aspects of the divine being that are presented objectively to our minds. This is the way that the school of thought called 'process theology' envisages the divine persuasion. All entities in the world, at whatever level they exist in nature, 'prehend' God who is conceived as dipolar, with one aspect of the divine being thoroughly independent of the world and another intimately related to it. In God's world-independent dimension, which A. N. Whitehead calls the 'primordial nature' of God and which Charles Hartshorne calls God's 'abstract essence', there is an infinite reservoir of possibilities for the world. From this store, God provides aims to guide all entities in the world on their path towards satisfaction, though they are free to reject them or to modify them.[31] In God's world-related dimension, which Whitehead calls the 'consequent nature' of God and which Hartshorne calls God's 'concrete states of experience',[32] God is perfectly related to all the reality there is; he receives the impact of all the actions, joys and tragedies of the world, so that he can be aptly called 'the fellow-sufferer who understands'.

From this brief sketch of process thinking about God, we can draw a significant insight about persuasion: it consists in being exposed both to the *purposes* of God for the world and to God's *sufferings* with the world. Worldly entities 'prehend' both aspects of the dipolar God, although process thinkers differ about how this happens, and about the way that the two 'poles' are integrated with each other. The impact of divine persuasion comes in the first place from the grasp of God upon the possibilities that will make for the greatest satisfaction, beauty and harmony in creation. Second, all entities are influenced as they feel the effects that their own choices and actions have upon God, and as they feel God's evaluation and transformation of these effects within the 'creative synthesis' of the consequent divine nature. We experience, as it were, God's experience of us, in an 'oscillation' of feeling. To take an illustration from family life, a child who has disobeyed and disappointed her mother may be influenced to behave in a different way when she feels *both* the strength of her mother's vision of what is possible for her, *and* the painful effect that her actions so far have had upon her mother.

In the next chapter I am going to defend the proposition that the world has an effect upon God and can even be said to 'condition' God. For the moment, we may recognise the importance of this process insight about the nature of persuasion, although I suggest that it should be set in a different context. Among several problems with the process concept of the dipolarity of God,[33] God is essentially envisaged as an object to be grasped, rather than as a triune communion in which we are involved. I do not disregard here the process view that when entities 'prehend' God, as well as other entities like themselves, there is a kind of 'presencing' of each in the other. Nor should we fail to acknowledge that the process view of the world is deeply relational and founded upon event rather than substance; its vision of the cosmos as a social organism, an interdependent whole growing towards its God-given goal through a network of mutual influences, has close affinity with the triune vision of creation I am commending. But despite various attempts to construe the 'primordial' and 'consequent' natures of God in terms of the Trinity,[34] it is hard to conceive of anything like inner mutual relationships between the different dimensions of God's being. Talk of 'participation' in God is thus limited, and it is participation rather than 'prehension' by which I suggest that we may best understand the persuasive activity of God in the world.

If 'persons' in God are relations in which created beings participate, they will be not only activities in God but actions in the world. In the previous chapter we considered the objection that the persons in the Trinity cannot simply be relations, because (supposedly) 'relations cannot act'; this critique, we saw, leads to the further objection that if the persons are relations, the acts of God in the world will be the unified act of a single divine substance.[35] In reply to these criticisms, we may now be able to see more clearly how 'relations' can be actions. Currents of relationship cannot, of course, have an impact in the sense of divine agents operating on worldly objects, causing things to happen mechanically and coercively; but they *are* actions in the sense that when we are involved in their movement, we are persuaded and moved to certain ends, caught up in their momentum. They are actions which are not characterised by domination, but by co-operation. In the Neo-platonic vision of the divine dance, the One Beyond Being moves finite beings without Itself being in movement; as the still centre of the dance It moves the dancers through their attraction to Its beauty. It is 'the love that moves the sun and the other stars' (Dante),[36] as – we might say – a beautiful person causes everyone in the room to circle around her or him without moving an inch. The divine persuasion I am describing is also based in attraction, but in the attractiveness of *movements* of love, patterns of the dance into which we are swept up, so that our actions follow the same divine aim. We are offered, or presented with, aims through being engaged in the purposeful flow of the divine love.

Now, to return to the issue of general and particular acts of God, there is room for both if the activity of the triune God is persuasive rather than irresistible. God can offer *general* aims to the whole of the world and humanity, and in *particular* events God can offer a special purpose, an 'elective purpose', designed to achieve something new and decisive. Let us consider once more the case of Cyrus. We may say that while God offers to Cyrus the same aims for truth and justice that are offered to all rulers, at this particular time in the history of Israel God also offers an aim that is not offered to other kings in the ancient Near East; this does not infringe Cyrus' freedom to exercise his skills in foreign policy, since he has to respond to this aim in order for it to come about – in order for the 'potential' to be 'actualised' (to use a technical language); he can also modify it in his own way. God's activity is thus blended with human action, giving us the two causes we thought about earlier.[37] But neither cause is mechanical, having inevitable results; one is persuasive, the other responsive. There is a co-operation, a working partnership between God and the world.

Here we may drawn upon a fruitful debate among the practitioners of process theology. The two formative thinkers mentioned earlier, Whitehead and Hartshorne, differ over the nature of the ground of possibility in the 'primordial nature' or 'abstract essence' of God. Whitehead thinks of God as having a perfect and eternal vision of all the possibilities whatever that might be actualised in the world ('eternal objects'); using a modern analogy from computers, we could say that all possibilities are contained in an eternal database or memory bank. Whitehead also thinks of God as ordering these possibilities into values which are relevant to any particular situations whatever, and selecting an 'initial aim' (or a narrow range of aims) for an entity as it begins its growth.[38] Hartshorne, however, thinks of the 'abstract essence' of God as like a person's character that endures throughout the many states of his experience; this abstract essence does not therefore contain a vision of detailed possibilities for the world, but is pure possibility itself, an open potential for definite possibilities that emerge in interaction between the world and God. The aim which God offers to worldly entities is therefore not specific, but a general setting of boundaries and limits for their decisions and actions.[39] As with the view of Maurice Wiles, God thus exerts only a general providence. Hartshorne is concerned that if God envisages all possibilities for the world, this will restrict the freedom of actual entities to contribute to the creation of new values. To adapt an analogy to which Hartshorne appeals, an artist might have a concept in her mind as to the colour she wishes to apply to her painting, but the exact fraction of colour will emerge out of the interaction of her intention with the actual composition of the pigments, the texture of the canvas, the nature of the brush. This particular shade of colour is not 'haunting reality from all eternity . . . begging for instantiation',[40] but emerges during the process of creation here and now.

Unhindered by a process metaphysic of dipolarity, we can learn from both streams of process thought. We can take Whitehead's insight into the particularity of divine action rather than Hartshorne's setting of general guidelines, and we can *also* agree with Hartshorne's insistence that the possibilities with which God persuades us can emerge in creative interaction between God and the world. In God's life of communion there are held 'outline' possibilities for the future, which will become more and more detailed as created beings make their contribution to God's purpose, as they (we might say) add their own character to the patterns of the dance; but then, from this ever-increasing store of possibilities for the flourishing of life, God can present particular as well as general aims to creatures. This is because God has given the world a genuine freedom, to share in creative activity. God has allowed the created community to be creative too, in God's own image. This also of course opens the terrible possibility that created beings will go their own way, thinking they know better – and so there is the possibility of evil, tragedy as well as triumph. Who could doubt that the mountain of evil of an Auschwitz represents a massive resistance to God's persuasive love, and on God's part an agonising frustration of the divine desire for human life?

In the light of the New Testament, we may say that this principle of co-working with God comes to its positive climax with Jesus. In Christ there is blended uniquely the divine call and the human response. He is the 'only-begotten' and 'beloved' Son; that is, an aim is offered to him by the Father to represent the Father's accepting love and liberating justice in a way that is given to no other.[41] But still he freely accepts this aim; as the author to the Hebrews says, 'he learned obedience through what he suffered', saying 'yes' to the will of the Father in Gethsemane. This is why, as we have already seen, his relation as 'Son to Father' is the means of our entering the same movement of mutual love.

Persuasion and Intercession

As with other views of divine action, we bring this understanding of persuasion to the test of intercessory prayer. This is not a difficult link to make, as the participation through which we come into the sphere of divine influence takes primary form in prayer. I suggest in fact that *only* the view that God's activity is persuasive makes sense of intercessory prayer.

If divine activity takes this form, then as we pray we can add the persuasive power of our love to God's. That is, in praying for others we are expressing our love and concern for them, and God takes that desire into the divine desire for their well-being. God wants to create a response within persons at every level (conscious and unconscious), to entice them into an openness to new possibilities that will promote healing, to woo them into co-operating with initiatives of grace. Our hopes, expectations and longings for someone are assumed into God's own persuasion, augmenting and amplifying the urgings of God's Spirit, so that together God and the interceders begin to work transformation. Whether we want someone to act justly and generously, or to be comforted, or to be strong in the face of adversity, God is the means of communicating this desire to them, and of making it effective within God's own pressure of grace where on its own it could achieve little. At the same time, of course, the one praying is becoming attuned to the desires of God, prompted to act appropriately, and where possible, to change the situation with practical deeds of help.

One way of understanding this effect of our prayers upon God's own persuasive action comes from the process perspective of the 'consequent nature' of God. Process thinkers, especially in the tradition of Whitehead, understand the aims of God as somehow being shaped by absorption of the human situation in God's world-related dimension.[42] Particular aims are woven from the realities of the world, and we are adding to that reality as we pray; as we offer ourselves in the adventure of empathetic concern for others, this adds to the experience of God which in turn gives a particular character to the initial aims God offers, so that – as Marjorie Suchocki suggests – those who are prayed for receive possibilities stronger than they would have been had there been no prayer.[43]

This is an important insight, not limited to the model of a dipolar God; our prayers shape God's own experience of the world, and so give divine persuasion a character which is 'fitted' to human life. In this way our prayers continue the path of God into creation that we perceive in the incarnation of Christ. This is perhaps what H. H. Farmer means when he proposes that our prayers enable God to 'get a purchase on the human scene in a way not otherwise possible'.[44] But such communication of our love to others through God remains indirect and rather remote if this is all there is to be said. The notion of participation in the triune communion does, however, say more. Sharing in the movements of God's relational life, our love and concern for others both touches them immediately and mediately, directly and yet also transformed through God. Like God's own presence in the world, there is a 'mediated immediacy' of our presence to others. Intercession becomes the enfolding of someone in the interweaving currents of the love of God, and encouraging them to find the movements of health and healing that are already there.

It is not enough, then, to think of our partnership with God in intercession as a matter of 'letting God into the situation', or 'giving permission' to God to enter human life. This has been proposed by the philosopher Eleanor Stump, who suggests that God shows a non-dominating relation of friendship with creation by refraining from 'doing what is possible' until requested to do so.[45] This retains the idea that the 'primary causation' of an event is a unilateral act of God, once human permission has been granted. It raises, however, the moral problem of whether it is justice that God should help one person because we remembered to ask God, and should leave another in trouble because we failed to ask. Does God really say (in effect), 'I would have healed Mary if you had only asked me, but I waited for all eternity to hear your prayer and it didn't arrive, so I decided not to build this into my plan for the world'? The view I am proposing affirms sovereignty in God, but not in the sense of unilateral activity. Rather, God takes the initiative in the project of influencing the world towards the flourishing of life and the maximal creation of values. Our prayer is not needed to get God started, after which we can stand back; God always draws near to people with persuasive love, with or without us, and God's grace will be the major factor in transforming human life; but our intercessions still make a difference to what God achieves, though we be the minor partner.

Healing for individuals and society comes through partnership between Creator and creation, and prayer is a means of entering such a partnership. If, however, the point of intercessory prayer is the transforming effect of our love for people, the question arises as to why our intercessions should take the form of a *request* to God. Why pray 'O God, give peace . . . give healing . . . give wisdom . . .'? Why ask God to do what we know God desires to do? Of course, intercessions often take another form, as language like 'We lift her before you, O God . . .' or 'we place him in your hands . . .' is also used in prayer. But for all that, it is quite proper for our loving concern for another to take the form of asking God for something; we are expressing what we fervently wish to happen within the context of a child–parent relationship where requests are natural. The form of a request belongs with the use of names for God in invocation, such as 'Our Father', which, I have already suggested, draw us into the movements of relationship in which God consists. In a similar way, our asking draws us into the dance of divine perichoresis where we can affect the lives of others. It is also appropriate for such asking to be informed by some detailed understanding of the situation for which we are praying, as long as the result is not a set of instructions for the way that God should operate. A realistic understanding of the needs faced by people will help us to empathise with them, entering imaginatively into their situation, and so enabling us to enter more deeply into God's transforming love towards them.

Problems with Persuasion

There are, however, more fundamental questions that may be posed about the proposal that the mighty acts of God are acts of persuasion alone, and here we may consider three.

First, the question arises as to whether God is powerful enough to be the Creator and sustainer of all, if indeed God works only by influence. In immediate response to this objection we might observe, as in the previous chapter, that we often project a worldly idea of power on to God. We attribute to God political notions of power, assuming that it means coerciveness, being able to compel others to do what we want. But the Apostle Paul reminds us that 'the weakness of God is stronger than human strength', that the true God is not Zeus the God of thunder but the God of the cross (1 Cor. 1:18–25). This divine weakness is also 'wisdom', for there is in fact no greater power than the ability to influence others through suffering love, that is, actually to change their minds and emotions. A dictator can force people to obey him in outward actions, but he can never force a change of mind and attitude. So, in George Orwell's novel *1984*, the dictator named 'Big Brother' has apparently unlimited power, but he is not content because he cannot get people to 'love big brother'.

But there is something we can say beyond this point I have already made. It is that, in divine persuasion, God always keeps the initiative. 'Influence' seems a weak method to us because when we have been rejected a few times there is nothing else we can do; we are left with a feeling of helplessness. But God retains the initiative; being related to all reality and present on all occasions, God can go on offering aims to creatures, in a myriad different ways. This is expressed in the faith of the Old Testament, in the willingness of Yahweh to remake the covenant when it has been broken by human unfaithfulness, finding new ways to 'woo' Israel as one lover entices another (Hos. 2:14–20).

In his book, *God's Theatre*, Timothy Gorringe draws our attention to the experience of a well-known theatre director, Peter Brook, on the subject of influence.[46] Brook reflects that that the relationship between the director and the actors is like that of a dance. The director must not, he maintains, manipulate or coerce the actors – rather as does, we may say, the author-producer at the close of the second act of Chesterton's play. But neither must the director be a merely 'honourable unassuming director' who just stands back and lets the actors get on with it, ad-libbing in a free style. This kind of unassuming director seems more like Wiles' picture of God's general purposiveness, where God is working without any script at all. Rather, Brook's experience of effective direction is that the director moves among the actors as in a dance, allowing freedom, but knowing where to guide the steps and take action to draw out an actor's right impulses: 'Deciding who's the leader depends on where you stand. The director will find all the time new means are needed.'[47] God, by analogy, can always find new means within the dance-drama of the triune life in which we participate.

But then, someone might pose a second problem about persuasion: can God ever be sure of fulfilling the divine purposes? If God's action is persuasive, and can be resisted, is the whole project of creation so open-ended that we cannot say (in the words of a well-known hymn) 'God is working his purpose out'? Might the whole universe drift off into nothingness, and evil triumph over the good? Is the risk of love a total one, so that love must face the real possibility that 'all will have been given in vain'?[48] I suggest that we should think of the risk as real, but not total. God can possess the divine life in joy because God can have a confident hope that the aim of bringing many sons and daughters to glory, the reconciliation of all things, will be achieved. This is because God knows the strength of persuasive love; we take a wager on the hope that 'the weakness of God is stronger than human strength', but God *knows* this is so. The issue is whether love is stronger than evil, and the resurrection of Jesus Christ in the middle of history gives us good reason to believe that this is the reality of creation. God is not the auto-victim of the universe. But taking this viewpoint on the destiny of the cosmos, we can also perceive a risk, the risk of tragedy *within* the triumph.

In fulfilling the divine purpose, God makes room for the response and co-operation of the created world. In the first place this means that the *route* to the destination depends upon our choices, our attunement to the purpose of God. Though the route to the end of this space of history may be a winding one, God will bring us there in the end through the gentle gambits of love. But this means, in the second place, that there is something open-ended about the *content* of the end. Because the project of God is the making of persons, the route and the destination are bound together. God is not manufacturing a standard product in a factory, but making free personalities, so that the kind of persons we become is shaped by the road we take, the decisions we make. There is the real potential for God to reap a 'tragic beauty' (Whitehead's phrase).[49] While God will finally reconcile all things, there is an openness about the nature of the world that will be reconciled. Doubtless, created beings will feel nothing lacking in their vision of God; they will be satisfied by the glory of their destination, deeper into God. But God may feel the tragedy that the world has not fulfilled all the divine aims for it, or has failed to realise them in the way that would bring about the maximum beauty and value. Such a possibility does not eternalise evil in God, because the reality which will be in existence will be wholly good, and the past marked by evil will have been transformed; yet God may still feel pain over the absence of some good that might have been achieved. In humility, God is prepared to know that there is a lack within the final reconciliation of the universe, where we are sublimely unaware of anything missing at all. This is a limited risk, but a real one.

Thus, in a blend of triumph and tragedy, God leaves things open, making space for our contribution to the creative project. This is surely why the predominant note of the Old Testament Scriptures is that of Yahweh's promises for the future, rather than exact predictions. There is room for the freedom of God, for God to fulfil promises in unexpected ways; there is also room for the freedom of human beings to contribute in their own way to this fulfilment. God's enterprise takes the form of a purpose, but not a detailed plan or blueprint, as Jeremiah's little parable of the potter makes clear ('The vessel . . . was spoiled . . . and he reworked it', Jer. 18:4).

But this vision of the pattern of history leads on to a third question about divine persuasion, a rather more philosophical one. Does God know the future, if it has an openness about it – even the limited risk I have described? With several modern philosophers of religion, I believe we may say that God knows at any moment *all that there is to be known* about the future.[50] That is, God knows it *as the future*, not as something that is either present or past to God, and knows it perfectly in this way as we do not. So God knows all the possibilities that exist for the world and its inhabitants, from the least to the greatest, which we do not. God also knows the strength of love to bring the best possibilities about, those which will make for the greatest flourishing of life and the richest emergence of values. But God knows these as possibilities, not as actualities, because they have not yet happened.

In making a free world which dwells in time, God has thus freely limited God's own self to knowing all that can be known, allowing for some things to be unknowable because they are not yet in existence. When they are, God will infallibly know them. Moreover, while God knows all the possibilities that there are, there are some possibilities which cannot yet be known, at least in detail, because God is going to imagine them in the future, or because they are going to emerge out of God's partnership with the world. Wonderfully, our imaginations too can play a part. The notion of 'primary causation' in Aquinas that we reviewed earlier assumes God must know all potentialities as eternally actualised; they have, as it were, already come to pass under the unmoving divine gaze. But if God is going to allow the world to be creative with some reflection of God's creativity, there must be some things which are possible but which have not yet become actual for God. Further, when they actually happen there will be something new about them, something contributed by the world.

To take a pastoral example of these rather abstract ideas, when someone sets out to build a community – say a local church congregation – she might know at least some of the possibilities for it, but when they actually happen there will be bound to be something new about them. A community is never quite the same in actuality as in possibility. New values are brought to it which we cannot imagine until people actually get together. Failures happen which we would not have predicted. But the sense of helplessness we feel in facing any project is made the more acute by other factors too: our knowledge of the possibilities for this group of people is very limited; we do not know them deeply even as they are now, in the present actuality of their lives; and we are all too sadly aware of the lack of strength of our love. It is otherwise for God. There will certainly be something new for God when the community comes into being, but God knows perfectly all the participants as they actually are now, many possibilities there are for them, and the power of divine love to transform them. In this sense God 'foreknows' what will be the finished project, and acts with a certain strategy.

To take another example, an artist sets out with a purpose for his picture, and knows in outline what is going to be in it. In this sense he 'foreknows' the end from the beginning. But as he paints, the density of the paint and the feel of the brushes and the texture of the canvas make their own impact, and his very materials make a contribution to the work in its actuality. So God has a 'real future' because of a real partnership with created beings, although we must remind ourselves again that as the only truly Original Artist God has freely chosen to create in this way.

Prayer and the Natural World

There remains, however, a final question which is highly relevant to intercessory prayer. Can an understanding of God's action as persuasion be applied to the world of nature as well as to the sphere of the human mind? Some Christian thinkers are happy enough to speak of God's loving persuasion in the human consciousness, but view God's action within the physical world as purely unilateral. From my previous comments on the dualism of an existential view, it should be clear that we can have no similar dualism here. If human beings are truly involved in their environment, it makes no sense to speak of persuasive action in human life and coercive action elsewhere. Within the realm of 'nature', after all, we must include the human body, and the physical brain as one component part of it. There must always be divine action and the response of the created world, so that grace transfigures nature.

If we are to restrict God's action among persons to persuasion, then we must also conceive God as working in this way within the whole of nature, guiding it patiently, offering innovation through the influence of the Holy Spirit and calling out response from it. If the world is an organic community, then all its members work together, affecting each other. If human beings are able to respond to God, then it is not unreasonable to think that there must be something at least akin to response to God at all levels of creation, some 'family-likeness' within the cosmos. Even if we cannot describe exactly how this relationship between God and the natural world works, we do have various kinds of language to point to the mystery.

Process theology offers one kind of language, in which all entities in the world have the capacity for feeling enjoyment, and all can reach after satisfaction. In the process vision, 'actual entities' are the smallest building-blocks of the universe, subatomic particles in the process of becoming; they aggregate together to form larger-scale objects or 'societies', whether persons or inanimate objects such as stones. All entities are 'dipolar', with a mental as well as a physical dimension, though at this lowest level of reality 'mind' has not yet reached consciousness as it has in persons. Individual entities and 'societies' work together in the organic community of the world, influencing and being influenced by others, moving towards the achievement of value and beauty.[51] God offers an aim – or at least parameters for development – to every entity in creation to enable it to grow into fullness of life, and because there is a mental element (or a 'feeling' aspect) in everything, all can accept, reject or modify the divine purpose.[52]

While thoroughgoing adherents of process philosophy take this picture of the world as a scientific description, I suggest that it may be better to regard it as metaphor, pointing to an inexpressible underlying reality. The vision of the whole environment being in some way alive and responsive does strike some chords with the biblical understanding of God's relationship to the natural world. According to the Old Testament, God makes covenant not only with human beings but with 'every living creature . . . the birds, the cattle, and every beast of the earth' (Gen. 9:10). Not only human beings but the world of nature sings praise to Yahweh; the waves roar before him, the heavens pour forth speech, the trees of the fields clap their hands as he comes to his world, and God plays with the sea-monsters in the deep.[53] In the New Testament, according to Paul in Romans 8:19–22, the whole universe 'groans as if in the pangs of childbirth'(*NEB*), waiting for God to set it free, with its destiny deeply bound up with the redemption of God's human children. This is certainly poetic language, but it offers testimony to some kind of response which the natural world can make, or fail to make, to the purposes of God; it also hints that this response is implicated in some way in the human response.

Another pathway of thought, based on more recent physics than process philosophy, observes that causality in the world is of two types: there is 'energetic' causality (where one thing makes a physical impact on another), and there is 'informational' causality, where the input of information into a system forms its patterns of behaviour. Some theologians, and notably John Polkinghorne, have suggested that while creaturely acts involve a mixture of energetic and informational causalities, God acts through making a pure entry of information into nature. This is a holistic kind of causation, affecting the patterns of whole, large-scale systems, which then have an influence on their smaller component parts.[54] Polkinghorne does not regard this forming of patterns by God as a persuasive activity which necessarily calls for response, but I suggest that we can in fact see it in this way, if we place this pattern-inducing activity in the context of the triune life of God.

As I have been proposing, the divine 'persons' act in the world through being in movement, and by drawing created realities into the momentum of their relationships. We can thus take up the insight of 'pattern-making', though without having to restrict it to the particular scientific language of an 'input of information'. We can envisage the influence of the patterns of the divine 'dance' of relationships on the patterns of behaviour of natural systems, human persons and human societies. If intercessory prayer 'works' through the influence of love which it adds into the dance (as I argued earlier), then our prayers can have some real effect on the forming of patterns in nature as well as in the human personal life.

Here then are three kinds of language which, taken together, begin to express the response of all nature to God – the capacity of all entities for feeling, the movement of all creation in praise, and a receptivity to the holistic forming of patterns. This wholeness of response to God can perhaps best be seen in the wholeness of the human being, in the mysterious psychosomatic unity of mind and body, and in the hidden interaction between what is conscious and what is unconscious. In praying for the healing of someone, for instance, we place our love in the midst of the dance of God's love, confident that God's persuasive lure towards life will reach into the whole pattern of the human being, crossing all boundaries between spirit and body. Correspondingly, we are hoping for a response to God's purpose which cannot be isolated in the mind alone but which somehow, at the same time, arises from the body which the mind transcends.

The result of such holistic response to the divine initiative may be an enriching of a pattern of nature that is already there, such as the receiving of a sense of peace despite the presence of disease and disability, or an easing of symptoms and pain though the cause of them is still there. But there is room in the partnership between God and nature for a something new to happen which is not already part of the regular flow of events; there might, for example, be some inexplicable remission in the onward march of a disease, or the extraordinary disappearance of damaged cells, or some hastening of a process that usually takes longer, or restoring of function to an area of the brain that seemed to have been defunct. We might call these events 'miracles', yet we should agree with Aquinas and Barth that these are not 'breaches' in nature, but grace finding new paths through nature.

God's persuasive love, augmented by our praying, may, however, be thwarted by resistances in nature, by lack of co-operation. We must take a very wide view of this failure in co-operation, being especially careful not to throw the burden of blame for its breaking down mainly – or indeed *at all* – upon the particular participants in any situation where healing is needed, and where people are called to be open in trust to God. To focus narrowly on their response will be likely to produce a mountain of false guilt. The resistance to co-operation that God meets in the world is a complex and tangled story, and one of which we usually catch only a glimpse. No doubt, God *can* be frustrated in the divine desire to bring healing through some lack of response that could have been offered in the immediate situation, either consciously or unconsciously by the individual sufferer, or by the community of carers around her. But this is only one small thread in a much larger tapestry. There is a whole network of factors, in the past and present, which combine to produce resistance to God's persuasive love: there are social pressures, genetic defects, the inheriting of the consequences of others' sins and failures, and interactions between people at a sub-surface level. Blockages may be there, deeply embedded in a world of nature which has for millennia been slipping away from God's purposes. When healing does not come, in physical recovery or spiritual well-being, there are hidden factors in the fallen world which for the moment the combined influences of divine and human love, united in prayer, cannot overcome.

We should not, therefore, be over-confident in our ability to unravel these elements, or to reduce them to a simplistic explanation that only feeds our ego or our sense of power over others. Neither, however, should we lose hope in the final victory of love in the new creation, and sometimes, for reasons we cannot discover, the resistances are overcome here and now. At such times we are inclined to say 'a miracle has happened in answer to prayer'. But it is the same miracle of love that happens every day in our intercession for others, the wonder of being pulled into the community of God's triune life, in which all kinds of connections can happen.

NOTES

1. Aquinas, *Summa Theologiae* 1a.22.3.
2. Aquinas, *Summa Theologiae* 1a.22.4.
3. Aquinas, *Summa contra Gentiles* 3.100.2.
4. Karl Barth, *Church Dogmatics*, trans. and ed. G. W. Bromiley and T. F. Torrance (Edinburgh: T. & T. Clark, 1936–77), III/2, 94.
5. Barth, *Church Dogmatics*, III/2, 125–8.
6. Isaac Watts, hymn: 'I sing the almighty power of God'.
7. E.g. John R. Lucas, *Freedom and Grace* (London: SPCK, 1969), 9, 31.
8. G. K. Chesterton, *The Surprise: A Play* (London: Sheed & Ward, 1952), 63.
9. So Austin Farrer, *Faith and Speculation* (London: A. & C. Black, 1967), 61–7, 83–5.
10. E.g. John Polkinghorne, *One World: The Interaction of Science and Theology* (London: SPCK, 1986), 62–85; Ian G. Barbour, *Religion in an Age of Science* (London: SCM Press, 1990), 23–30; Arthur R. Peacocke, *Creation and the World of Science* (Oxford: Clarendon Press, 1979), 14–38.
11. Aquinas, *Summa Theologiae* 2a2ae. 83.2; translation in Blackfriars edition, 53.

12. Brian Davies, *The Thought of Thomas Aquinas* (Oxford: Clarendon Press, 1993), 184.
13. Aquinas, *Summa Theologiae* 2a2ae, 83.2; translation in Blackfriars edition, 53.
14. C. S. Lewis, *Mere Christianity* (London: Geoffrey Bles, 1952), 133.
15. Ann and Barry Ulanov, *Primary Speech: A Psychology of Prayer* (London: SCM Press, 1985), 90.
16. See Anthony Kenny, *The God of the Philosophers* (Oxford: Clarendon Press, 1969), 39–48.
17. See Richard Swinburne, *The Coherence of Theism* (Oxford: Clarendon Press, 1977), 225.
18. E.g. Genesis 21:33; Isaiah 26:4, 40:28; Psalm 89:2. See Nelson Pike, *God and Timelessness* (London: Routledge & Kegan Paul, 1970), 184; Richard Swinburne, *The Christian God* (Oxford: Clarendon Press, 1994), 138–44.
19. Barth, *Church Dogmatics* I/2, 45, II/1, 611f.; cf. I/1, 426–7.
20. See Aquinas, *Summa Theologiae* 1a.39.8.
21. Aquinas, *De Malo* 6.
22. Rudolf Bultmann, *Jesus Christ and Mythology* (London: SCM Press, 1960), 62, 65–8.
23. See John Polkinghorne, *Belief in God in an Age of Science* (New Haven, Conn.: Yale University Press, 1998), 51–4, 60–6.
24. Maurice Wiles, The Remaking of Christian Doctrine (London: SCM Press, 1974), 38; cf. Wiles, *God's Action in the World* (London: SCM Press, 1986), 28–30, 79–81.
25. Wiles, *God's Action in the World*, 61–2.
26. Gordon Kaufman, 'On the Meaning of "Act of God" ' in Owen Thomas (ed.), *God's Activity in the World: The Contemporary Problem*, AAR Studies in Religion 31 (Chico, CA: Scholar's Press, 1983), 147–57.
27. See Schubert Ogden, 'What Sense Does it Make to Say, "God Acts in History"?' in *The Reality of God* (London: SCM Press, 1967), 187–8; *The Point of Christology* (London: SCM Press, 1982), 65–8.
28. Wiles, *God's Action in the World*, 89.
29. Polkinghorne, *Belief in God in an Age of Science*, 34.
30. H. H. Farmer, *The World and God* (London: Nisbet, 1935), 24; cf. 70.
31. Alfred North Whitehead, *Process and Reality: An Essay in Cosmology* (New York: Macmillan, 1929, repr. 1967), 69–7, 373–5, 521–3; Charles Hartshorne, *Creative Synthesis and Philosophic Method* (London: SCM Press, 1970), 68; *The Divine Relativity: A Social Conception of God* (New Haven, CT: Yale University Press, 1948), 72–4.
32. Whitehead, *Process and Reality*, 46–7, 523, 529–32; Hartshorne, *The Divine Relativity*, 80–81; *A Natural Theology for Our Time* (La Salle, IL: Open Court, 1967), 27, 40.
33. In the next chapter, I consider problems with a dipolar view of the suffering of God.

34. See John B. Cobb, 'The Relativization of the Trinity' in Joseph Bracken and Marjorie Suchocki (eds), *Trinity in Process: A Relational Theology of God* (New York: Continuum, 1997), 20–2; David Griffin, 'A Naturalistic Trinity', ibid., 35–8.

35. See above, pp. 83–9

36. Dante, *The Divine Comedy: Paradiso*, 33.145.

37. A complementary approach here is that of Vincent Brümmer, *Speaking of a Personal God* (Cambridge: Cambridge University Press, 1992), 113–15, who distinguishes between the necessary and sufficient causes for an event, the former being God and the latter including the world.

38. Whitehead, *Process and Reality*, 69–73; John B. Cobb, *A Christian Natural Theology: Based on the Thought of Alfred North Whitehead* (London: Lutterworth, 1966), 151–8.

39. Hartshorne, *Creative Synthesis and Philosophic Method*, 58ff., 68; cf. *The Divine Relativity*, 70ff.

40. Hartshorne, *Creative Synthesis and Philosophic Method*, 59.

41. See David R. Griffin, 'Schubert Ogden's Christology' in D. Brown, R. James and G. Reeves (eds), *Process Theology and Christian Thought* (Indianapolis, IN: Bobbs-Merrill, 1971), 347–61; *A Process Christology* (Philadelphia, PA: Westminster Press, 1973), 143–6.

42. Whitehead, *Process and Reality*, 524. But *how* the 'weaving of God's physical feelings upon his primordial concepts' happens is not clear: see Paul S. Fiddes, *The Creative Suffering of God* (Oxford: Clarendon Press, 1988), 127–9.

43. Marjorie Suchocki, *God, Christ, Church* (New York: Crossroad, 1989), 217–24.

44. Farmer, *The World and God*, 239.

45. Eleanor Stump, 'Petitionary prayer', *American Philosophical Quarterly* 16 (1979), 381–91.

46. Peter Brook, *The Empty Space* (Harmondsworth: Penguin Books, 1972); cited in Timothy Gorringe, *God's Theatre* (London: SCM Press, 1991), 77–82.

47. Brook, *The Empty Space*, 138.

48. So W. H. Vanstone, *Love's Endeavour, Love's Expense* (London: Darton, Longman & Todd, 1977), 77.

49. A. N. Whitehead, *Adventures of Ideas* (London: Cambridge University Press, 1933, repr. 1939), 356, 380–1.

50. See Richard Swinburne, *The Christian God*, 131–4; Keith Ward, *Religion and Creation* (Oxford: Clarendon Press, 1996), 275–7.

51. Whitehead, *Process and Reality*, 27–39, 163–6, 373–5.

52. Lewis S. Ford, *The Lure of God: A Biblical Background for Process Theism* (Philadelphia, PA: Fortress Press, 1978), 82–5; Hartshorne, *The Divine Relativity*, 134–8.

53. Psalms 19:1–4; 29:5–6; 96:12–13; 98:7–9; 104:26.

54. Polkinghorne, *Belief in God in an Age of Science*, 62–4; also, Arthur Peacocke, 'God's Interaction with the World' in R. J. Russell, N. Murphy and A. R. Peacocke (eds), *Chaos and Complexity: Scientific Perspectives on Divine Action* (Vatican City State: Vatican Observatory/ Berkeley: Center for Theology and Natural Sciences, 1995), 263–4, 272–5, 285–7.

5

The Vulnerable God
and the Problem of Suffering

Is a Theodicy Possible?

Some while ago I was talking to a young woman who was suffering from a continual illness that sapped her strength, and which showed no sign of remission after some eight years. We spoke about her spiritual journey in this situation, and she said strikingly, 'I have come to a tacit agreement with God that we just don't talk about this any longer.' She had come to realise that in her case at least there was going to be no intervention, no miraculous cure, and the way she was coping with this was to treat the subject as unmentionable, as if God might be embarrassed by its being raised. So, 'we just don't talk about it'. But we *do* need to talk *to* God and *about* God concerning suffering; suppression is unhealthy, and any burying of resentments and protest will only break out in destructive forms later on. The Christian pastor will want to help the sufferer to express how she feels. When sufferers are driven into silence and brooding, the pastor will want to help them to re-establish communication with others and with God.

The moment of acute suffering, such as the loss of a child in an accident or the sudden death of a partner in middle life, is not of course the time for the pastor to offer theological arguments about the problem of suffering. But I suggest that the way pastors act and react in this situation *will* be guided by the image of God that they hold. Even more profoundly, it will be influenced by what they believe can become possible through participation, or deeper participation, in the triune God. Sometimes these beliefs may even guide the words they speak when they are asked a direct question like 'why has God done this to me?' So developing a theological approach to suffering is a critical part of pastoral theology.

How shall we think and speak responsibly about God in the face of suffering in our world – the pain of individuals, the ethnic cleansing of a Bosnia or a Kosovo, the genocide of a Rwanda or a Holocaust? I want to state immediately that no argument finally convinces. We cannot rationalise God, or fully explain suffering and evil. There cannot be a totally satisfactory theodicy, in the literal sense of the word, which is an intellectual 'justification of God'. We can no longer embark on Milton's kind of grand project, to 'justify the ways of God to men'.[1] But I believe that we can at least work *towards* a theodicy with the more modest aim of thinking of God and suffering together. I am thus using the word 'theodicy' in the softer sense of thinking consistently about God and suffering *in one perspective*. It is possible then to move by responsible argument to the edge of a great gap which we finally have to leap by faith; theodicy can enable us to identify where the abyss is, and even the direction in which we need to leap.

Basic to any understanding of the problem of suffering is, I suggest, the idea of the suffering of *God*, or the self-emptying (*kenosis*) of God. In recent years it has seemed to many theologians and ordinary Christians that an essential element in any theodicy is the belief that God suffers with creation.[2] It seems to fit particularly well with a move away from an interventionist or coercive picture of God's activity, to the picture we were considering in the last chapter – that is, one in which God acts with loving persuasion on the inside of nature, luring creation from within towards a fullness of life. Centuries of traditional belief about the impassibility of God have been overturned in our age, whether by theologians or devotional writers. I believe that this revolution has been right and necessary. Yet, I want to place a warning sign early on. Much talk about the suffering of God is merely sentimental, even romantic, and does not face the real problems it raises.

For example, those who write about the suffering of God often repeat the moving story of the hanged boy in a Nazi concentration camp.[3] One day the SS guards hanged two Jewish men and a young boy in front of the whole camp. The men died quickly, but the child being lighter did not. The Jewish writer Elie Wiesel who witnessed the scene and survived the camp tells how, as the boy hung in agony, he heard a man asking 'Where is God now?' and he heard a voice within him answer, 'Here he is, hanging on this gallows.'[4] It is hard to talk about such a story; merely discussing it seems to diminish it and the participants. But we have to observe that this story has been retold many times as an illustration of the truth that God is present, suffering with us. This, for instance, is the way that Moltmann uses the story in his book *The Crucified God*; because God was identified with the suffering of the crucified Jesus, says Moltmann, he is also with all who suffer on the crosses of our world.[5] Elie Wiesel himself, however, drew a different conclusion; this experience had, he says 'murdered my God and my soul and turned my dreams to dust'.[6] For him, God was truly hung – that is, dead, not involved in the world any longer.

So as soon as we dare to speak of a suffering God, the theologian is faced with some hard questions. Is the belief that God suffers with the world really a theodicy, or is it a despairing view of God who is just as much of a victim of evil as we are?[7] If we approve Moltmann's interpretation, we shall need to think about how a suffering God might not be a helpless God, but victorious over evil *through* weakness. There can be no theodicy without an end to evil.

Theodicy and Divine Suffering

What light, then, is cast on the problem of evil by affirming that God suffers with humanity? How does it help us practically in our experience of suffering to say that God suffers too? Here we may consider four kinds of theodicy, all of which, I suggest, are strengthened immeasurably by a belief in the suffering of God.

A theodicy of consolation

A first kind of theodicy aims at consolation, and is sometimes called a 'practical' theodicy. No attempt is made to *explain* the existence of evil, or to *excuse* the goodness of the Creator, or to *justify* the mountain of human misery represented by the names of Auschwitz or Babi Yar, Hiroshima or Rwanda. Instead, it is simply being claimed that it is consoling to those who suffer to know that God is with them, that suffering has not cut them off from God. People who are healthy and prosperous often abandon those who suffer, through sheer embarrassment, through a feeling of not being able to cope, through fear that associating with the sufferer will bring similar disaster, or because the suffering of another brings too painfully to mind the fragility of life and one's own vulnerability. 'My friends and companions stand aloof from my affliction', laments the psalm-writer (Ps. 38:11 *NRSV*). In this situation, it is affirmed, God does not abandon the victims. It can readily be seen that this theodicy is strengthened by the affirmation that the God who is with them also suffers alongside them, and so understands their situation from within.

This is really less of a rational argument than a picture of God that has psychological effect upon the sufferer. No attempt is being made to argue that the suffering of God somehow accounts for human misery. But believing that God suffers in God's own self and so understands their predicament at first hand may in the end be more convincing to sufferers than any formal theodicy can be. So Moltmann remarks that 'the Shema of Israel and the Lord's

prayer were prayed in Auschwitz', and that 'there would be no
"theology after Auschwitz" . . . if there had been no "theology in
Auschwitz" '.[8]

The Book of Job fits into this kind of practical theodicy. It does
not as yet hint at the idea that God suffers in God's own self, but
the only answer it offers to the problem of suffering is that of
consolation: God is still with Job. In his sufferings, Job has not been
deserted. What satisfies Job in the end is not that he has solved the
mystery of suffering, but simply that he has met God. In his solilo-
quies Job demands that God should break the divine silence and
come into court as the just judge, to hear the supposed case against
his servant. Job is confident that if only he can appear before God,
he will be acquitted of the charge voiced by his 'friends', that he
must have sinned grievously; since Job shares with his friends a
rigid view of retribution, he assumes that this acquittal will mean
that God will be obliged to put an end to his suffering. But when
God does appear to him, he repents of trying to force God into a
corner; it is enough simply to know that God is with him, that
God has not abandoned him. So he exclaims:

'I had heard of you by the hearing of the ear,
   but now my eye sees you . . .'
           (Job 42:5–6 NRSV)

This is not yet a theodicy of a suffering God, but it is the foundation
for one. It affirms that God is present with Job, and it leaves open
the possibility of saying that this divine presence takes the mode of
suffering, that God is present in the deepest sense of sharing Job's
pain. When someone says to us, 'Why has God done this to me?'
the only possible reply at that time may fail as an answer, but still
be a response: 'God is suffering this with you.'

A theodicy of story

There is, second, a more modern version of the 'practical approach to theodicy', that we might call the theodicy of story. Again there is no attempt to produce a rational argument about the problem of evil and suffering, but instead an appeal is simply made to the power of stories of others who have suffered, which can help us to find some meaning in the story of our own lives and our own suffering.

Much of human suffering appears meaningless. It is not heroic, not part of a great crusade, not the death of a martyr giving herself for a glorious cause. Suffering just befalls us, and because we cannot see the sense of it we are driven into silence. We are numbed by suffering, paralysed in our will and our emotions. We have to say that most of those who died in the Holocaust died like this – not as martyrs, not knowing why they died. We may, then, be helped to cope with suffering and find some hope in the midst of it, if we place alongside our story some greater story, a story of suffering which *does* have meaning. Dorothee Sölle puts it this way in her book on suffering:

> Those who suffer in vain and without respect depend on
> those who suffer in accord with justice. If there were no
> one who said, 'I die, but I shall live' then there would be
> no hope for those who suffer mute and devoid of hoping.[9]

This is why we like to go to the theatre and watch the tragedies of Shakespeare; they give us a story in which we can find ourselves, by which we can interpret our lives. Our suffering appears meaningless, perplexing and even absurd, but in the moment of death Mark Antony and Lear affirm love and Hamlet affirms loyalty even in the face of the mess they have made of their lives, fallible heroes as they are.

We find in the Gospel passion narrative that Jesus himself depends on a story like this. In the midst of his agony, he recalls the little story of the righteous sufferer in Psalm 22, and out of his silence he speaks the words from that story: 'My God, why have you forsaken me?' It is a cry of protest (and I shall have more to write about protest shortly), but even in that cry he is beginning to relate his experience of death to God. In turn, the story of the cross of Jesus itself becomes a paradigm that we can place alongside our suffering, to see what meaning emerges.

For the death of Jesus, experienced in the moment of its happening as apparently senseless and useless, 'acquires a meaning'[10] with the resurrection of Jesus from the dead, so that we can perceive by faith in this event nothing less than *the story of God*: 'God was in Christ, reconciling the world to himself.' Beyond all human stories we find that the suffering of God in the cross of Jesus has a purpose and a plot, and from this climactic point we can also read the story of God's suffering in the world before and after the cross. In this story God has an aim in view, to transform human life by the power of sacrificial love, and to bring resurrection life out of the worst kind of death. Telling the story of the suffering of God might then help us to find a path *through* our suffering, to enable us to use suffering in a way that will enhance life and overcome evil. We can choose to make our sufferings serve the sufferings of God, or as one New Testament text puts it, to 'complete what is lacking in Christ's afflictions' (Col. 1:24).

The story of the suffering of God which reaches its greatest height and depth in the cross of Jesus may then help to give words to those who are struck dumb by suffering, may help them to start speaking about what they are feeling and enduring, even if at first they simply cry in protest at the unfairness of it all. Those who are their pastors must not react in shock at the accusations and bitterness that flow out; at least they have come out of silence and dark brooding, to speak to God and to others. So it is that the Jewish poet Paul Celan breaks out of the silence, the 'terrible dumbness' which the Holocaust has inflicted on human language itself. The story of Jesus, as – for Celan – a purely human victim of violence gives him images with which he can talk about the millions of other murdered Jews. It also gives him a metaphor for the God whom he must address, not in quiet trust but in savage irony; he speaks to God as a dead body tumbled among the many other discarded bodies, at Golgotha and at Auschwitz:

> We are near, Lord,
> near and at hand.
>
> Handled already, Lord,
> clawed and clawing as though
> the body of each of us were
> your body, Lord.[11]

As Oliver Davies comments, 'There is a sense that Celan can only speak to God in this way at this time; no other speech is possible.'[12] Yet through this broken, negative appeal to the tragic story of God, Celan finds his voice as a poet, finds it possible to do the impossible thing of *being* a poet after the Holocaust which took the lives of his own parents among so many others.

Telling the story of the suffering of God can help us to find meaning in our stories. But if we follow this line of thought we must be very careful to stress that we are talking about each person's *finding* a meaning for himself or herself, not having some meaning thrust upon him or her. Pastors must not say to someone suffering, 'in the light of the suffering of God, this must be the meaning for your suffering', or even 'God's suffering tells us that he must have some reason for your suffering that we cannot know.' There can be no question of God's having sent suffering to a person to work out some greater *plan*, however mysterious to us. That would be to make God an authority-figure who inflicts suffering and to whose omnipotent choice of meaning we must simply submit. Such a concept does not fit in with the character of a God who suffers. Rather, the power of the story of God's suffering is that we can *make* a meaning for our suffering, rather than uncovering some hidden meaning that already lies behind it. That is, suffering (like the cross of Jesus) can *acquire* a meaning. We can put the story of God's suffering alongside our apparently senseless suffering, and see what meaning *emerges*. We can see how a terrible situation can be redeemed, and good even be brought out of evil.

To succumb to the temptation of *imposing* meaning on the suffering of others is to diminish the horror of their suffering; it is to fail to take their experience seriously. For this reason, some Christian thinkers like Kenneth Surin have avoided any talk of meaning at all, and prefer to speak of letting stories 'interrupt' our lives.[13] We must simply allow the stories of those who have suffered grievously to break into our lives, making us face the truth, whatever the consequence. Elie Wiesel, from his first-hand experience of the death camps, urges:

> Let us tell tales . . . all the rest can wait . . . tales of children so wise and old. Tales of old men mute with fear . . . Tales of immense flames reaching out to the sky, tales of night consuming life and hope and eternity.[14]

So we might also say of the story of God's suffering that we should simply allow it to 'interrupt' our lives, to jerk us out of our complacency or out of our despair; '*all the rest can wait*'. However, if approached with caution, I believe that it is important to talk about the making of meaning, or other meanings will soon flood in to fill up the void. What matters is to work together with God to *make* that meaning, as something new for us and God, rather than simply receiving it in a passive way.

But if meaning is to be made like this, then the story of the divine suffering must itself have meaning, and so we must be able to perceive that through suffering God will overcome evil and put a final end to human pain. We have already reflected on the power of love to fulfil God's purposes,[15] and in the next chapter we shall be exploring one insight into the way that the experience of pain in forgiving love can achieve transformation.

A theodicy of protest

Still in the area of what we might call practical rather than theoretical theodicies, there is the theodicy which is characterised by
protest. Rather than finding an intellectual explanation for suffering,
we engage in protest against it and against those who inflict it. This
can be called a 'theodicy' rather than 'protest atheism', when protest
and resistance arises from the conviction that God too protests
against the dealers in pain, and is on the side of the victims. The
theologians of liberation have been particularly critical of Western
theology in this respect; what is important, they insist, is not to
explain suffering but to change the factors in society that cause it.
Indeed, the development of arguments which justify a God who
has created a world with suffering in it often end up by justifying
suffering itself, making it 'reasonable' and acceptable.

Now, a belief that God suffers can be a strong support to this
kind of theodicy. If God suffers then God too, as Leonardo Boff
points out, is to be numbered among the victims and not among
the torturers, murderers and oppressors.[16] Belief in a suffering God
forbids us to structure any theological argument where God directly
causes suffering, even (as popular piety sometimes says) for 'reasons
which he knows best'. It even forbids the scholastic refinement of
God's being the primary cause of suffering within secondary causes
in the world. The concept of a suffering God cuts away the ground
from beneath an atheism of protest, because protest atheism envisages God as a cruel tyrant who manipulates people and moves
them around like pieces on a chessboard – sacrificing a pawn here,
a knight there, for the sake of the strategy of the game. If the cross
of Jesus tells us that God is in pain, then God's power can hardly
be that of the human absolute monarch who shows his supremacy
by avoiding pain; it can only be the power of a love that is made
perfect in weakness.

Sufferers rightly protest against their suffering. God protests with
the protesters because God too suffers. There is a mutuality
between the two experiences: if God suffers then God too protests,

and a God who protests against suffering cannot be the cause of it, or God would be protesting against God. At times, then, when someone says 'Why has God done this to me?' it *may* be appropriate to say 'God hasn't: but God is suffering with you'. At other times, however, a pastor will be sensitive to know that the first phrase cannot be heard, and only the second is necessary.

A belief in the suffering of God thus strengthens three kinds of practical theodicy – those of consolation, story and protest. Moreover, I want to suggest that each of these becomes even *more practical* when we affirm that the suffering God exists in triune relationships, and that God has made room for us to participate in these movements of relationship. As with our discussion of God's action in the world in the previous chapter, the invitation to participate more deeply in the interweaving patterns of the divine life is at the heart of the matter. If, to begin with, we take the theodicy of consolation, the affirmation that God is 'alongside us' in our suffering may be understood as our involvement in currents of relational love that are already there before us. God is present because we are present in God. We are not simply accompanied by another individual who suffers, but embraced by movements of suffering love – like those, for instance, between a father who has lost a beloved son and a son who has been forsaken and abandoned by all whom he loves. There are a myriad aspects of loss and alienation contained in these currents of relationship which surround us, permeated by the movement of a Spirit of hope, opening up the future in the midst of pain. Prayers of the church community for those who suffer can help to draw them deeper into an awareness of this communion of consolation (2 Cor. 1:3–5).

This means that the story of God's suffering is not only a narrative to be told, 'once upon a time', but an ongoing story in which we can participate. The experience of those who have suffered and found meaning in their suffering, and above all the experience of Christ, is held eternally within the patterns of the divine dance, bringing richness to the life of God and shaping the pattern of our own life. Hearing the story told, or seeing it displayed in broken bread and outpoured wine, can thus draw us into a deeper awareness of the divine fellowship and the 'communion of saints', so that we can live in a larger story.

A significant theme in that story is protest against suffering, whether suffering comes directly from human oppressors, or from aspects of a broken and distorted cosmos that can wreak terrible damage on sentient life. I have already suggested that our participation in a God who makes space for created beings within the relations of the divine life alerts us to ways in which we can co-operate with God in making spaces of freedom in the world.[17] The black theologian, James Cone, suggests that the image of God is most clearly seen in the struggle for liberation: 'The image is human nature in rebellion against the structures of oppression. It is humanity involved in the liberation struggle against the forces of inhumanity.'[18] Sharing in God's own protest against suffering should mean that our protest is turned outwards from the temptation of nursing an internal grudge to actions in the world that can begin to create space for others. Participating in the protest which is voiced in the triune communion makes our protest creative rather than cynical.

For God to protest against something that occupies God's own creation might, however, be thought to need some explanation. Moreover, the need for explanation becomes more acute if we want to go on and say that God *allows* suffering to befall us without actually inflicting it. If we wish to grapple with these issues we must move on from practical theodicies to theodicy in the sense of a reasonable argument. The most adequate – or the least inadequate – theodicy is, I believe, the argument from free will; the theodicy of a suffering God is, I suggest, necessary to strengthen the free-will defence of the existence of evil. It is needed to make this defence credible.

A Theodicy of Free Will

The argument of a free-will theodicy runs something like this:

> *God's purpose in creating the universe was to make a world of personal beings with whom God could enter into a relationship. For them to be real persons they must have been created free to do either good or evil; the only other option was a world of puppets and robots. If doing the right is to have any meaning, there must be the alternative of doing the wrong (evil), with all the suffering this entails.*

There have been attempts by philosophers to show that this argument is neither a logical nor necessary one,[19] and equally strident defences of it.[20] In brief, it seems to me that it is difficult to maintain that God cannot create some world somewhere which contains free beings for whom *only* good is an option. The point, however, is whether God could have created *our particular world* of personal beings like that, and it appears that the personal characteristics and values we actually have require a choice between good and evil for us to be truly free. The moral question, then, is whether it was *worth* God's creating this particular world (and so, probably, this particular universe), and this is a question to which we shall have to return. I am not concerned now to give an elaborate account of what has often been called the 'free-will defence' of the occurrence of evil and suffering in the world, but to show that belief in a suffering God strengthens the argument. Indeed, it seems essential for it to have any explanatory power at all.

The central point is that, if created persons are to be given a genuine freedom to make real choices, then God must limit God's own self. In allowing persons to grow and develop as adults, God must give them room to be themselves. God must take a risk on them, so that they can 'come of age'.[21] This is the experience of all parents with teenage children, and similarly God must refrain from intervening in a way that would interfere with the growth in responsibility of God's human daughters and sons. God cannot control but only guide, acting to persuade but not coerce. Thus God must limit God's own self in the act of creation. The technical term usually applied to this is *kenosis* – the self-emptying of God. Freedom for the world therefore means self-limitation for God. While this has been increasingly accepted by Christian theologians today,[22] not all draw the conclusion that this must also mean suffering for God. We can, however, see that this is bound to be true in at least three ways.

In the first place, the giving of freedom to created beings means that God is going to suffer some *frustration* of the divine purposes and desires. As I have argued, although God will fulfil the project of creation, there is room in this triumph for frustrations and reversals in the intermediate scope of things, and for some loss in the long term. This is a painful experience for God that the Old Testament prophets describe in colourful language. As Hosea, Jeremiah and Ezekiel paint the picture, for example, God is like a husband suffering the agony of having an unfaithful wife. His purpose was that she should love him and enjoy marital intimacy with him, but this has been frustrated as she has gone her own way and taken other lovers.[23] Hosea, Isaiah and Jeremiah also present God as speaking in the hurt tones of a disappointed parent – a mother, perhaps:

> When Israel was a child I loved him
>   and out of Egypt I called my son.
> The more I called them
>   the more they went from me . . .
> Yet it was I who taught Ephraim to walk,
>   I took them up in my arms,
>   but they did not know that I healed them . . .
>
> (Hosea 11:1–3)[24]

There is the pain of God's frustrated purpose in every line of this poem. A loving relationship allows the risk of freedom to the other, and therefore involves pain. In our time, who can doubt that God's aims for human life were savagely frustrated by Auschwitz, and that God suffered all the pain of a parent who sees her children hurting not only themselves but inflicting terrible damage on others?

A second reason why self-limitation means suffering is because this humility of God allows something strange and alien to emerge from God's own creation. There is something that God has not planned, something to be confronted, something therefore to be suffered. Since the thought of the early church fathers – Athanasius in the East and Augustine in the West – evil has been named 'non-being'.[25] This is to assert that it has no real existence of its own. It is not an eternal reality alongside God who is Very Being, but is simply a turning away from the Good; it is a free turning from Something (God) to Nothing. Like the darkness which comes when the light is turned out, it is what happens when God's creation slips away from the divine aims. To call evil 'non-being' or 'the nothingness' (*nihil*) does not therefore deny that it is powerful, or pretend that it is some kind of illusion. It simply has no power of its own: it is a parasite, drawing its energy from preying on what is good, as a fungus draws its vitality from the life-giving trunk of a tree. Evil always perverts what is good, and twists what is full of life into what is destructive. Augustine added that since evil is 'nothing' it cannot, strictly, have a cause; while human freedom gives evil opportunity, it does not *create* evil any more than God does.[26]

All this is familiar enough territory in presenting the classical free-will defence. But the implication not always drawn is that if evil issues from creation through the free will of the creatures, it is something that *happens* to God; it *befalls* God. The Creator does not make it, and so has to endure it.[27] God takes the risk in creation that non-being will emerge, and suffers its impact. Augustine did not draw this conclusion, but then he was working within a framework of thought (influenced by Neoplatonism) in which God was assumed to be invulnerable.

We shall see shortly that this view of non-being as 'befalling' God is in fact formative for our understanding of God's vulnerability.

A word, however, is needed about the way the word 'evil' is being related to suffering in this discussion. The distinction is usually made between 'moral evil' – resulting from free human choices – and 'natural evil' – damage caused to humankind and sentient animals by events in the order of nature. While much suffering is inflicted by the immoral acts of human beings against each other, a great deal of suffering among both humankind and sentient animals is caused by what may be called natural evil, whether it be a large-scale flood or a microscopic virus. It may be said that it is a mistake to call the latter kind of damage 'evil' at all, since a certain amount of such suffering seems to be needed for the development of more complex forms of life out of simple organisms. Evolution requires there to be victims; it is just 'nature', it may be concluded, not natural evil. But the world in which we actually live contains a wholly excessive amount of suffering caused by non-human means as well as human agents, far beyond what seems to be needed for growth and education.

All of life, not simply human life, is thus marked by 'non-being' and associated suffering. All the blame for this cannot be laid at the door of human beings, though they have certainly made things worse – or failed to make them better. Earthquakes, for instance, have a far more disastrous effect when cities, for the sake of human greed, are built over fault lines. Floods are more destructive when those who own the wealth in society force the poor to live on coastal flood plains. The AIDS virus may have leapt the species gap to humans through the hunting of monkeys for food. But I suggest that there is still such a thing as 'natural evil' in the sense that the *whole* of creation has drifted (or 'fallen') from the divine purpose, and does not function exactly as God intends. The capacity of nature at every level to respond to the creative lure of God may offer a clue to this defectiveness;[28] failure in response may mean that there is something corresponding to a 'free-will defection' at every level of nature, though not in the same way as human moral evil. Anyway, in one way or another, the *kenosis* of God will result in suffering 'befalling' God through the non-being which pervades creation.

This leads to a third reason why the self-limitation of God entails the suffering of God. The emergence of non-being raises the matter of divine *responsibility* for a broken world. While the free-will defence argues that the emergence is not absolutely necessary in our world, it is very likely to develop through free choices when human beings are immature and the divine glory is veiled. As Reinhold Niebuhr puts it, sin is 'inevitable, but not in such a way as to fit into the category of natural necessity'.[29] It is, we might say, practically inevitable but not logically necessary. In short, God took a *considerable* risk in granting radical freedom to creation. While not directly creating evil and suffering, God puts the world into this situation. In the Hebraic-Christian tradition, God is not then absolved from final responsibility in choosing to make a free world at all, and in taking such a severe risk.

To assign ultimate responsibility to God is thus a healthy religious feeling which ought not to be suppressed. The Old Testament prophet Jeremiah did not shrink from being angry with God,[30] and the modern Jewish poet Paul Celan finds his voice in the silence following the Holocaust by blaming God. The irony of a well-known aphorism addressed to God catches the point: 'It's no wonder that you have so few friends when you treat those you have so badly.' The feeling of protest is complex; we have seen that God shares our protest against suffering, and has not inflicted it in any particular circumstances; yet as the Creator who has chosen to make free worlds, in some sense God is the target of protest.[31] Now, if God is finally, though not immediately, responsible for the way that the world is, a God of love will *take* responsibility. As a faithful covenant-partner, God must share the suffering that flows from the risk. Only the fact that God suffers can make credible the tracing of suffering to the free will of creation.

If God exposes a creation to the high risk of slipping into non-being, God too will face the outcome of the risk. But then this is what the Christian story of the cross of Jesus tells us. God does take responsibility; in the cross 'God was in Christ, reconciling the world to himself'. As the theologian Karl Barth puts it,

> The fact that from all eternity God resolved to take to Himself and bear man's rejection is a prior justification of God in respect of the risk to which he resolved to expose man by creation – and in respect of the far greater risk to which he committed him by his permitting of the fall. We must insist upon man's responsibility . . . But much more must we insist upon the responsibility which God himself shouldered.[32]

These convolutions of careful thought about 'prior justification' are given a different tone by Sydney Carter in a song called 'It was on a Friday morning' in which the singer is complaining about all that is wrong in the world. The refrain runs:

> It's God they ought to crucify instead of you and me
> I said to the carpenter, a-hanging on the tree . . .[33]

and the hearer says to herself: God *was* crucified. 'It's God they ought to crucify . . .' This sentiment becomes unhealthy, of course, when it is used to excuse human beings from their responsibility for their own free choices. It is also misleading if it is taken to mean that God directly causes suffering. Evil emerges from the creation as something strange to God, something that befalls God, as I have been arguing. The Creator does not design evil and suffering as a great educational opportunity. The epitome of *that* kind of thinking is found in the work of the psychologist Carl Jung, when he argues that the cross of Jesus was the way in which God cleared his guilty conscience for the wrongs he had done to human beings. Jung particularly had the story of Job in mind, judging that God owed something to Job for the way he had used him.[34] Nevertheless, the urge to trace responsibility for suffering to God in an ultimate manner is an essential part of a free-will theodicy, and it can only be met by the conviction that God also suffers.

I have been arguing so far that a belief in the suffering of God is essential to any theodicy, to any attempt to understand the love and justice of God in a world of pain. The belief that God suffers strengthens a theodicy of consolation, a theodicy of story, a theodicy of protest and most important, a free-will theodicy. They are only made credible by the assertion that God in God's own self shares the risk of creation and suffers with a broken world. But the question remains as to what kind of 'suffering' we are talking about, and whether the concept of divine suffering we have is adequate for theodicy. In what sense is God vulnerable?

The Vulnerability of God

Why were the fathers of the early church, and the schoolmen of the Middle Ages, so opposed to saying that God suffers? Often, today, religious writers express astonishment that their ancestors in the faith could have been so blind to what seems obvious to us. But as soon as we go beyond a merely sentimental belief in the suffering of God, we can see why they thought divine passibility to be so dangerous a heresy. When we think at all carefully about it, suffering must involve *being changed* by something or someone outside oneself. It means being affected, conditioned and even afflicted by another. A suffering God must be 'vulnerable' in the strict sense of 'open to being wounded'.

Aquinas speaks on behalf of the Christian philosophy of the Middle Ages when he binds together suffering with change, and therefore excludes God from both. To suffer, he argues, even to have the feeling of suffering, one must have the potential to receive some impact from outside oneself. One must have the potential to receive an injury, whether it is the physical blow from a fist or the emotional blow of feeling rejected. But as pure actuality (*actus purus*), he maintains, God cannot have any potentials that God does not eternally realise.[35] From a reflection on the nature of love, a modern Christian thinker (Daniel Day Williams) equally links together suffering and change, though by contrast with Aquinas he ascribes both to God: 'There can be no love without suffering.

[For] suffering in the widest sense means the capacity to be acted upon, to be changed, moved, transformed by the action of, or in relation to another.'[36]

To love is to be in relationship where what the loved one does alters one's own experience. Love is the sharing of experience and mutuality of feeling. Sympathy must be taken in its literal sense of 'suffering with'; as Charles Hartshorne puts it, simply to be aware of the suffering of another will mean a 'participation in that suffering'.[37] Hartshorne points out that involvement in the feeling of others means to be influenced and so altered by them: 'to love is to rejoice with the joys and sorrow with the sorrows of others. Thus it is to be *influenced* by those who are loved.'[38] Moreover, the person who loves is also changed by taking the other into account as he or she is, gladly receiving what he or she has to contribute to the relationship.

Thus, if we say that God loves, it seems we must say that God not only suffers but is changed by those whom God loves. Several theological strategies have, however, been developed to avoid this conclusion. First, some Christian thinkers have exempted God from change by developing a concept of love which does not involve any suffering at all. If suffering implies being changed, then love cannot suffer. Aquinas, notably, maintained that love could be a purely 'intellectual appetite'. In this, he stood in a long tradition of regarding love as the merciful willing and doing of good to another, without involving the sharing of feelings in literal 'compassion'.[39] Augustine, for example, had already asserted that when we talk about the 'pity' of God we are not saying that God grieves, or has 'the wretched heart of a fellow-sufferer'; his pity really means 'the goodness of his help'.[40]

But if we bring this view of love as beneficence or goodwill up against the test of practical theodicies, we find it sadly lacking. It scarcely seems, for instance, to meet the demands of a theodicy of consolation. If love does not involve sympathetic suffering then we can only say that God is present with us in the manner of doing good to us. But in our society there is a reaction against people dismissed as 'do-gooders', precisely because they do charitable deeds without any real empathy with those whom they are helping.

There is moreover a problem with the affirmation that 'God loves the whole world' if that love is understood simply as 'doing good'. God's equal love for all does not seem to issue at present in all equally being-done-good-to. This problem has been sharpened by contemporary Black theology which observes that it is not just random individuals who have lost out on being-done-good-to, but a whole ethnic group. Black theologians are less concerned with the problem of suffering as a theoretical problem, than with the unjust distribution of suffering so heavily among black people. James Cone, for example, concludes that the question 'Is God a white racist?' is an urgent one, and is only made absurd by the fact that God suffers with black people.[41] Thus a theodicy of protest can hardly be supported by the restricting of love to doing good. Divine love must include a sympathy that suffers with the oppressed, and so protests against suffering with them. You protest *against* a do-gooder God; you protest *with* a suffering God.

A more modern version of love without suffering, and so without change, runs like this: unlike us, God knows that evil will finally be overcome, and so cannot share the anguish that we feel. Charles Creel, for example, gives the example of a mother who (supposedly) does not share emotionally in the distress of a child when she knows that the child is being frightened by a danger which is only imaginary. So, Creel argues, 'we cannot rule out the possibility that God knows something about our destiny that renders it inappropriate for him to be disturbed by our suffering in this life.'[42] In reply, we may return to our earlier consideration of God's knowledge of the future;[43] if there can be unknown elements for God in a future whose outline God is nevertheless certain about, this gives plenty of room for genuine empathy with us. But we may also notice that Creel's argument depends quite largely upon whether we are convinced by his illustration of what *human* love is like. The picture of the unperturbed mother misses, I suggest, the nature of sympathetic suffering as a necessary form of *communication* between persons. Whatever superior knowledge she has, for the mother to be truly in contact with her child it is quite appropriate for her to share the child's feelings of distress. When we apply this analogy to God, we can see again how theodicies of consolation and protest require this intimate communication through suffering; indeed, communication with the triune God means nothing less than participation in God.

Human love always involves some suffering in sympathy with others, and this in turn means being changed by others; it seems meaningless to apply the analogy of love to God unless we are willing to affirm these characteristics in God also. A merely beneficent love does not, in any case, meet the test of theodicy. Nor does a second strategy which has been adopted to avoid the conclusion that suffering involves change of some kind. That is, it may be suggested that God feels the *emotion* of suffering without this having any effect upon God's very *being*. For example, H. P. Owen proposes that God's experience of suffering takes the form of an imaginative response.[44] That is, God *imagines* what it would be like to experience the suffering that the world actually *knows*. It is hard, however, to see the difference for God's being between suffering in imagination and experiencing the actual mental pain which Owen denies to divinity. As Aquinas points out, any emotion is a movement from one state to another, and so involves change.[45] Further, if we apply the tests of the theodicies of consolation and protest, it is unlikely that sufferers will feel comforted by the notion that God is just imagining what it might be like to be them, while knowing nothing of it. This is God the romantic dreamer, not the sympathiser. Nor does such a speculative involvement in suffering support the theodicy of divine protest.

A third strategy for moderating the vulnerability of God accepts much of the linkage between love, suffering and change. But it is suggested that while God is indeed affected by human suffering, God still remains in total control of these effects upon the divine life. As Marcel Sarot puts it 'God may be influenced by the world, as long as this influence is subject to his will', so that 'God remains master of his own passibility'.[46] When Sarot writes of the divine suffering being subject to the will of God, he does not mean suffering which flows from a once-for-all willing self-limitation of God in creation which God cannot go back on. He means a continuous 'self-restraint' of God, which God 'can end . . . whenever he wants to, and this means that he can interfere whenever he wants'.[47] Sarot thus affirms a 'qualified form of passibility' in God in which God is passible but never passive, since God has command over any impact from outside.

A similar theory of 'semi-passibility' is the view that God, while not subject to change by the world, voluntarily changes the divine self in response to the suffering in the world.[48] Only God, as it were, makes God suffer in order to be able to sympathise with us and comfort us. In the words of Moltmann, God's suffering is 'the supreme work of God on God himself'.[49] Sarot takes a step further into passibility by proposing that God is indeed affected by created reality, but still keeps a kind of filter on the nature of this influence. He argues that this has some analogy with human experience, since he believes that in personal relations both partners have the 'ability to choose freely how they will act and react towards the other . . .' Personal relations are thus completely different from 'causal relations', which he defines as those 'in which "passion" is caused within the being by something outside the being overpowering its will'.[50] This means that the subject experiencing such an impact upon herself is 'nothing more than a passive victim'. Thus, Sarot argues, personal and causal relations in human life exclude each other, and only personal relations are suitable for God.

But if God thus has 'complete control' over the reception of influence from outside, this makes God's experience of suffering very different indeed from ours. Central to suffering as we know it is a feeling of helplessness. To some extent we do fall victim to what we cannot regulate. A God who simply devised all God's own suffering, or had total command over how much should impinge upon the divine life, would have a suffering difficult for us to recognise. This in turn would undermine any theodicy of story, as this kind of story of divine suffering could not provide an occasion for us to make meaning out of our own suffering. Moreover, such an image of God comes perilously close to divine masochism, and so to condoning and glorifying human suffering as an offering required in imitation of God. It is feminist theologians who have particularly drawn attention to this latter danger, perhaps because it is often women who have been expected to sacrifice themselves in imitation of a God for whom sacrifice seems to be the last word.[51] This picture of a God who produces and controls divine suffering therefore also fails to meet the requirements of a theodicy of protest. Indeed, protest is undermined in several ways. It is not only difficult to conceive of God protesting against a suffering under divine management; if God can end self-restraint 'whenever he wants to', the urgent moral question arises as to why God does not 'interfere' in an Auschwitz or Rwanda and so whether God can be conceived as in protest against them.

We notice that Sarot's exclusion of any causal effect of the world on God, in which things 'happen' to God, depends upon his definition of causation as something which always simply 'over-whelms' the recipient. God clearly cannot be overwhelmed by the world, or simply be its 'passive victim'. But this absolute distinction of 'causal' from 'personal' relations in human life seems to polarise our own relations quite artificially; our experience of human relations, even the most healthy ones, may contain a mixture of influences, some of which we can control, and others which we cannot. What 'happens' to us, as opposed to what we allow to happen, does not necessarily overwhelm us. So we can conceive of suffering 'befalling' God without thereby making God a total victim of the universe.

Indeed, the 'free-will' theodicy seems to require, as I have argued, precisely this kind of contingent happening in the divine life. When evil is defined as non-being, it emerges from God's creation through creaturely free will, as something strange to God. We may say that it 'befalls' God. The suffering which it causes in the world also 'happens' to God in the sense that it causes God to suffer through the deep sympathy of love. It is not sufficient to say that God changes God, that God adapts the divine being to the actions of our world. In the humble act of creation, God freely chooses to be open to the hurt that will befall, with its unpredictability. God willingly faces something unknown and alien on the journey of love for the sake of creation.

Christian thinkers in the past who denied that God can be changed or affected by the world, and therefore cannot suffer in the divine nature, certainly did not intend to create an image of a remote, dictatorial and non-compassionate God. That would be a travesty of their faith in the biblical God of love, with whom they knew themselves to be intimately related, as is witnessed for instance in the intensely personal *Confessions* of Augustine. Nor is it fair to suggest that their thought had been completely taken over by the philosophy of their time, although the presuppositions of Platonism, Neoplatonism and Aristotle did undoubtedly exercise some influence on the early church fathers and the medieval theologians. In particular, it seemed to them that the only possible cause and ground for the world in which we live – a world of change, flux and decay – must be a world which is an unmoving and unchanging perfection. In terms of Platonic philosophy, the necessary basis for a world of Becoming (our world, always in development and becoming something else) must be a world of pure Being. Such Being was therefore defined as the opposite of Becoming. It followed that God as Absolute Being must be absolutely unaffected and unconditioned by the world of Becoming. In the technical terms of philosophical theology, God was Necessary Being and the world was contingent; that is, the world was vulnerable to what happened to it and so was in a process of change, while God was not.

At the same time, however, the earlier theologians had their own inner dynamic of faith which came from the reading of Scripture and the worship life of the church. This led them to offer resistance to the inroads of philosophy, and most notably in their persisting with the scandal that God had become a human being in the incarnation, and could be said to suffer in the human nature of Christ (though not in God's own nature). We must always remember that they were not concerned so much to present a philosophical picture of God, as to do justice to their beliefs 'from within' that God was the sole origin of all reality and had created *ex nihilo*; that God was unchanging in moral character, unlike the arbitrary and cruel gods of Greek and Roman mythology; and that God was unique and not to be made one of a class with anything or anyone else. God was the ultimate Mystery who could only be addressed by 'saying' and 'unsaying', by using negative language as well as positive images. The word of the prophet Isaiah, 'Truly you are a God who hides himself' (Isa. 45:15 *NRSV*), was taken immensely seriously. The human mind could only begin to grasp the mystery and wonder of God if it remembered that in many aspects God was 'not like' the world; God was, for instance, imperishable, incomparable, inexpressible. It was perhaps inevitable that in the context of the thought of their time, the only way that all these intentions could be expressed was by using the negative attributes of impassibility and immutability. So there was a tendency for the God of Scripture to take on the colours of philosophy; God's unchanging faithfulness became an unchanging immobility, and God's moral otherness from the world (holiness) became a philosophical otherness that effectively excluded God from the turmoil of history.

Language is not merely descriptive but performative. In the setting of this present study, we may say that it is also pastoral. One can easily see that in a certain cultural context the denial that God changes or suffers could have the performative function of enabling participation in the triune God; to be fair to our ancestors in the faith, this might now be taken as shorthand for saying that God does not suffer and change *in exactly the same way as we do*.[52] In our time, however, we must also be sensitive to the performative nature of language. In an age after the Holocaust, and in an age of sensitivity to the problem of human suffering in general, I suggest that to state 'God does not suffer' will inhibit participation in God. To say this to a suffering person will send all the wrong signals in the way that it did not do in the past, when it could be used but then modified and checked by being placed in a context of other language about God's caring presence with us and intimate relation to us. I have been suggesting that in our time the requirements of theodicy, both practical and theoretical, will only be met by talking about the suffering of God in a way that has a recognisable connection with our own suffering.

We could not speak in this way, of course, unless we had good theological reason for thinking that the fundamental concerns of earlier theologians were also being met – for God's faithfulness, sovereignty, uniqueness and mystery. In the previous chapter on God's action in the world, I suggested that God can still be God when divine potentials have not yet been actualised, as long as God freely chooses to be limited by the act of creating. This addresses the objection of Aquinas that suffering means having unrealised potentials: God remains God in suffering, if this too is freely chosen. Such a choice should be understood as a once-for-all resolve of God in creation, binding God's self to a way of acting ever afterwards. The notion that God *chooses* to suffer may, however, be open to the same allegation of divine masochism as the notion that God *controls* divine suffering. We might end up once more by glorifying suffering as a way of life, and forcing self-sacrifice on others. It is essential then to place this choice in the context of suffering 'happening' to God, or 'befalling' God, which is consistent with the free-will theodicy in which evil emerges from creation as something strange to God.

By saying that God chooses to suffer, we thus mean that God chooses to be in situations where suffering can be inflicted upon God, with all its unpredictability. God opens God's own self to the world in vulnerability. God sets out on the road where hurts will happen, as Jesus set his face to go to Jerusalem, the place where prophets had often been killed. God opts to be in the way of being injured. We too can, for the sake of love, choose a path where it is likely that suffering will be imposed upon us, even though we have no desire for suffering in itself.

This leads us to another aspect of God's 'choosing' to suffer, by analogy with a healthy way in which we can 'choose' suffering.

When suffering does befall us, we can choose it for ourselves in the sense of taking hold of it, accepting it as our own and doing something with it. We do not resentfully regard it as something alien to us, but boldly take possession of it; as Dorothee Sölle perceives, 'what I take belongs to me in a differing sense from what I only bear'.[53] This is what the philosopher Kierkegaard called 'active suffering', which is 'the highest action in inwardness'.[54] So sufferers from cancer, or from a cruel bereavement or from debilitating unemployment may take hold of their suffering, and speak of 'my tumour', 'my loss', 'my poverty'. We have not chosen these things in the first place, but when they happen, we can choose them as our own. This acceptance does not mean passivity, mere resignation or Stoic toleration. Once we have accepted ownership of our suffering, we are free over it, to see where it can be ended, and where causes of suffering can be dealt with. Moreover, when someone accepts as her own the suffering inflicted upon her, the oppressor loses all power over her, all ability to dominate. When a sufferer has lost her fear of suffering as something strange to her being, she has the strength to resist and rebel against the tyrant. This is the strong mood of protest, not the weak mood of petulance and self-pity.

Active suffering like this would even 'de-throne' God, if God were the one inflicting suffering on us. But in fact God is not the oppressor. God too protests against suffering, and does so by choosing suffering as God's own. When suffering happens to God, then God lays ownership to it. The triune God who thus chooses to be open to suffering is not subjected to it; it has no power to overwhelm God since it has been freely grasped as belonging within the interweaving relations of love.

God Suffers as Trinity

The strongest challenge to these ideas about the suffering of God comes not from philosophy, but from the very same place that seems to call out for God to suffer. That is, it may be said that pastoral experience itself demands that there be at least some dimension of God that is invulnerable. The most impressive statement of this case in recent times appears in the book by Frances Young titled *Face to Face: A Narrative Essay in the Theology of Suffering*. The challenge is not so much in the argument as in the life-experience that underlies the book, for it is a story of bringing up a severely brain-damaged child, Arthur. The author honestly and painfully recounts the way that this experience brought her into religious doubt and perplexity, even while she was functioning successfully as a professor of theology and a Methodist minister. From this experience she has come to the conclusion that we can only cope with suffering if there is some aspect of God which is immune from suffering – which is detached, impassible, invulnerable.

Frances Young marks the turning point in her spiritual journey towards a new sense of the reality of God as being a moment when she heard a voice within her saying, 'It makes no difference to me whether you believe in me or not.'[55] She interprets this inner voice as meaning that in one dimension of God's being, it makes no difference whether the world rejects God's love and suffers the inevitable consequences of its refusal of God's purposes. God is untouched. However at the same time she does want to say that there is another aspect of God's being which is immersed in the world, and which does suffer. The image of the sea sums up for her this duality in God, unsuffering and suffering, detached and involved:

> That *passionless* deep beyond all sense
> That rages with *passion*, deep and intense,
> Mercy in wrath's serenity.[56]

This duality in God is, as we have already seen, expressed in process theology with the distinction between the 'primordial' and 'consequent' natures of God. For Frances Young, this double-sidedness is illuminated by the 'mystery of the Trinity'. She appeals with approval to the view of the Greek fathers of the church, who taught that God 'is impassible in his "essence" but became "passible" in Christ, who as both divine and human, "unsufferingly suffered" '.[57] In the second person of the Trinity God draws near and feels our pain, suffering in the human nature of Christ but not in his divine nature; in God's eternal being, God is immune. Perhaps the strongest alternative to a radical binding together of suffering and change in God is to make this distinction between the immanent being of God and divine activity in the world (or the *oikonomia* of God). The argument runs that in God's actions and energies towards us, and especially in God's encounter with us in the incarnate Son, God is vulnerable and passionate; in God's inner being, however, there is invulnerability and passionlessness.

Frances Young thus speaks of the 'dark side' of God which is both beyond knowledge and 'beyond passion'. We notice that here she follows the scholastic tradition of regarding impassibility as a form of *lack* of knowledge of God; it attempts to respect the mystery of God by not positively ascribing passion to God's inner being. In this way of thinking, to speak of God as 'impassible' is not to be mistaken for a description or a characteristic of God; it is, rather, refusing to shrink God within the bounds of human knowledge and language, such as our perception of suffering. God cannot be put in the class of those who suffer. Yet the term 'impassible', I suggest, cannot be evacuated of all descriptiveness, as is shown by Frances Young's own forming of an image of God's essence, as an 'ocean of love that can absorb all the suffering of the world and purge it without being polluted and changed by it'.[58] I have myself been urging the mystery of God, but not through the negative attributes of impassibility and immutability; rather, the mystery of God is in the hidden depths of what we *do* know of God through revelation. That is, it is impossible to turn the triune movements of suffering love into objects that we can observe; we cannot grasp them, but only participate in them. This is the true darkness of God, the hiddenness of God's being.

However, what is so challenging about Frances Young's account is not her appeal to a negative theology, but her own story. She has found a reason for this picture of God in her own experience that it helps to find people who seem to be detached from your own suffering, in the sense that they are not overwhelmed by it. They stand firm like granite, or they are as stable as the depths of the ocean. This has been her experience as someone who has both received care and offered care to others. Faced by the sorrow of some friends whose baby had been stillborn, she relates how she found that she could be of no help while she was 're-living her own pain', her own 'protest at the suffering of the world'. She discerned that she was 'too involved', and it was only when the self-involvement was purged that she could become of any use to her friends. So God, she concludes, 'is not emotionally involved [with us] in a self-concerned way'; he assures us that 'It makes no difference to me . . .' while at the same time in Christ 'he subjected himself to personal involvement in pain and anguish'.[59]

I feel a sense of presumption in daring to comment upon such a testimony, born out of so many years of self-giving love. However, I want to suggest two responses to this witness, while thoroughly respecting its integrity. We can surely sympathise with the desire for a God whose existence is not threatened by suffering, as ours is, and this can be considered from the two perspectives of origin and destination. First, as the only 'unoriginate' reality, God owes nothing to anyone or anything for the origin of God's existence. Traditionally, this has been called the 'aseity' of God; God exists from no one except from God's own self (*a se*). However, we need not equate self-existence with self-sufficiency. A God who exists from nothing but God's self can still choose to be fulfilled in the manner of that existence through fellowship with created beings, to be open to being affected and changed by them. If we dare to comment on the comforting words that Frances Young heard, I suggest that while we might indeed hear God saying 'It makes no difference *to my reality or my love* whether you believe in me or not', it would still make a difference to God in the richness of divine life, its bliss and satisfaction.

Second, Frances Young is rightly pointing out that a sufferer will not be helped if the one caring for her is overwhelmed by his or her own feelings of distress, or becomes erratic in response because of these emotions. But, with regard to God as the supreme carer, this need is not best met by keeping back an area of God's life that is invulnerable, an untouched reservoir of bliss. I do not think that we can speak of a God who shares the risk and responsibility of creation – an essential part of theodicy – if God puts part of the divine being into a zone of immunity. The need for a carer who is not herself broken by suffering is surely best met by showing how a suffering God will finally bring about the end of evil, and will achieve the fulfilment of divine purposes. I sketched an outline of this goal of God's love in the previous chapter, and I intend to return to it in thinking about the power of forgiveness. *Human* carers need to learn some non-involvement, as they will otherwise be overwhelmed and incapacitated by the pain of others; but it is the power of *God's* love to absorb suffering, to be changed and yet not degraded by it.

Yet there still remains a challenge in what Professor Young proposes, and this is further to do with the doctrine of the Trinity. If we do distinguish between an untouchable 'essence' of God and a divine Son who suffers with us in a human nature, we are also of course distinguishing between a Son who suffers and a Father who does not; the Holy Spirit is usually also exempted from suffering. The persons are, in this, distinct. If we affirm, by contrast, that God suffers with the world in the whole of the divine life, without reservations, then we seem to have a lost a way of 'telling the difference' between the divine persons. Moreover, the particular role of the Son in incarnation may appear to have been undermined. This was one reason, in fact, why the fathers of the early church maintained the impassibility of God. They were faced by opponents – 'monarchians' – who claimed the suffering of God the Father in order to deny any particular existence of three persons and to affirm one supreme divine subject in three modes of successive activity. God was portrayed as acting first in the mode of Father, then Son and then Spirit. In the memorable words of Tertullian, they 'put the Paraclete to flight and crucified the Father'.[60] Much of the rejection of patripassianism (the suffering of the Father) was simply an attempt to deal with this monarchian heresy.

In response to this ancient anxiety, we may now be able to see that it is *only* by speaking about the suffering of the Father and the Spirit as well as the Son that we can discern the true nature of relationships within God. Within the divine perichoresis, all three persons suffer, but in different ways according to the distinction of relations. Putting it more dynamically, we may say that there is suffering within all three movements of relationship. The holding of created beings within the pattern of movement of the divine life will mean suffering for God, in so far as this embraces the refusal of love by the creation. There is the pain of rejection, and the pain of empathy with the results of this rejection in the lives of creatures. The difference between modes of suffering in God is brought to light when we ask *where* this creaturely 'no' to God can be located. Here the theologian Hans Urs von Balthasar offers a crucial insight: since 'there is nothing outside God', there is only one place where our 'no' *can* be spoken, and that is – ironically – within the glad response of the Son to the Father. Just as our 'yes' to God leans upon the movement of thanksgiving and obedience that is already there in God, like the relation of a son to a father, so we speak our pain-giving 'no' in the same space. Our 'no' is a kind of 'twisted knot' within the current of love of the Son's response.[61] So von Balthasar says: 'The creature's No, its wanting to be autonomous without acknowledging its origin, must be located within the Son's all-embracing Yes to the Father, in the Spirit.'[62]

The drama of human life can only take place within the greater drama of the divine life. Our dance of relationships can only happen within the patterns of the larger Dance. 'The creature's No resounds at the "place" of distinction within the Godhead.'[63] That is, von Balthasar affirms, there is already an infinite distance between the Son and the Father through the pouring forth of the Son from the being of the Father. What greater distance could there be than a giving away of Godness by the Father in begetting the Son? While the Father does not cease to be God, such an infinite self-gift amounts to a gulf of 'Godlessness'. This distance has room for all the distances between persons that there are within the world of finitude, including those of sin.[64] In von Balthasar's vision of God, the role of the third divine Person, the Holy Spirit, is that 'he maintains the infinite difference between [Father and Son], seals it and bridges it'. We must surely add, however, that the Spirit continually 'opens up' the divine space into new dimensions of love. Later we shall see how all this comes to a focus and to a resolution in the cross of Jesus; but this is only possible because the story of creation from the beginning is God's carrying a creaturely 'no' within the divine life.

We may take von Balthasar's picture of 'distances' in God and interpret them in terms of spaces within and between the interweaving currents of relational love in God. They are spaces in a dance of perichoresis. When God enters with deep empathy into the experience of the human movers and dancers, God will identify with the lives of human sons and daughters in different ways according to modes of being as Father, Son and Spirit. First, in the movement of fatherhood, God has the particular kind of suffering that comes when a pouring-forth of selfhood is met not by a glad 'yes' of receptivity but a 'no', when 'the recklessness with which the Father gives away himself encounters a freedom that, instead of responding in kind to this magnanimity, turns it into a calculating, cautious, self-preservation'.[65] Yet such is the fatherly love of God that God will suffer *with* a human son or daughter, just as a human parent enters with sympathy into the pain of a child, feeling the hurt they have caused themselves. Second, in the filial movement of love, God will be identified with human sons and daughters, so that there will be the suffering of bearing the 'no' of created beings within the 'yes' to the Father, of taking all those movements of resistance up into the pattern of the dance. While in fatherhood God suffers *with* created persons, in the movement of sonship (and daughterhood) God will suffer *as* the human son or daughter does, damaged as they are by their own refusal of love or by the sins of others. Third, as Spirit, God is wanting to open up the space within the dance in creative ways; this involves the particular suffering that comes from the 'no' which is one of self-preservation, or the hoarding of space. God as Spirit will then suffer *in* creatures, suffering at the depths of human life and nature, crying out in the birth-pains of creation (Rom. 8:22–3).

God is always entering with sympathy into the life of creatures. It is not only in the particular point in history of the cross of Jesus Christ that God makes a journey into human life and is changed by the experience. But the Christian story is that in Christ God goes furthest on the journey into the creation for which space has been made in the fellowship of the divine life. God has never been drawn further into flesh than here, giving God's own self without any reserve at all. In the cross the divine Father suffers *with* this human Son (Jesus) more fully than with any other; the divine Son suffers more completely *as* this human son than as any other sons and daughters. In the mystery of incarnation, the movements of divine and human sonship towards the Father can be identified as exactly the same. Since nothing is held back in this sameness, it is not just functional, but a matter of divine being. Because of this identification, we too can lean our sufferings upon those of the Son, so that God suffers not only 'with' but 'as' and 'in' us in the interweaving relationship of the divine dance.

The Limit of Theodicy

But I must end with the same word of caution with which I began this chapter. There can be no complete theodicy. There can be no completely rational defence of God in a world of pain. If there could be, it would justify suffering on the one hand, and destroy faith on the other. In argument we may talk of the risk that God took in creation, and the way God shares that risk in suffering. Rational theodicy is thus not divorced from practical theodicy: they are both concerned with a suffering that 'befalls' God or 'happens' to God. But it still remains open to decide whether God's creative decision that set all this off is worth the cost.

In Dostoyevsky's novel *The Brothers Karamazov*, one of the characters (Ivan) asks the question: 'Is the whole universe worth the tears of one tortured child?'[66] He has in mind the story of a rich landowner who threw a peasant child to his hunting dogs to be torn apart because the child had thrown a stone and broken a dog's leg. Is it all worth the tears of one child, let alone the millions in Auschwitz? Even if God suffers, is it worth it? Ivan thinks not, and says that he is 'returning his entrance ticket to God with the polite observation that the price is too steep'.

The belief that God suffers with us may help us to say that the making of persons is worth all the tears. But only faith can answer the question, 'is it worth it?' after all reasonable arguments have fallen silent.

NOTES

1. John Milton, *Paradise Lost*, Book 1, 26.
2. For reviews of recent writing on the passibility of God, see Paul S. Fiddes, *The Creative Suffering of God* (Oxford: Clarendon Press, 1988), 16–45; Marcel Sarot, *God, Passibility and Corporeality* (Kampen: Kok Pharos, 1992), 1–30; Thomas Weinandy, *Does God Suffer?* (Edinburgh: T. & T. Clark, 2000), 1–25.
3. The camp was Buna, although Moltmann, *The Crucified God*, trans. R. A. Wilson and J. Bowden (London: SCM Press, 1974), 273–4, wrongly identifies it as Auschwitz.
4. Elie Wiesel, *Night*, trans. S. Rodway (Harmondsworth: Penguin Books, 1981), 76–7.
5. Moltmann, *The Crucified God*, 277–8, cf. 252, 255.
6. Wiesel, *Night*, 45. For accounts taking Wiesel's conclusion seriously, see K. Surin, *Theology and the Problem of Evil* (Oxford: Blackwell, 1986), 116–32; Marcel Sarot, 'Auschwitz, Morality and the Suffering of God', *Modern Theology* 7/2 (1991), 137–9.
7. This is the view of Herbert McCabe, *God Matters* (London: Chapman, 1987), 92; also John K. Roth, 'A Theodicy of Protest' in Stephen T. Davis (ed.), *Encountering Evil: Live Options in Theodicy* (Edinburgh: T. & T. Clark, 1981), 121.
8. Moltmann, *The Crucified God*, 278.

9. Dorothee Sölle, *Suffering*, trans. E. Kalin (London: Darton, Longman & Todd, 1975), 150.

10. Hans Küng, *On Being a Christian*, trans. E. Quinn (London: Collins, 1977), 433.

11. *Poems of Paul Celan*, trans. Michael Hamburger (London: Anvil Press Poetry, 1995), 'Tenebrae', 115. I am indebted to Oliver Davies for drawing my attention to this poem.

12. Oliver Davies, 'Soundings: Towards a Theological Poetics of Silence' in Oliver Davies and Denys Turner (eds), *Silence and the Word: Negative Theology and Incarnation* (forthcoming, 2001).

13. Surin, *Theology and the Problem of Evil*, 162.

14. Elie Wiesel, 'Art and Culture after the Holocaust' in Eva Fleischner (ed.), *Auschwitz, Beginning of a New Era?: Reflections on the Holocaust* (New York: Ktav Publications, 1977), 403.

15. See above, Ch. 4.

16. Leonardo Boff, *Passion of Christ, Passion of the World*, trans. R. Barr (Maryknoll, NY: Orbis, 1987), 111–12.

17. See Ch. 3 above, pp. 97–8.

18. James Cone, *A Black Theology of Liberation*, revised edn (Maryknoll, NY: Orbis, 1986), 94.

19. E.g. J. L. Mackie, *The Miracle of Theism* (Oxford: Clarendon Press, 1982), 162–76.

20. E.g. Alvin Plantinga, *The Nature of Necessity* (New York: Oxford University Press, 1974), 173–89.

21. 'The world come of age' is a phrase made famous by Dietrich Bonhoeffer, *Letters and Papers from Prison*, enlarged edn, ed. Eberhard Bethge, trans. R. Fuller and others (London: SCM Press, 1971), 326–7, 360–1; cf. 279–80.

22. See e.g. Maurice Wiles, *God's Action in the World* (London: SCM Press, 1986), 21–5; Keith Ward, *Religion and Creation* (Oxford: Clarendon Press, 1996), 167–71, 258–61.

23. E.g. Hosea 2:1–10; Jeremiah 12:7–11; Ezekiel 16:1–34.

24. Also Isaiah 1:2; Jeremiah 31:20.

25. Athanasius, *De Incarnatione* 4–5; Augustine, *De Civitate Dei* 11.9; *Enchiridion* 4.13–14; cf. Origen, *De Principiis* 2.9.2.

26. Augustine, *De Civitate Dei* 12.6–8.

27. For extensive argument of this point, see Fiddes, *The Creative Suffering of God*, 210–29.

28. See Ch. 4 above, pp. 144–7.

29. Reinhold Niebuhr, *The Nature and Destiny of Man*, Vol. 1 (London: Nisbet, 1943), 279, cf. 257.

30. Jeremiah 15:18.

31. This is stressed by Roth, 'A Theodicy of Protest', 14–18.

32. Barth, *Church Dogmatics*, II/2, 165. At this point, I am drawing on material from my book, *The Creative Suffering of God*, 34–6.

33. Song, 'Friday Morning' in *Sydney Carter in the Present Tense*, Book 2 (London: Galliard, 1960).

34. Carl G. Jung, *Answer to Job*, trans. R. F. C. Hull (London: Routledge & Kegan Paul, 1954), 91–2.

35. Aquinas, *Summa Theologiae* 1a.2.3; 3.1; 9.2. Thomas Weinandy also bases his argument for divine immutability and impassibility on God's being pure act: *Does God Suffer?*, 123–7.

36. Daniel Day Williams, *The Spirit and the Forms of Love* (Welwyn: James Nisbet, 1968), 117.

37. Charles Hartshorne, *A Natural Theology for Our Time* (La Salle, IL; Open Court, 1967), 105.

38. Ibid., 75.

39. Aquinas, *Summa Theologiae* 1a.20.1; 1a.21.3; *Summa Contra Gentiles* 1.91.16. Cf. Anselm, *Proslogion* 8.

40. Augustine, *Contra Adversarium Legis et Prophetarum* 1.40.

41. James Cone, *God of the Oppressed* (London: SPCK, 1967), 163, 166–7.

42. Richard E. Creel, *Divine Impassibility* (Cambridge: Cambridge University Press, 1986), 117.

43. See Ch. 4, pp. 142–4.

44. H. P. Owen, *Concepts of Deity* (London: Macmillan, 1971), 23–4.

45. Thus, Weinandy, *Does God Suffer?*, 168–70, proposes that grief and sorrow can be ascribed to God in the sense that he is 'intensely concerned' about human suffering, but not as any kind of emotion. Even if this is coherent, I suggest it similarly fails the test of practical theodicies.

46. Sarot, *God, Passibility and Corporeality*, 66, 41.

47. Ibid., 55.

48. E.g. Jung Young Lee, *God Suffers For Us: A Systematic Enquiry into a Doctrine of Divine Passibility* (The Hague: Martinus Nijhoff, 1974), 41.

49. Jürgen Moltmann, *The Trinity and the Kingdom of God*, trans. M. Kohl (London: SCM Press, 1981), 99.

50. Sarot, *God, Passibility and Corporeality*, 34.

51. See Sölle, *Suffering*, 25–7; Mary Grey, *Redeeming the Dream: Feminism, Redemption and the Christian Tradition* (London: SPCK, 1989), 13–14, 122–4.

52. E.g. Justin Martyr, *Apologia* 1.20; Tertullian, *Adversus Hermogenem* 12; *Adversus Marcionem* 1.8; Aquinas, *Summa Theologiae* 1a.9.1–2; 1a.20.1.

53. Sölle, *Suffering*, 103.

54. S. Kierkegaard, *Concluding Unscientific Postcript*, trans. D. F. Swenson and W. Lowries (Princeton, NJ: Princeton University Press, 1941), 386–8.

55. Frances Young, *Face to Face: A Narrative Essay in the Theology of Suffering* (Edinburgh: T. & T. Clark, 1990), 81, 248.

56. Ibid., 242. My italics.

57. Ibid., 274.
58. Ibid., 245.
59. Ibid., 239.
60. Tertullian, *Adversus Praxean* 1.
61. Hans Urs von Balthasar, *Theodrama: Theological Dramatic Theory*, Vol. IV, *The Action*, trans. G. Harrison (San Francisco, CA: Ignatius Press, 1994), 330.
62. Ibid., 329.
63. Ibid., 333–4.
64. Ibid., 323–4.
65. Ibid., 328.
66. F. Dostoyevsky, *The Brothers Karamazov*, trans. D. Magarshack (Harmondsworth: Penguin Books, 1982), 287.

6

The God of Love and the Practice of Forgiveness

In 1995 the author Salman Rushdie was interviewed for the *Guardian* newspaper about his then most recent novel, which had just been shortlisted for the Booker Prize.[1] The interviewer naturally took the opportunity to ask him about his experience of having to go into hiding for six years because of the threat on his life arising from the sentence of blasphemy (the *fatwah*) passed on him by Iranian Muslim clerics. It seems that his wife, who was also a novelist, had at first shared his forced seclusion with him, but had left him after five months, subsequently giving several unflattering accounts in the press about their life together. In this interview, Rushdie declared that 'I will not forgive her'. Yet the novel for which he was being interviewed was about love, with the main character (the 'Moor') defining love as a 'flowing together' and 'the dropping of the boundaries of the self'.[2] As we shall see, these images are – perhaps ironically – highly illuminating for the practice of forgiveness.

What then stops someone forgiving? Or what stops someone *accepting* forgiveness? How can the unhappy cycle of lack of forgiveness, both offered and taken, be broken? In this chapter I want to consider insights that the experience of human forgiveness offers into the nature of the triune God of love, and conversely I want to explore the way that participating in God's threefold movements of love can create human forgiveness.

There is something else to consider too. Those who offer pastoral care are dealing all the time with people who need forgiveness, people who crave forgiveness and people who cannot forgive. Christian ministers, in addition, lead prayers of confession in public worship, and some hear confessions privately; all offer absolution or an assurance of God's forgiveness. How can these pastoral acts be in tune with the rhythm of God's forgiving love and communicate this love to those who need to feel it? In seeking to answer these questions we should begin with reflections on the human experience of forgiveness.

The Two-Stage Journey of Forgiveness

I have long been haunted by a phrase about forgiveness, which comes from a fine book written on the theme some sixty years ago by H. R. Mackintosh: 'How true it is that in heart and mind the forgiver must set out on *voyages of anguish*! It is an experience of sacrificial pain, of vicarious suffering.'[3] In this chapter I want to explore this metaphor of forgiveness as a painful journey. Though Mackintosh employs it only in a passing way, it is worth dwelling upon and unpacking.[4] I suggest that when forgiveness is understood as a journey into the experience of another person, a costly voyage of empathy and identification, then we begin to understand the creative power of suffering. The *voyage* of forgiveness has the power that flows from participation. It points to the transforming effect of sharing the experience and feelings of another. Whatever Rushdie says about forgiveness, the character in his novel has a similar perception about love when he finds it to be an event in which 'the boundaries of your self begin to dissolve'.[5]

Forgiveness, writes Mackintosh, is a 'shattering experience' for the one who forgives as well as for the one who is forgiven. This is because forgiveness, unlike a mere pardon, seeks to *win the offender back* into relationship. And reconciliation is a costly process because there are resistances to it in the attitude of the person who has offended; the one who sets out to forgive must aim to remove those blockages and restore the relationship. Forgiveness, then, involves an acceptance which is costly. Forgiveness as an act creating response is bound to be expensive in time and effort, requiring mental and physical anguish. But the suffering it calls for is creative.

If we think carefully about the journey of forgiveness, we notice that travelling this path means that a change takes place in *both* the participants, in the forgiver as much as in the one who is forgiven. For true reconciliation there must be a movement from both sides. Naturally, the offender has to move in sorrow and repentance towards the person he has hurt, but the forgiver also needs to move and experience change within herself, even when she is totally willing to forgive. In human acts of forgiveness this movement is often partly a matter of the one who wants to forgive recognising that she herself has contributed something to the breach. In situations where an established relationship has been broken – in the family, between friends or colleagues – the forgiver may have been the one mainly injured, but in human relationships no one is an entirely 'innocent party'. So the forgiver also needs to be forgiven, and must move in her attitude to accept this. However, there is another kind of 'change' in approach to the other, which belongs to the act of empathy itself. Forestalling our later discussion, we may find this is also appropriate for God who is perfect in relationships, as we are not. Borrowing Mackintosh's phrase, we can say that the forgiver must 'set out on voyages of anguish'; she must make an agonising and costly journey in experience. This journey, we notice, is in two stages.

The first part of the journey of forgiveness is a *voyage of discovery*, an active movement in which awareness is awakened. If the forgiver is aiming to heal a broken relationship, she cannot just forget about the offence done to her. In fact it would be far more comfortable to put the hurtful affair out of mind and to resolve never to meet the offender again. Perhaps separation may be necessary for a while, in order to see things straight and to see the other as he is; she may have demonised the other in bitterness, and a gap is necessary to clear her sight of distortions. But separation cannot last for ever. There is a brokenness in relationship that has to be faced up to if it is going to be healed, and so the forgiver needs to bring the injury done to her back to mind, and has to live again through the pain of it.

Honest and open feelings of anger are not only appropriate here, but in many cases they are necessary for the forgiver to confront the reality of the situation.[6] Suppressing anger, pretending that what happened 'didn't really matter', not only undermines self-respect: concealed emotions will be likely to break out in more violent forms later, as William Blake perceived:

> I was angry with my friend:
> I told my wrath, my wrath did end.
> I was angry with my foe:
> I told it not, my wrath did grow.[7]

But this voyage of discovery must go further, beyond feelings of hurt and anger to the very point of thinking herself into the mind of the offender, feeling with the guilty person, standing in his shoes and making a deep effort to understand why he said or did what he did. Only when the forgiver has made this costly journey of sympathy into the experience of the other can she go to him and say 'I forgive you'.

As soon as she says this, she has brought the offence out into the open, pulling it from the darkness in which it has been festering into clear daylight. Now the offender must embark upon his own voyage of discovery; he has been shaken into awareness of what he has done, and there can be no healing unless it is faced up to and sorrowed over. There is no need for the forgiver to utter words of recrimination; the word of forgiveness itself is a word of searching judgement, reminding them both of the hurt and wrong that lies between them.

The first stage, then, in the voyage of forgiveness is the journey of discovery – both for the person offering forgiveness and for the person seeking it. But then comes the second stage for the forgiver: the journey of endurance. This is a passive mood, submitting to the consequences of acting to awaken the sleeping wrong. The forgiver must absorb the hostility of the other, to bear it and receive it into herself. By offering the word of forgiveness she has taken the first step across the gulf which separates the two who are apart, and so she has exposed herself to attack. She has made herself vulnerable, laying herself open to aggressive reactions. The offender is resentful at having the offence recalled; he fears blame and so wants to justify himself by blaming the other. He is angry with the one who offers forgiveness, saying (or at least feeling), 'How dare you say that you forgive me! What presumption! It's as much your fault as mine.' Unlike the one offering forgiveness, he cannot get beyond the feeling of anger, which is now possessing and driving him. If there is to be reconciliation, the forgiver must not react to justify herself or to accuse the other; she must not argue the case, but rather bear patiently the hostility of the other, drawing out the venom of his anger. She has acted to bring the matter out into the open in the first place; now she must neutralise the hostility by submissively bearing with the other in love.

Through the twofold journey of action and submission, provoking and absorbing, the forgiver is actually discovering how to win the offender back into relationship. Through identification with the feelings of the other, she is learning how to enable the other to accept her forgiveness. The inner 'change' the forgiver undergoes is thus an empathetic entering into the other's life, and her approach to him is shaped by this experience. Forgiveness takes the form of a painful voyage like this because of the nature of the problem to be dealt with; there is a blockage in the offender's attitude to the relationship which makes it hard for him to accept forgiveness. As we shall see, there are several dimensions to the journey of empathy which is at the heart of forgiveness, but one key aspect is its transformative effect upon the other person, empowering him to overcome obstructions that lie in the path towards restoration.

I have stressed, as Mackintosh does in his account, the hostility that blocks forgiveness. This is what a modern psychotherapist would call 'split feelings'; that is, we locate our own 'nasty' feelings in others, and this makes us even more angry with them.[8] But as Paul Tillich reminds us, this is often mixed with a second blockage, that of our anxiety. We cannot believe that we can be acceptable, given what we have done; in Tillich's fine phrase, we need to gain 'the courage to accept that we are accepted'.[9] These feelings of anxiety may sometimes be due to the experience of a dominating parent; especially, they may have their roots in an implacable and demanding father for whom the child was never good enough, and who has now been internalised as a constant critic, whether or not we give this inner voice the Freudian name of the superego.

This fear that we are unacceptable is often directed towards God, created in the image of the Super-Father. The continual ritual of confession may, if we are not careful, simply become a framework for keeping someone in a state of anxiety like this. Confession can be a point of development, but it can also simply be a reinforcement of the harsh feelings that people have towards themselves. Hostility or anxiety may then block the entrance to forgiveness, and usually we have a blend of both surging within us.

There is also however a third blockage to receiving forgiveness, and this is the self-indulgence we are prone to in accusing ourselves. The seeking of forgiveness from another often begins by being driven by a personal need, a need to feel better inside, to reach 'closure', or to be free of forces that threaten to tear us apart. It is healthy enough to begin here, but unless we can truly enter into the life of persons we have offended and be concerned for them, our supposed 'openness' and 'honesty' about ourselves may simply be an infantile self-unburdening for our own sake. We may appear to be openly admitting our fault and seeking reconciliation, but in fact we are hurting the other for the benefit of getting relief ourselves. It is more difficult to ask ourselves, 'How will it affect her if I confess this?' We need to be drawn by the person offering forgiveness along the pain-filled journey of truly sharing her feelings.

As Mackintosh puts it, then, forgiveness is a 'shattering experience' for the one who is forgiven as much as for the one who offers it. It is a humbling and disturbing gift, and it is not at all surprising if it is declined. This is why forgiveness is a voyage of empathy which the forgiver willingly undergoes. The offender will only be enticed and enabled to accept forgiveness if he experiences the forgiver as a certain kind of person, not as a harsh critic or judge of his actions, but someone who has truly drawn alongside him and feels with him. Forgiveness is a creative act, 'calling a fresh situation into being' (Mackintosh).[10]

The Journey of Forgiveness Made by Christ

The experience of forgiveness in human relationships helps us to interpret God's great offer of forgiveness to human beings, creating a new situation universally. When salvation is understood as an act of divine forgiveness like this, it overturns any idea of atonement as a legal transaction or commercial arrangement. In the history of Christian doctrine, forgiveness has unfortunately *not* been usually understood as a journey of experience. It has been interpreted as a legal pardon, or a 'remission' of sin and so has been associated with the so-called Latin model of atonement, in which the justice of God is somehow satisfied in the death of Christ. But the *voyage* of forgiveness points to atonement as having the power that flows from participation. It points to the transforming effect of sharing the experience and feelings of another. It alerts us to creative suffering.

The profound experience of forgiveness has too often been reduced in Christian doctrine and preaching to the idea of a mere legal pardon. In different ways this appears in the rather transactional accounts of atonement in Anselm and Calvin, the former stressing remission from debt and the latter remission from punishment.[11]

Popular evangelistic preaching has often, moreover, depicted a prisoner languishing in a condemned cell on the eve of execution, and then suddenly receiving a free pardon from the Monarch or President. All the prisoner needs to do, it is urged, is to accept what is offered. But this legal illustration loses the personal nature of forgiveness. The picture of a pardoned criminal fails to communicate the painful relational experience which lies at the heart of forgiving and being forgiven. On its own, the issue of a notice of pardon cannot touch a person deeply: in life a prisoner can accept a pardon and go free, hating the authorities who gave it and the judge who sentenced him – or perhaps laughing at them. At its best, such remission might be called 'mercy', a public act of deciding not to inflict a penalty. In social polity it may be useful, with Jeffrie Murphy and Jean Hampton,[12] to distinguish this from 'forgiveness', which is an attitude of heart and mind, and which can in fact accompany the imposing of just punishments.[13]

When transferred to theology, at its worse such public mercy may degenerate into the view of the poet Heine as he lay dying that God would 'of course' forgive him, since 'it's his business'. But forgiveness is no business. It is a 'shattering experience' for the one who forgives as well as for the one who is forgiven. This is because forgiveness, unlike a mere pardon, seeks to win the offender back into relationship. And it *is* hard to accept forgiveness, whether from God or other people; as we have seen, there is so much in human emotions and reactions that resists it.

For Christian faith the life and death of Christ focuses God's journey of forgiveness. While God has always been voyaging into the world to share human life, nowhere is God seen as penetrating more deeply into creation than here. Later in the chapter we shall consider more exactly *how* the costly forgiveness offered by Christ is actually identical with the redemptive suffering of the triune God. For the moment, we can at least see clearly *revealed* in the ministry of Jesus the twofold journey of discovery and endurance made by God's own self.

In the first place there is the voyage of discovery, as Christ the true Son enters into the experience of human sons and daughters who have offended against God and life itself, and have propelled themselves into a situation of estrangement. This pattern of identification is characteristic of the whole ministry of Jesus. He offered God's forgiveness of sins and acceptance into the coming Kingdom of God. Even if we had no examples of Jesus actually speaking about forgiveness,[14] the offer would be unmistakable in the way he acted. Without waiting for them to repent first, he welcomes into his company those whom the respectable religious establishment reckoned as grievous sinners or definite outcasts from God's Kingdom.

Then in death Christ identifies himself with human beings at the lowest point of their existence, immersed into utter forsakenness. Though himself living in tune with the Father's mind, he consents to participate in the alienation which is the lot of a humanity which has lost communion with God. The various words of Christ from the cross which the Evangelists place in their narratives interpret the event: the plea 'Father, forgive them' does not conflict with the awful cry 'My God, why have you forsaken me?'[15] but brings out its meaning, since forgiveness is nothing less than a voyage into the dark void of another's guilty life.

So the Apostle Paul affirms that Christ shares our death, so that we might rise to new life with him (Rom. 6:1–11). When we analyse the act of forgiveness we find the *power* of this participation; the forgiver enters the experience of the guilty, identifying with their predicament, in order to create change and draw them into reconciliation. Paul Tillich rightly sees this journey of empathy as lying at the heart of atonement, when he says: 'The suffering of God, *universally and in the Christ*, is the power which overcomes creaturely self-destruction by participation and transformation.'[16]

At the same time the cross brings all humankind into the journey of awareness, into discovery of its condition, bringing clearly out into the open the vicious nature of human sin, and the end to which it leads. This is what it looks like for people to sin against their neighbours, to crucify love. Further, this is what death looks like when humankind is estranged from the source of its life in God. As the Forgiver plumbs the depths of the offenders' lives, he provokes the guilty into noticing the wrongs they would prefer to hide. The initiative he takes in identifying with them calls for a response; empathy becomes judgement.

So we come to the second stage of the journey of forgiveness as I have described it – the voyage of endurance. This is no less characteristic of the ministry and the death of Jesus. Through participating in the lives of sinners, Jesus evokes resentment and antagonism from the religious authorities. It seems that Jesus also shared table fellowship with scribes and Pharisees, but on the whole it appears that they refused to accept a forgiveness pronounced by one who believed in sharing the banquet table of the Kingdom with those who were still outcasts and ritually unclean. A simmering hostility comes to a head with the trial and crucifixion, where we see Jesus drawing out the venom of hatred from priests, soldiers and the crowd. Having provoked antagonism, he absorbs it – for the most part in patient silence: 'Consider him who endured from sinners such hostility against himself' (Heb. 12:3). The fact that the common people consented to the death, despite the frequent popularity of Jesus with the crowds, shows how vulnerable someone becomes when he identifies with others. Jesus developed no demagogic mystique to protect himself, as the temptation narratives in the Gospels illustrate;[17] thus, by his openness he was the more in danger of rejection.

The life and death of Jesus thus reveals and focuses the twofold journey of creative suffering in forgiveness that always characterises God's engagement with the world. It is the testimony of Christian people that the path of Jesus, our own acts of giving and receiving forgiveness, and God's being as triune love interact in one event of participation. But before developing this doctrine of God, we need to explore further the nature of the human journey of forgiveness, and especially the role of empathy within it.

The Human Journey of Discovery

We have seen that the empathy exercised by one who embarks on the journey of forgiveness has the power to remove blockages in the attitude of the offender; but empathy in forgiveness has other dimensions as well.

First, forgiveness is a voyage of memory, a calling to mind. As a path of discovery, forgiveness is not forgetting. Memory is subversive, calling the present situation into question. This theme has been taken up recently by a number of feminist theologians, including Mary Grey.[18] As a woman theologian, she feels keenly that women have always been expected to be the forgivers in family and society, and that this has been taken to mean a passive function, a self-denying victim role. But there can never be a restoring of relations, she believes, unless women take an active role of self-affirmation. Central to this movement for reconciliation is memory; this is 'dangerous memory' (in the phrase of Johannes-Baptist Metz),[19] a memory which brings judgement and awakens us to the truth, when it is memory of the suffering, exclusion, oppression and degradation of women. We may add that where there has been an abusive relationship of any kind, including the sexual abuse suffered by children within the family, it is essential for any healing that this should be brought to mind and named.

Memory is not only a function of the individual, but may be held corporately by communities. Those engaged in movements for reconciliation in Northern Ireland, for example, are aware that it is only through reviving the memory of the whole people, rather than the selective memory of sectarian groups, that the truth can be faced and forgiveness achieved. In a collection of essays called *Reconciling Memories*, one contributor, Joe Harris, writes on 'reconciliation as remembrance'. He tells how his own experience of growing up in the gospel hall, living in Sandy Row in Belfast, attending Protestant Orange parades, was challenged by a growing sense of a wider memory. Even as a child, standing on the Orange field, he felt a 'disturbance', a sense of large gaps in the story he was being told; later he reflected that 'what I had resisted all those years was a recognition of the intertwining of all the history of this land'.[20]

Now, empathy is cultivated through this sharing of stories. Empathy, as Donald Shriver puts it in his study of *Forgiveness in Politics*, means 'the appropriating of each others' memories'.[21] Cultural expectations, he observes, often inhibit this process of empathy, pointing out that forgiveness following the Second World War has been easier to achieve between America and Germany, who share a culture of repentance, than between America and Japan. An opportunity for the latter two peoples to listen to each other's stories was, he judges, missed at the time of the fiftieth anniversary of the bombing of Pearl Harbor. This event, he feels, rendered a disservice 'in the excuse it gave to the American memory to cover over the complexities and mutual culpabilities of the Pacific War', including the bombing of Hiroshima.

There is some hope that a more effective sharing of memories, and so the achieving of a deeper empathy, has been happening in the 'Truth and Reconciliation' process in South Africa since 1996. Attempting to unify a nation following the dismantling of apartheid, the Government was faced with the apparently stark alternatives of either imposing widespread penalties on those who had committed human rights violations from a political objective, or granting a blanket amnesty automatically. Neither course seemed likely to promote social harmony. With daring imagination it chose a third way: violators would be eligible for amnesty if they appeared before the commission, made a full disclosure of the truth of what they had done, explained from their point of view why they had acted as they had, and listened to the testimony of those whom they had abused and injured. We notice that the legal structure itself was one of amnesty, or public 'mercy': to fulfil legal requirements no remorse or repentance was necessary, only the telling of the full truth (and the establishing of political motivation). But the aim was to create a space for the developing of what people really needed; as expressed by the Commission Chairperson, Archbishop Desmond Tutu, they were 'engaging in what should be a corporate nationwide process of healing through contrition, confession and forgiveness'.[22] According to the National Reconciliation Act (1995), victims were to be given 'civil dignity' in being able to relate their own accounts of their suffering. The sharing of stories between abusers and abused would be, according to Tutu, 'something that is ultimately deeply spiritual, deeply personal'. One of the very first hearings offered hope that this could happen, when a woman whose husband had been imprisoned, mutilated and then killed by the state security forces spoke movingly about the importance of facing the truth and understanding the other person:

> As a mother I always had to play the roles of both parents, but I'll be really glad if I can know what happened so that my children can get an explanation from me, so that I can say it is so and so, and so and so. This will probably make me understand. I do not know the reason for their cruelty, but I just want to know and my family will also be happy to know who really cut short the life of my husband. Not to say that when they are old I'm just teaching them to retaliate or to be revengeful, it's just to know who's done this and who changed our lives so drastically.[23]

If 'memory, suffused by moral judgement' (Shriver)[24] is an essential aspect of the journey of forgiveness, a second is the discovery of the mixed feelings that exist within ourselves. We contain a complex mass of good and bad feelings about other people, a mixture of love and hate, an emotional condition perhaps never better expressed than in the inner reflections of characters in D. H. Lawrence's novels. In her book about forgiveness, Mary Ann Coate traces this inner state to the experience of childhood, and following Melanie Klein she focuses on the child's experience of the mother, rather than that of the father as Freud had done.[25] According to this kind of psychoanalytic diagnosis, the child first experiences the mother as someone wholly good, the provider, the satisfier of bodily needs, the generous breast flowing with milk. But then mother disappoints; the food does not arrive on time, or the mother's attention is not devoted wholly to the child but turns elsewhere. The infant reacts with frustration, fear and rage. It seems she has *two* mothers, the good and the bad. She has feelings of love and hate, and she tries to cope with this by projecting them on to the other. She regards the *mother* as the one who both hates and loves.

There can be no growth in maturity, stresses Mary Coate, unless we stop denying these mixed feelings and face up to them. A beginning of responsibility is to recognise the damage we do to others through our feelings, even to our mothers.[26] According to Klein, we make 'reparation' – for the harm we have done – through empathetic identification with others, through 'putting ourselves in the place of other people' and a 'genuine sympathy with other people and . . . the ability to understand them, as they are and as they feel'.[27] So we play the roles both at once, of the good child and the good parent, and reverse the previous situation of resentment. As we do this, we also see others – starting with our mother – as 'whole' rather than as two good and bad 'part-objects', and so come to see ourselves whole as well; we discover that our good and bad feelings coexist, but that love is always stronger than hate.[28] Coate adds to Klein that there can be no forgiveness unless we come to this point of maturity, recognising our darker side and believing that it can be integrated with the light.[29] This need for growth in understanding and love surely applies both to those who offer and those who receive forgiveness.

If the journey of empathy deals with the *past* by sharing memories, and with the *present* by making us aware of the light and dark within us, it also has a part to play in creating the *future*. The political philosopher Hannah Arendt finds a place for forgiveness within public life and politics, affirming that only forgiveness can deal with the apparently irreversible actions of the past and so open up the future. Such forgiveness, discerns Arendt, springs from the power of love (in private relations) or respect (in public relations) to be 'fully receptive to who somebody is, to the point of always being willing to forgive him whatever he may have done',[30] and she credits Jesus with discovering the role of forgiveness in social life. We can only restore a sense of community by recognising the people who have hurt us as fellow human beings; as Shriver puts it, one 'mild move' on the road to reconciliation is the forgiveness that restores at least a 'civil relationship' or a willingness to coexist with 'some level of mutual affirmation'.[31] Now, it is the empathy in forgiveness that enables us to give others this respect (Arendt) or affirmation (Shriver). On the journey of discovery we put ourselves in the place of other persons, give them value in themselves, and so envisage a future community in which they play a part with us. To achieve this imaginative vision, we need at the most basic level to know who the person is who has damaged us, and this is why the Truth and Reconciliation Commission in South Africa has placed such weight on the disclosure of the truth. Archbishop Tutu's insight that 'to be able to forgive one needs to know whom one is forgiving, and why'[32] has been amply confirmed by the hearings. 'Would you like to know the identity of these persons?' one member of a panel asked a young woman whose father had been brutally murdered. She replied:

> I would love to know who killed my father, so would my brother. I suppose, because it's very hard for us right now to do anything, because in order for us to forget, and forgive – we do want to forgive – but I mean . . . we don't know who to forgive, we don't know the killers, you know. And I must say we're all upset about this . . .[33]

To sum up, the empathy which is exercised on the journey of forgiveness enables us to listen to each others' stories as if they were our own, to give respect to the other, and to discover the power of love in our divided selves. All this contributes to the power of empathy in removing the blockages in another person to the reception of forgiveness.

The Transforming Power of the Divine Journey

In the last chapter I urged that if God suffers then God also endures change. There can of course be no alteration in God's character of goodness and faithfulness, or we would no longer be talking about 'God' at all, but we can conceive of God's taking new experience into the divine life for the sake of creation. Now, this is exactly what the voyage of forgiveness expresses. In our experience of human forgiveness we know that through the twofold journey of awakening awareness and absorbing hostility, a forgiver is *learning how best to win* an offender to himself or herself. The fruit of this agonising journey of empathy is the ability to draw a hostile and stubborn heart into forgiving love.

Though talk of *God's* 'learning' can only be a metaphorical way of speaking about the taking of new experience into God, yet it gives a hint that God's Spirit is able to wrestle with recalcitrant human spirits today and draw them into reconciliation because God has made a journey of discovery, above all in the cross of Jesus. It is as if God's approach to us as a forgiver is shaped to our needs because it is marked by the experience of Christ's own journey of forgiveness through life and death. To speak of this as 'new experience' in God's triune life does not deny that God has always been offering forgiveness to created persons. If the divine nature is love, then throughout history God has been sharing in the darkness of human experience, and through continuous participation has been creating change in human hearts and human society. God is always moving on the journey of forgiveness and so absorbing painful new experience; the Hebrew Bible, with its story of the God who goes into slavery and exile with his people, tells us no less. But the Christian story is that the cross of Jesus was the deepest point of descent for God into the alienation of human life, that nowhere else has God journeyed as far into the despair and nihilism of his creation. At the cross was a new situation for the forgiving God; there was a unique experience of human hostility – expressed *towards* Christ – and a unique human response – expressed *by* Christ.

Thus here, to a degree which has happened nowhere else, God is drawn into human flesh and stands where humankind stands.

In this past event the God who was and is always willing to forgive gains through the cross that experience of the human heart that gives a new way into our hearts. A change in God (in the sense of new experience) thus makes change in us. We experience God as the one who empathises with us, and so we are enabled to face up both to judgement and to acceptance. The conditioning of God by the world creates a new condition for human response, and opens up the future. As Karl Barth puts it, celebrating the radical freedom of God as Lord:

> According to the biblical testimony, God has the prerogative
> to be free without being limited by His freedom from
> external conditioning, free also with regard to His
> freedom . . . God must not only be unconditioned but, in
> the absoluteness in which He sets up this fellowship [with
> humankind], *He can and will also be conditioned.*[34]

Such an understanding of the freedom of God makes it quite coherent to say that God is changed through suffering with the world, and that this contributes to the glory and completeness of God's own being.[35]

If it be protested that God is less than omnipotent if God is indeed conditioned and affected through journeying on the path of forgiveness, we may recall our discussion of divine power earlier in this book. We must abandon worldly ideas of power – the power to make other people do what we want. Divine power is the ability to transform human hearts, to re-create human society. When we explored issues of theodicy (Chapter 5), we began to see that *only* a suffering God can fulfil purposes and overcome evil. The journey of forgiveness exemplifies this in a striking way: it is only through a painful, empathetic entering into the experience of another that reconciliation can be achieved. The power to incite human response to divine forgiveness, to prompt human persons to forgive one another, and thus to expiate evil, comes from taking the humble journey of identification. Only a wounded God can heal.

This portrayal of the divine forgiveness envisages an interaction of journeys of experience: those taken by God, by Jesus of Nazareth, and by ourselves. Only a doctrine of God which is participatory, and thus – I suggest – triune, can properly express this. In his study of *Divine Empathy*, Edward Farley constructs a doctrine of God based on empathy which has some affinities with my own proposal (he writes, for instance of a 'merger of empathies'),[36] but like process theologians he regards the divine empathy as only one aspect of God: empathy is a world-immanent and creative dimension of God's being, which is matched by a transcendent, holy otherness. The divine empathy which is united inseparably with the human empathy of Jesus can thus, he maintains, be symbolised (if we wish to employ the traditional symbolics of the Trinity) indifferently as either 'word' or 'spirit'.[37] I suggest, however, that an interweaving of divine and human empathy is best understood in terms of human participation in a God whose *whole being* is empathetic without reserve, as a triune event of relational love.

The perichoresis, or dance of relations, in God is like the movement of three persons deeply searching each other (cf. 1 Cor. 2:10–11), standing in each other's place and living each other's life. At the same time these inner journeyings of love take the form of voyages of forgiveness, not because there needs to be forgiveness within God's own self, but because they are always generously open to include human relationships, and are open to being conditioned and even hurt by them. Thus they are journeys of forgiveness into the world which is in God. This means that wherever there are movements of empathy between human persons, these are leaning upon perfect empathetic movements which are there already before them. Using trinitarian symbols, we may describe these movements as being like the entering of a father into the feelings of a son, or of a daughter into the feelings of a mother, and a continual expanding of this shared experience through a spirit of empathy which is always provoking new depths of fellow-feeling. Unlike our faltering steps into the life of another, the journey of forgiveness of Jesus which was his life's journey can be *exactly* mapped on to the journeys of God, and so it is fitting to use a description such as 'union of being'. In consequence, we are as dependent upon his journey at one particular moment in history as we are upon the eternal currents of love in God.

Participation in God like this corresponds to our experience of forgiving. We know that we cannot be commanded or admonished to forgive as a duty, but can only be drawn to forgive. William Countryman aptly writes that the gospel 'delivers us from an unforgiving spirit . . . by overwhelming us with love, by drawing us towards the One who loves us and towards the community of the new age'.[38] But we must add that we are moved to forgive, not just in a subjective, emotive way, but by living in God in the midst of actual movements of love where boundaries are always 'dissolving' and persons are always 'flowing together' (Rushdie's phrases again).

Moreover, when we recognise our participation in God and each other, we begin to see a way through some of the problems associated with a forgiveness which is characterised by empathy. If we place such a weight on mutuality, on the creating of a new situation in which response to forgiveness is enabled, what happens when response is not forthcoming? If forgiveness aims at reconciliation, is it meaningful to speak of forgiveness when someone refuses to be reconciled, or is not present to be reconciled because we have lost contact with them, or they have died? This problem becomes particularly acute in instances of abuse long ago as a child, when an abusive parent is no longer living. In such cases, the one who forgives can still set out in spirit and imagination on the path of empathy towards the other, so becoming the kind of person who is freed from the chains of the past. The forgiver can still benefit himself or herself from the attitude of forgiveness, 'moving on' from the prison of bitterness and resentment, even where this does not reach destination and closure in reconciliation. Moreover, because we make this movement *in God*, then, like the intercessory prayer that we considered earlier, it can have incalculable effects in the lives of others. The journey of our forgiveness becomes part of God's journey, and so has persuasive power in creating reconciliation in the world; we cannot know what this will achieve, either in the one with whom we desire to be reconciled, or in others who need to be reconciled and of whom we are quite unaware.

Finally, we have seen that the journey of forgiveness is a process of discovery, bringing to light the truth of a situation and so provoking sorrow and repentance in the offender. Empathy in this way becomes judgement. Even in face of lack of response, the one who truly sets out on the road of forgiveness in God may hope for discovery in the end. The symbol of the Last Judgement in Christian eschatology assures us that where truth has not been exposed in this life, even in such forums as the Truth and Reconciliation Commission, it will nevertheless be made plain before the audience of the whole cosmos. Judgement, then, is not an image of exclusion but of healing, brought about through the painful act of admitting what is true about ourselves and others.

Forgiveness and the Love of God

Forgiveness, whether or not it succeeds in gaining a response, brings some benefit, some true realisation of self, to the one who forgives. Whether or not the other is won, forgivers win themselves anew on the pilgrimage of discovery and are now ready for fresh voyages, for new roads to be trodden. By analogy, I have been proposing that God suffers change in experience, in order to draw us into forgiving and being forgiven. But if this be accepted, the triune God also will become more fully God's self, more enriched in beauty and love. Indeed, God – to remain God – cannot be degraded through change but can only move from one degree of glory to another. Here we may distinguish between divine per-fection and divine completion: while never less than perfectly related to everything God has made, God in sovereign freedom may choose to be completed through relating to it. God will be perfect in relation to amoral organic life at the amoeba stage, in a different way from being perfect in relation to persons in need of forgiveness.

This vision of God offers a sharp challenge to a distinction between two kinds of love which has become conventional in Protestant theology, that is between self-affirming and self-giving love. In self-affirming love, which is usually called *eros*, we search for an object of love to satisfy our own being; love is desire, and the object of desire fulfils the lover. In contrast, self-giving love, which is usually called *agape* (following the New Testament term for love), is understood as spending ourselves freely and carelessly for the other person, sacrificing ourselves without any hope of gain. It is then often argued that God's love must be purely agape with no hint of eros, and that the best kind of human love will approach the heights of divine agape.[39] Correspondingly, a God who finds self-fulfilment in creation will – it is protested – be making creation into a self-serving act. Even though God suffers to bring many daughters and sons to glory, the divine glory is thereby completed as well. Critics of the notion that God gains satisfaction through creating the world, such as E. L. Mascall, therefore object that 'creation, while it might be an act of love, would certainly not be an act of purely unselfish love'.[40] Surely, he argues, the highest form of love is totally disinterested, a love in which the lover 'gains nothing for himself'.

But if we explore what seems to be the nature of love in our experience, we find that true lovers do not in fact assume a rigid stance of refusing to receive anything from those they love. They become truly personal through the very act of giving value to the other, so that, as Eberhard Jüngel discerns, in giving themselves away to the beloved and becoming alien to themselves, lovers come close to themselves in a new way:

> For when love is fulfilled, then that peculiar alienation is transformed into an intensity of self-relation and world-relationship which was never there before. Lovers are alien

in the world and yet more at home in it than others . . .
The loving I has itself only as though it did not have itself.[41]

This self-realisation is not selfish, since it is not the aim but the mysterious by-product of losing ourselves in love for another. In the words of the Gospel text, 'the one who loses his life will gain it'. The purest human love thus has a proper element of eros, and we might think of agape as a 'a power which integrates eros'.[42] Since love is essentially mutuality, there will be a harmony between 'other-regarding love' and 'self-love'. The attempt at a purely self-giving attitude which insists, 'I can do everything for you but you can do nothing for me', and which meets every gift from the other with the retort, 'You shouldn't have done it', is at best a cold kind of do-gooding, and at the worst a kind of tyranny. True lovers will affirm the identity of those whom they love by receiving gladly the other's contribution to the relationship; they will gladly be enriched by new values brought about by the other.

By analogy, God's love for us is also receptive, delighting in response. As Eberhard Jüngel expresses it again, God experiences a 'still greater self-relatedness' through ever-greater self-giving.[43] Since the 'self' of God is communion, the relations in which God lives in the dance of perichoresis will be eternally renewed on the basis of self-giving love to others. Humankind is the object of God's searching love and fulfils the desire of God as 'the creative Eros',[44] in Whitehead's telling phrase. Yet at the same time this must include self-giving love, for in the quest for humankind God is giving God's own self to the utmost, willingly being constrained and hurt by the world. The quest of eros is itself the journey of sacrificial and forgiving love. In the paradox of divine love God is supremely selfless although – indeed, *because* – God is fulfilled through the pilgrimage of suffering love.

One reason why theologians have shrunk from recognising eros-love in God, however, is that in human experience it has an inescapable element of need in it. Of course, a relationship based on one person's attempts to satisfy his or her own needs at the expense of others is an unhealthy one. Nor, if we love truly, do we offer love in expectation of earning a response that will affirm us and validate us. The love which motivates forgiveness is given without calculation as to the gain that might be achieved, and with the humility of knowing that we might be rejected. But for all that, there is a proper place for needs in love. We do need to be valued for who we are, to be confirmed in our personal identity, and these needs are satisfied as an unmerited gift precisely as we bestow value on others by our unconditional love of them. While there can be no exact transfer to the love in which God lives and acts, it seems possible that there is an analogy in so far as our response to God gives God praise and glory, adding the particular kind of value to God's life that only a created world can produce. The philosopher Vincent Brümmer claims a role for the satisfying of 'need-love' in healthy relationships with others, and dares to find an analogy in God:

> We long for the love of others because as persons we
> necessarily need to be loved. But can we say the same of
> God? . . . If, as we have argued, God desires our love, it
> would seem to follow that he needs our love, for this desire
> to be fulfilled.[45]

Much earlier, the seventeenth-century poet and mystic Thomas Traherne had declared of God that:

> He is from all Eternity full of Want [i.e. need]: or els He
> would not be full of Treasure . . . had there been no Need
> He would not hav created the World . . . Infinit Wants
> satisfied Produce infinit Joys.[46]

He is making the point that the joy of God, divine 'felicity', springs from the meeting of needs and the satisfying of desires through a loving companionship with creation. Thus he urges his readers to learn how to have needs as God does, rather than to adopt the Platonic stance of pretending that we need nothing: 'God made us to Want [i.e. need] like Gods, that like Gods we might be satisfied.'

His plea is for us to enjoy the natural world and each other as God does, and this involves recognising our needs. Until we learn what our needs are, he reflects, we will never be happy.

Yet God, unlike us, does not have needs imposed from outside, cannot be subject to external necessity, since God exists *a se*, from God's self. We can, I suggest, only reconcile the needs of God with the divine freedom by appealing to the willing self-limitation or *kenosis* of God which has already been a central part of our discussion about the suffering of God. God freely determines the kind of God that God wills to be,[47] and God chooses to be completed in love and joy through a created universe – or perhaps several universes. With regard to love as eros, it follows, then, that God needs the world because God freely chooses to be in need: 'God needs our love, because he is the loving God that he has freely decided to be.'[48]

Talk of God's 'deciding' to be in need does at first seem to strike a jarring note, especially in the context of love where we do not usually speak of 'deciding' to love someone. We should notice, however, that we may have to begin the process of *forgiveness* with a deliberate decision. Moreover, any talk about God is going to be odd, stretching the resources of human language, using a cluster of metaphors and images in order to enable us participate in the reality of God's life, not to observe it. Here it is helpful to place the language of 'desire', which is naturally associated with eros, alongside that of willing, deciding and choosing. Divine desire cannot be an alternative to the divine will, but expresses something of its settled quality. It hints at something about God's choice that makes it infinitely different from our own choosing between this and that, which might well be an arbitrary and unstable decision. If God is choosing God's own being when God chooses us as covenant partners then – as Karl Barth puts it – 'in the free decision of love God is God in the very fact that he *does* stand in this relationship with the other', so that 'we cannot go back on this decision if we would know God and speak of him'.[49] Julian of Norwich perceived 'a desire, longing and thirst' in God 'from eternity',[50] and when we speak like this we are recognising that God's decision to be in need of created persons is the furthest frontier of our knowledge of God. We cannot go behind it and say, 'if God had not created, then this would have happened instead', or 'God would be this other kind of God'.

Using the active language of 'willing', 'choosing' and 'desiring' about God evokes the nature of God as event and happening, as an interweaving of currents of love; we find that we are being summoned to participate in this threefold movement of relations, and being drawn along the journeys of forgiveness of the God of love.

The Announcement of Forgiveness

In this pastoral theology of God, let us return to Christian pastors. In their counselling they will be probing many situations where forgiveness is needed or is blocked, but some will also be involved in occasions where forgiveness is actually offered. I mean the giving of absolution, or announcing of an assurance of forgiveness, in public worship or in private confessions. Whenever pastors speak the words, 'You are forgiven, go in peace', they are participating in the rhythm of God's forgiveness, travelling the road of God's empathy, in a privileged way; they are making incarnate in their own flesh and blood the forgiving offer of God. They are daring to act for God. It is as if God knows that people need to hear the word of acceptance spoken in an audible voice as well as silently in their hearts; they need acceptance embodied in a person whom they can grasp with their senses.

This is not a mere psychological extravaganza. There is good warrant for it in the Gospels. In Matthew 9, the scribes are scandalised when Jesus assures the paralysed man, 'Your sins are forgiven'; but the Evangelist finishes the story by commenting that the people praised God for granting 'such authority to *human beings*' *(NRSV)*. As Hannah Arendt notices in her political philosophy,[51] forgiveness is no longer being reserved to God or even to Jesus, although the Evangelists portray him as focusing the accepting love of God.

Others too can speak the word of forgiveness, as Jesus makes clear when he passes to his disciples generally the 'power of the keys' of the Kingdom (Jn 20:22; cf. Mt. 18:17–18).

Not only ordained ministers may dare to speak for God in this way; all disciples surely can, and may at times be called upon to do so. But those who are ordained have a commission to speak for God regularly, given them by Christ and by the congregation. As Donald Shriver has shown,[52] the institutionalising of forgiveness in the sacrament of penance unfortunately led, in the history of the church, to the privatising of forgiveness, and the loss of the function of forgiveness in building society. How then shall pastors speak for God? How shall they speak to make forgiveness real for both individual and community? What is happening as they do?

First, the pastor must speak with as much generosity as God, that is with the shocking generosity displayed by Jesus. For Jesus, the announcement of forgiveness came *before* the evidence of repentance; in fact, it enabled the response of penitence. As we have seen, forgiveness takes the initiative and is a creative act, entering into the experience of another to draw out response. Jesus takes the initiative, entering sympathetically into the lives of tax-collectors (extortioners and quislings as they were), prostitutes, beggars and those who were too ignorant to keep the religious laws properly, in order to entice them to an obedient response to God's purpose. By sharing table-fellowship with them he is sharing their life, and offering them a place at the Messianic feast, the festival of joy that would be ushered in by God's new creation of all things at the end of the age. Though Jesus hopes the sinners will repent, he offers forgiveness on God's behalf without prior conditions.

Forgiveness takes a risk; it calls out and enables the response of goodness but cannot guarantee results. When Jesus asks for hospitality from the notorious tax collector of the Jericho area, Zacchaeus, he does not first require him to return what he has gained through fraud and extortion, though this is the happy outcome.[53] He accepts from a prostitute the intimate act of her anointing his feet and wiping them with her hair, without first establishing whether she has given up her trade, and pronounces the forgiveness of God without further enquiry.[54] This does not mean that forgiveness, in the sense of reconciliation, can be *completed* without any response. Forgiveness must be received, and reception means a whole change of being, a journey of growth. But the announcement of God's *offer* of forgiveness can be made unconditionally.

Some logical objections can be made to this sequence. Richard Swinburne, as a philosopher of religion, insists that forgiveness must logically follow repentance.[55] Indeed, it is also in his view 'morally appropriate' that it should follow reparation as well (an effort to repair the damage done).[56] In our relation with God, he argues that reparation is not 'logically necessary' for God to forgive us, but that because it is appropriate God has provided it vicariously in the death of Jesus. Through repentance, then, we enter the moral realm of forgiveness. My own argument has been that the nature of loving relationships prevents us from keeping the word 'forgiveness' for the end of the process of reconciliation and restoration. However untidy it appears, we find that the initiating act of identification and empathy with a wrongdoer *is* forgiveness. We cannot hold back the generous utterance 'I forgive you' until the end of the road. In this untidy, extravagant quality of forgiveness lies its transformative power. Forgiveness enables penitence, drawing out response which will be manifest in acts of sorrow. This view of forgiveness is supported by the insights of Melanie Klein, to which I have already drawn attention. She discerns that we feel a profound need to offer 'reparation' for our destructive and aggressive instincts, stemming from our childhood experience, and that this making of reparation is a fundamental part of all human relationships. But she also, in her own way, disturbs the neat sequence between reparation and forgiveness. She claims that reparation can only take place through identification with others; the very act of sympathy with another *is itself* a kind of reparation.[57] A loving concern which sets out to feel as another person feels – as I have characterised forgiveness – is what sets things right and frees from guilt.

The generous announcement of forgiveness by the pastor thus precedes a repentant response and penance. It may sometimes, indeed, precede it by a considerable gap of time. The pastor may be aware that the maturity needed for true repentance, the awareness of conflicting good and bad feelings and the capacity for growth, may not yet be present. Some people will be at the stage, as Mary Ann Coate urges, when spiritual counselling is more appropriate than confession.[58] It is more urgent for them to come to understand themselves. The making of a confession may only drive them into repeating patterns of self-hate and self-loathing. For others it may have no meaning at all. But the pastor will still take opportunities to declare the forgiveness of God, whether ritually in worship or more individually. Declaration is not advice, such as 'God will forgive you if you repent'; it is the courage to speak on behalf of God where the pastor believes that this will create a healing process, to say 'Your sins are forgiven you . . . go in peace'.

When pastors do so, in the second place they are speaking with *consent* to God's forgiveness. Following the rhythm of God's love, they involve themselves as far as they can in the offer; they do not speak with the grudging reservation: 'God will forgive you but I cannot'. They must incarnate the forgiveness of God in flesh and blood, so that people can be assured they are forgiven. The unspoken 'I forgive you' lies beneath the declaration 'God forgives you.'

But this then raises the problem: how can we pronounce forgiveness for wrongs not done to us personally? This is not just a difficulty faced by pastors. It is memorably expressed in a story by Dostoyevsky, writing out of his experience of the terrible suffering of the peasants in nineteenth-century Russia. In the story of the boy torn to pieces by a pack of hounds that I related in the previous chapter, Dostoyevsky's character protests:

> I don't want a mother to embrace the torturer who had her child torn to pieces by his dogs! She has no right to forgive him! If she likes, she can forgive him for herself, she can

> forgive the torturer for the immeasurable suffering he has
> inflicted upon her as a mother; but she has no right to forgive
> him for the sufferings of her tortured child. She has no
> right to forgive the torturer for that, even if the child were
> to forgive him! . . . Is there in the whole world a being who
> could or would have the right to forgive?[59]

The problem is how one can forgive on behalf of others, to forgive
injury done not alone to oneself, but to someone else. Surely, only
the person who has actually been injured has the right to forgive.
Jewish people have felt this acutely when asked whether they
forgive those responsible for the horrific suffering of Holocaust
victims. Many respond like Simon Wiesenthal, who relates in his
autobiography how he was asked for forgiveness by a senior Nazi
officer on his deathbed. He describes how he walked silently out
of the room, believing that forgiveness was not his to give.[60]

'Is there anyone who has the right to forgive?' cries Ivan.
Christian faith (as Dostoyevsky knew) replies that there is God. All
the suffering of victims has taken place within the interweaving
relations of the triune God, and has hurt God. The growing pains
of creatures, and the sacrifices of evolutionary development, have
happened within the fatherly movement of God, in which a creative
imagination goes out beyond itself in the risk of making something
new. The movement in God which is like the response of a daughter
or son to the love of a parent has been marked by the suffering of
all those in our world who are forsaken and treated in a way that
denies love. In the movement of the Spirit God shares in the birth-
pangs of creation, the painful longing for the liberation which is to
come. Through creation and cross the triune God has gained the
right to forgive.

The follower of Christ also gains the right to pronounce this
forgiveness. This is what it means to 'forgive' the one who injures
someone other than oneself. We may forgive directly for the hurt
caused to ourselves, and for the rest we may say, 'God offers you
forgiveness through Christ, and I consent willingly to that offer.'

Justice is then not neglected, for we have seen that forgiveness must be completed in the repentance of the offender; the offer is unconditional, but the offer is itself a form of judgement, awakening the wrongdoer to his offence. Forgiveness aims at reconciliation, and that requires the offender to come back into the relationship in sorrow and penitence.

How then shall pastors speak the word of forgiveness? Generously, with consent, and finally listening to it for themselves. This is a disturbing process. Because pastors are speaking for God they are travelling God's own path into the lives of others, and their own inner world is going to be awakened and even turned upside down. They are going to be painfully aware of their own failures in forgiveness, their own grievances against others, their own causing of hurt to others. Pastors may seek to avoid this searching experience in several ways: by not listening to the words they are speaking, by becoming judgemental of others, or by accepting a role of magical power which others will readily give them, and which will arm them against the impact of God's offer of forgiveness.

But the Christian pastor is summoned to share the journey of forgiveness with God. To give absolution is not to wield a weapon, but to be summoned to sacrifice.

NOTES

1. Interview with Suzie Mackenzie, *Guardian Weekend*, 4 November 1995.
2. Salman Rushdie, *The Moor's Last Sigh* (London: Jonathan Cape, 1995), 433.
3. H. R. Mackintosh, *The Christian Experience of Forgiveness* (London: Nisbet & Co., 1934), 191. My italics.
4. In the following pages I follow quite closely a section on the meaning of forgiveness from my book *Past Event and Present Salvation: The Christian Idea of Atonement* (London: Darton, Longman & Todd, 1989), 173–8, with the kind consent of my publisher.
5. Rushdie, *The Moor's Last Sigh*, 193.
6. See L. William Countryman, *Forgiven and Forgiving* (Harrisburg, PA: Morehouse Publishing, 1998), 49.
7. William Blake, 'A Poison Tree', from *Songs of Experience* (Etched 1789–1794).

8. See Mary Ann Coate, *Sin, Guilt and Forgiveness: The Hidden Dimensions of a Pastoral Process* (London: SPCK, 1994), 91.
9. Paul Tillich, *The Courage to Be* (London: Collins/Fontana, 1962), 159–71.
10. Mackintosh, *The Christian Experience of Forgiveness*, 211.
11. Anselm, *Cur Deus Homo* 1.7–8, 11; Calvin, *Institutes of the Christian Religion* (1559), Book II, 16.5.
12. Jeffrie G. Murphy and Jean Hampton, *Forgiveness and Mercy* (Cambridge: Cambridge University Press, 1988), 157–9, 166–8.
13. This, however, leads Jeffrie Murphy, ibid., 94–8, 163–4, to separate Christian forgiveness from mercy in the public realm, and to affirm 'retributive hatred'. See critique by Duncan Forrester, *Christian Justice and Public Policy* (Cambridge: Cambridge University Press, 1997), 235–7, 242.
14. Mark 2:1–12, Luke 7:36–50. Joachim Jeremias, *New Testament Theology*, Vol. I, trans. J. Bowden (London: SCM Press, 1971), 114, refers also to pictures of forgiveness: debt remitted, the stray brought home, the lost found, the child accepted into the father's house.
15. Compare Mark 15:34/Matthew 27:46 with Luke 23:34.
16. Paul Tillich, *Systematic Theology* (London: Nisbet & Co., 1968), Vol. II, 40.
17. This lies at the heart of the temptation narratives: see Matthew 4:1–10.
18. Mary Grey, *Redeeming the Dream: Feminism, Redemption and the Christian Tradition* (London: SPCK, 1989), 61–3, 95–7.
19. J. B. Metz, 'The future in the memory of suffering', *Concilium* 8/6 (1972), 9–25.
20. Joe Harris, 'Reconciliation as Remembrance' in Alan D. Falconer (ed.), *Reconciling Memories* (Dublin: Columba, 1988), 44.
21. Donald W. Shriver, *An Ethic For Enemies: Forgiveness in Politics* (New York: Oxford University Press, 1997), 139.
22. Desmond Tutu, 'Address to the First Gathering of the Truth and Reconciliation Commission', 16 December 1995, published on the website of the Truth and Reconciliation Commission, www.truth.org.za.
23. Testimony of Nomonde Calata, Hearing of the Human Rights Violations Committee at East London, South Africa on 16 April 1996; published www.truth.org.za.
24. Shriver, *An Ethic For Enemies*, 7.
25. Coate, *Sin, Guilt and Forgiveness*, 117–19; see Melanie Klein, 'On Observing the Behaviour of Young Infants' in *Envy and Gratitude* (London: Virago Press, 1988), 100–6.
26. Coate, *Sin, Guilt and Forgiveness*, 119–23.
27. Melanie Klein, 'Love, Guilt and Reparation' in *Love, Guilt and Reparation, and Other Works 1921–1945* (London, Virago, 1991), 311–12.
28. Klein, 'Psychogenesis of Manic-Depressive States' in *Love, Guilt and Reparation*, 288–9.
29. Coate, *Sin, Guilt and Forgiveness*, 166–8.

30. Hannah Arendt, *The Human Condition* (Chicago: University of Chicago Press, 1958), 236ff.
31. Shriver, *An Ethic For Enemies*, 8–9.
32. Tutu, 'Address to the First Gathering of the Truth and Reconciliation Commission'.
33. The testimony of Nombuyiselo Mhlawuli, Hearing of the Human Rights Violations Committee at East London, South Africa on 16 April 1996; published www.truth.org.za.
34. Karl Barth, *Church Dogmatics*, trans. and ed. G. W. Bromiley and T. F. Torrance (Edinburgh: T. & T. Clark, 1936–77), II/1, 303. My italics.
35. For detail, see my study *The Creative Suffering of God* (Oxford: Clarendon Press, 1988), Chs. 3–4.
36. Edward Farley, *Divine Empathy: A Theology of God* (Minneapolis, MN: Fortress Press, 1996), 282.
37. Ibid., 283, 295–6; cf. 36–38, 144–8.
38. Countryman, *Forgiven and Forgiving*, 114–15.
39. E.g. Anders Nygren, *Agape and Eros*, trans. P. S. Watson (London: SPCK, 1953); Barth, *Church Dogmatics*, IV/2, 727ff.
40. E. L. Mascall, *He Who Is: A Study in Traditional Theism* (London: Longmans, Green & Co., 1958), 108–9.
41. Eberhard Jüngel, *God as the Mystery of the World*, trans. D. Guder (Edinburgh: T. & T. Clark, 1983), 318, 320.
42. Ibid., p. 338.
43. Ibid., 317, 298, 374–5.
44. A. N. Whitehead, *Adventures of Ideas* (London: Cambridge University Press, 1933), 356, 380–1.
45. Vincent Brümmer, *The Model of Love* (Cambridge: Cambridge University Press, 1993), 236.
46. Thomas Traherne, *Poems, Centuries and Three Thanksgivings*, ed. Anne Ridler (Oxford: Oxford University Press, 1966), *The First Century*, 42–3.
47. So Karl Barth, *Church Dogmatics*, II/2, 271–2; but he does not draw my conclusions.
48. This is a quotation from Brümmer, *The Model of Love*, 237, in a passage where he is commending and adopting the approach I had developed in my book *The Creative Suffering of God*, 66–8.
49. Barth, *Church Dogmatics*, II/2, 6.
50. Julian of Norwich, *Revelations of Divine Love*, trans. E. Spearing (Harmondsworth: Penguin Books, 1998), ch. 31, p. 84.
51. Arendt, *The Human Condition*, 214–15.
52. Shriver, *An Ethic for Enemies*, 50–5.
53. Luke 19:1–10. Even after his repentance, Zacchaeus does not make an offering as the law required.
54. Luke 7:36–50.

55. Richard Swinburne, *Responsibility and Atonement* (Oxford: Clarendon Press, 1989), 83–5.

56. Ibid., 148–52, 160–2.

57. Klein, 'Love, Guilt and Reparation', 309–12.

58. Coate, *Sin, Guilt and Forgiveness*, 168–70, cf. 159.

59. F. Dostoyevsky, *The Brothers Karamazov*, trans. D. Magarshack (Harmondsworth: Penguin Books, 1982), 287.

60. Simon Wiesenthal, *The Sunflower: On the Possibilities and Limits of Forgiveness*, revised edn, trans. H. J. H. Cargas (New York: Schocken Books, 1998).

7

The Living God and the
Threat of Death

The Denial of Death

'How would you like to die?' This is a question regularly included
by the *Guardian* newspaper in the questionnaire that various famous
people are asked to answer in its weekend colour supplement. The
light-hearted way that the question is asked, and the usually flippant
answers (including, recently, 'while reading a book of jokes'[1]) seem
to support the observation of Freud that 'No one really believes in
his own death'.[2] While we know intellectually that everyone born
also dies, we often do not feel it *emotionally* as something that will
happen to us. When we hear the news of people killed in floods,
aircraft accidents and wars, we think it is always 'the other person'
for whom death calls. There is a good deal of evidence that in the
final stages of moving towards death most people know they are
going to die, and a high proportion of these accept the fact peace-
fully;[3] but while in the midst of life, we tend to feel we are immortal.
Even those with fatal illnesses will harbour a hope for a miracle
cure that will appear in the nick of time. In face of the threat of
death the universal human response is some form of denial.

We might speculate on the causes of this phenomenon. Some
(such as Freud) think that the unconscious mind is simply unable

to perceive the death of the self, while it can perceive the deaths of others. Another suggestion is that we cannot relate to death because we cannot 'find' ourselves in it.[4] It is the nature of the human person to try to find our way out of every situation that confronts us, and we establish our identity or 'find ourselves' by imagining the ways we might deal with a problem; but we cannot resolve the problem of death and so we cannot recognise ourselves within it. It is alien to us.

Whatever the deep-laid reasons for this reluctance to accept the reality of death, it has certainly been fostered by the customs of our present society. We stave off ageing and the evidence of approaching death with cosmetics, plastic surgery, hormone replacement therapy and finally the most desperate means of deep-freeze storage of the body (cryogenics). Dying happens more frequently in hospital wards than at home; funeral rites have largely been removed from the home, and children have been removed from funerals. Doctors often go to great lengths to conceal from patients the fact that they have a fatal illness, and relatives often feel obliged to sustain the pretence.[5] The result of all this denial of death is not only a decreasing ability to face death with dignity, and a lack of truth in relationships between the dying person and those whom he or she loves: it may also result, as Elisabeth Kübler-Ross suggests,[6] in increasing violence in our society. Perhaps we are projecting our infantile wish for immortality outwards by inflicting destruction upon others, to reinforce our conviction that death is something which happens to others and not ourselves.

Those exercising pastoral care will be called upon in many situations to help people face death, either their own or that of others in bereavement. We need, then, to reflect on the healing power of accepting death; but we must also notice the *ambiguities* of acceptance. Resistance, fighting against death, even denial are not *always* an unhealthy reaction to the threat of death. A fatalistic submission may not be serving life. The Apostle Paul after all names death as 'the last enemy' (1 Cor. 15:26), a mood that the poet Dylan Thomas echoed with his defiant, 'Do not go gentle into that good night'.[7]

A doctor with many years experience in hospices, while urging that some terminally ill patients are at the point when 'the healthy thing to do is to die', also remarks that 'for others the dignified way to die will be in fighting to the last'.[8] We need a theology, and especially a doctrine of God, that will be a resource as we face the complexity of situations in which either acceptance or refusal might be appropriate, or a blend of these reactions.

The Ambiguities of Acceptance

I have already indicated that *total* denial of death is damaging to well-being, whether in healthy life or in moving towards death. The need openly to face the fact of our death is clear from many witnesses. First there is the experience of those who work in hospices or among the dying in the wards of hospitals. The pioneering study in Britain by John Hinton, *Dying* (first published in 1967), concluded that the opportunity to talk about the possibility of dying was viewed very positively by patients. Far from upsetting them by doing so, Hinton found that most patients were glad to talk about their fears with someone who was not just humouring them or offering false reassurance.[9] Elisabeth Kübler-Ross was doing similar studies in the USA at the same time, bringing patients with fatal illnesses into seminars with doctors and theological students to talk about their feelings.

In her resulting book, *On Death and Dying*, Kübler-Ross gives a graphic illustration of an elderly woman with abdominal cancer, faced by doctors and relatives who refused to accept what she knew to the case, that she was close to death.[10] Kübler-Ross records that she had faced her illness with courage and dignity and had 'impressed the staff . . . by her ability to face her impending death with equanimity'. In her final admission to hospital, the surgeons decided on a further operation that could possibly prolong her life, and the husband pleaded with them to do everything in their power to 'turn the clock back'. As she was being taken into the operating theatre she suddenly manifested a severe psychotic state; she was clearly delusional, was having visual hallucinations and was paranoid. She was returned to her room, and husband and staff were bewildered by the 'crazy' behaviour of a woman who had previously been so dignified and self-possessed. The woman's own comment was simply, 'Talk to this man [her husband] and make him understand.' As soon as the husband was able to acknowledge the impending death and the operation was permanently cancelled, the psychotic state disappeared. The woman actually had less pain, and moved towards her end with her former dignity.

This kind of incident could be repeated many times. It confirms a more general sense that death provides a boundary that makes sense of life. Any story needs an end as well as a beginning and a middle, and the conclusion of death makes human life into a meaningful story rather than just a succession of incidents or a 'tale/ Told by an idiot, full of sound and fury/ Signifying nothing'.[11] Novels and plays bear abundant witness to the tragedy of those who cannot face death and find they have no story. In Ursula Le Guin's science fiction novel *The Farthest Shore*, the corrupt wizard called Cob secures immortality for himself by giving up his name, which symbolises his particular existence between birth and death; he is told:

> 'You exist without name, without form. You cannot see the light of day; you cannot see the dark. You sold the green earth and the sun and the stars to save yourself. But you have no self . . . You have given everything for nothing.'[12]

In Oscar Wilde's Parable, *The Doer of Good*, the miracle-worker sees seated by the roadside a young man who is weeping: 'And the young man looked up and recognized him and made answer: "But I was dead once and you raised me from the dead. What else should I do but weep?" '[13]

The tragedy of those who have lost their boundary-marker for life is given a philosophical explanation by Martin Heidegger. He maintains that the self finds its unity by being confronted with the shock of non-being that death delivers. He diagnoses the self as being broken into fragments by the passing of time; it will only establish its identity by achieving a sameness through past, present and future, and concentration of the will upon the fact of our own death will have this unifying force. Theologians like John Mac-quarrie and Paul Tillich have opposed Heidegger's claim that death should therefore be the 'master concern' of our will, since God alone is our final concern; but they agree that the shock of non-being, of ceasing to be, can awaken us to the power of Being and can integrate our experience of the self in time.[14]

Medical, literary and philosophical witnesses thus urge us to face the fact of death, to accept. But, as I have already hinted, things are not as simple as this. In cultures where there is a strong fatalistic acceptance of death, there may be less effort to create public health and welfare provision that can hold death back. On a more personal level, it is well known that the resistance of the will to the advance of cancerous cells can cause remission. While people can certainly suffer lack of dignity when doctors fight heroically to keep them alive on drips, intravenous tubes and ventilators, sometimes those who have survived, even for a brief while, will express satisfaction in their extra lease of life.

In her book, Kübler-Ross suggests that through all the stages she identifies in approaching death – denial, anger, bargaining, depression, acceptance – there is one attitude that persists, that of hope. She writes:

> In listening to our terminally ill patients we were always impressed that even the most accepting, the most realistic patients left the possibility open for some cure, for the discovery of a new drug . . . It is this glimpse of hope that maintains them through days, weeks, or months of suffering . . . for [some] it remains a form of temporary but needed denial.[15]

She points out that the patients showed the greatest confidence in the doctors who allowed for such hope – realistic or not. This does not mean that doctors have to tell lies, she stresses; it merely means that 'we share with [patients] the hope that something unforeseen may happen, that they may have a remission, that they will live longer than expected'.[16] Doctors, she adds, do need some humility to qualify their assumed omniscience. She tells the story of one 28-year-old woman with terminal liver disease, who accepted her approaching death with one part of her being, but also believed she had been healed by a faith-healer, saying 'I am going to show the doctors that God will heal me.' Kübler-Ross's conclusion, looking back on what she calls a 'long and meaningful relationship', was that good co-operation between patient and hospital staff was possible only because those dealing with her respected her wish to deny her illness as long as possible. Kübler-Ross even says, 'This patient made it quite clear from the very beginning that denial was essential in order for her to remain sane.'[17] Hinton draws a similar conclusion from this kind of experience, urging that there is no reason why the dying should not have the comfort of 'toying with light hopes and fantasies', even when at other times they show a fuller insight into their condition.[18]

There has been a good deal of reflection by doctors and counsellors on ways to support the patient on the path towards death in an honest way without utterly excluding hope. Some commend a practice of allowing an awareness of the outcome to grow gradually, letting patients know that some of their surmises are true and assuring them that other fears are unjustified, while always being ready to answer straight questions openly.[19] Richard Lamerton advises that 'in all such conversations the patient leads the way', with the doctor or counsellor giving a choice of directions for the conversation to move, so that 'it is almost like a dance'.[20]

This period of anticipating death, in which acceptance and denial are blended in ambiguous and complex ways, is a kind of boundary or threshold situation. Beverley Raphael uses the image of a 'no man's land' between life and death, in which relationships need to be developed which are particularly geared to an awareness of 'fragility of existence'.[21] The carer may be called to stay alongside the potentially dying person for a considerable period, through remissions, returns home from hospital and re-admissions; but they remain on the threshold together. Indeed, this period may be experienced by both as focusing more sharply the general liminality of human existence, trembling as it does on the borders between being and nothingness, between 'being-at-home' and 'not at home' (as Heidegger describes it).[22] In the midst of life we are in death.

My purpose in this chapter is not thoroughly to examine methods of counselling that might be practised with those near death, but to explore a doctrine of God that arises in this situation, which will make sense of it and guide us in the process. In particular there are two sets of pastoral-theological questions faced by Christian believers who offer care to the bereaved, and to the dying who are in the 'threshold' period when acceptance and denial are mixed together. The questions call for a doctrine of God both as Creator of death and Redeemer from death. First, if death is God's gift in creation for human life, why should we resist death and fight against it when it seems a likely outcome? Moreover, if we believe that God gives life beyond death, why should we not invariably welcome it without resistance as a door to greater life? Second, if death is God's gift, and God also offers life beyond death, why should we grieve for those whom we have lost? Or, putting it more in the form people ask, is it a lack of faith to grieve *deeply*, protesting against death?

Actually, both sets of questions are really about grief. We do not only grieve for *others* who have died; when we approach our own death we grieve over our impending departure from life, a grief which sometimes takes the form of depression.[23] To help find an answer to these questions we turn first to the view of death in the Hebrew and Christian Scriptures.

Death as Enemy and as Boundary

It is has often been supposed in Christian tradition that physical death is the result of human sin, so that it was never part of God's intention in creation.[24] Actually, the biblical picture of death, in the faith of Israel and in the early Christian church, is more complex than this. There is an ambiguity about experience of death which matches the kind of ambiguous mix of acceptance and denial we have been charting so far.

In the first place, death is presented as a destructive force in much of the Old Testament, an enemy threatening life, which is of the highest value. There is a finality about death, putting an end to relationships within the family and the nation and between persons and God:

> The dead do not praise the Lord,
>   nor do any that go down into silence.
>
>   (Psalm 115:17)
>
> Is your steadfast love declared in the grave,
>   or your faithfulness in Abaddon?
> Are your wonders known in the darkness
>   or your saving help in the land of forgetfulness?
>
>   (Psalm 88: 11–12 NRSV)

Death also puts an end to personal identity. There is no idea of an immortal soul which leaves the body behind and lives a vital existence somewhere else; body, mind and soul are a psychosomatic unity, and at death the vitality or energy (*nephesh*) seeps out of the body like water spilt from a bucket – or, as we might say today, like air leaking from a tyre: 'We must all die; we are like water spilt on the ground, which cannot be gathered up again' (2 Sam. 14:14). The result of this loss of *nephesh* is that the body collapses into an utterly weak version of its former self, all strength and vitality gone, and this pale reflection of a person lingers out a shadowy existence in Sheol. It is not really alive; it exists in a land of forgetfulness. This is no afterlife in a meaningful sense at all. Moreover, the power of death as an enemy reaches back into life; if people are ill then their *nephesh*, their soul or vitality, begins to seep out. So they are entering the sphere of influence of Sheol; death is getting hold of their throat like water threatening to drown them (Ps. 69:1–3,

14–15). As in the perceptions of modern medicine, death is regarded as a process, not as a single point, and to be ill is to begin the journey of going down into the pit. This is the vivid portrayal of a 'threshold' situation, but what waits at the entrance is something hostile.

> My soul is full of troubles,
>> and my life draws near to Sheol.
> I am reckoned among those who go down to the Pit;
>> I am a man who has no strength.
>
> (Psalm 88: 3–4)

In the Old Testament Psalms, to be rescued from Sheol means to be restored to health, to have *nephesh* returning into the body, to be saved from dying, to be snatched from the jaws of death. It does not mean life beyond death, but the regaining of life before death.

All this depicts death as an enemy to life, which is viewed as a positive good, a blessing from Yahweh. There is no yearning to escape this life for an existence in another world, as may be found in other ancient Near Eastern religions. But there is another side to death which can be glimpsed from time to time. The destructive force of death is lessened when it comes in old age, though even here there is still a tinge of regret:

> You shall come to your grave in ripe old age,
>> as a shock of grain comes up to the threshing floor in its season.
>
> (Job 5:26)

Here it seems much more like a *natural* boundary to life, though there is still some pain promised in the threshing. Similarly, a prophet who stands in the tradition of Isaiah has a vision of the ideal city when God restores his people:

> I will rejoice in Jerusalem . . .
> No more shall there be in it

an infant that lives but a few days,
or an old man who does not fill out his days,
for the child shall die a hundred years old . . .

(Isaiah 65:19–20)

There are, then, two faces of death: the enemy and the boundary-marker. Perhaps the best interpretation of this duality is to be found in the Yahwist's account of the man and the woman in the garden in Genesis 3. If we listen carefully to the story, we find no hint that the man and woman would not have died if they had not disobeyed God. They are said to be taken from dust, and to return to dust (Gen. 2:7; 3:19). They have not yet eaten the fruit of the 'tree of life' by which they might gain immortality. Although God warns that they will die the very day they eat the fruit of the tree of the knowledge of good and evil, they do not in fact die physically at that moment; either the serpent is correct when it says 'you will not die' (Gen. 3:4), or the 'death' which comes upon them cannot be taken literally, as if it were the sudden onset of mortality. Of course, the story has been compiled from a number of sources, and different motifs have been woven together, but taken in the final form the storyteller gives us, it does not deny that death was originally part of creation. What it does underline is that the result of turning away from God's purpose is that death becomes an enemy to life.[25] It threatens to make all work futile; it makes the work of the garden into an experience of struggling with thorns and thistles:

In the sweat of your face
   you shall eat bread
till you return to the ground,
   for out of it you were taken;
you are dust,
   and to dust you shall return.

(Genesis 3:19)

Thus death in the experience of Israel was something natural, but a good thing spoilt. It was now an enemy, within which God's original intention could nevertheless still be glimpsed. The Apostle Paul in the New Testament confirms this mixed nature of death, observing that death is the last enemy because the sting of death is sin (1 Cor. 15:26, 56). He significantly puts law and death together (Rom. 7:13–25); in his view, they are both good things corrupted. In abstract essence they are good gifts, but as we actually know them in existence they have become 'another law' (Rom. 7:23) and another death, oppressing and life-denying. They share in the slipping of the universe away from God's creative purpose. This is a fair description of our experience of death as well. 'Ripeness is all,' says Edgar to his suicidal father in Shakespeare's *King Lear*,[26] but as a matter of fact much of death in our world is not in the ripeness of old age or fulfilled achievement. Even in rare cases where it is, it is still felt as an offence against love; it takes away from us the opportunity of spending love on another. While death still retains the feel of a neutral boundary, in reality we always experience it as a mixture, in varying proportions, of natural limit and hostile force.[27]

There is, moreover, a third element in this mixture if we follow the biblical picture. There is a clue in the Genesis story that while death is a natural limit, it was not to be permanent in God's creative intention. The presence of the tree of life in the garden which the man and woman are now prohibited from eating is a symbol that natural death was a provisional stage within God's purpose for maturing of humankind. As Irenaeus read the story, even natural death is provisional.[28] This idea is supported by the biblical symbols of the resurrection of the dead and the *eschaton* when 'death will be swallowed up for ever' (Isa. 25:8; 1 Cor. 15:54; Rev. 21:4). Even as a natural boundary, death is finally to be abolished and so has the status of the penultimate. But death as we actually know it is interfused with frustrations, untimeliness and regrets of which human beings are victims, whatever their own sins might or might not contribute to the tragedy.

These elements of natural boundary, hostile force and provisionality are woven together in the experience of death. It cannot be simply regarded as a punishment for sin. Any view of creation which conceives the Spirit of God as working within and influencing the evolutionary development of life must allow for death as a biological necessity in the process, since 'the death of old organisms is a prerequisite for the appearance of new ones'.[29] When death is experienced as a hostile force this may well be the consequence of sin and evil, but even here it may not be so; it may sometimes be the sheer provisionality of death that we feel. This ambiguity of death from a theological perspective begins, I suggest, to explain why our approach to death has the multi-dimensional character of denial and acceptance. But it also makes clear that God in God's own self is faced by something strange and alien in God's creation, something that God sorrows about and protests against.

In a previous chapter, when considering the doctrine of God in the context of the problems of suffering, I maintained that any free-will defence must allow that the excessive and intolerable amount of suffering in the world befalls God as something alien within creation, not as an educational enterprise God has planned. What befalls God as strange is the *disproportionate* nature of pain and natural evil, beyond what might be claimed by any stretch of the imagination to be helpful for the development of human character. In the same way we may say that death 'befalls' God − not the death within God's creative intention but death as it has *become*, another death. It is vital to maintain the distinction between these aspects of death − death as a boundary and death as an enemy, or in more philosophical language, between neutral 'non-being' and non-being which is aggressive towards being, the distinction Plato made between *ouk on* and *me on*.[30] The first is simply bare nothingness; the second is an annihilating power. Augustine made a similar distinction between the nothing from which we are made (*ex nihilo*), and the nothingness of evil which is a turning away from something, the Good.[31] In Augustine's view, since God as the Supreme Good has raised created beings from nothing, they only have to let go of God to slip back back down towards nothing again. If we follow his thought carefully, we should say that the nothing from which we have come and to which we tend to return is not evil in itself; but it is the *movement towards nothing*, the dynamic tendency to turn from the Good, which is a hostile nothingness. It is strictly nothing because it is parasitic upon Something, the Good.

Theologians are not always careful in making this distinction between two kinds of 'nothing' or non-being. It is with some surprise, for example, that we find Jürgen Moltmann writing that 'by yielding up the Son to death in God-forsakenness on the cross, and by surrendering him to hell, the eternal God enters the Nothingness *out of which he created the world*.'[32] (I have a similar criticism to make of Eberhard Jüngel below.) Of course, the Christian understanding of atonement is that in the cross of Jesus God indeed confronts death and overcomes it; the resurrection of Jesus from among the dead witnesses to this victory. But there seems to be a sliding here from one sense of nothingness to another, from the neutral non-being from which creation emerged, to the annihilating Nothingness which is hostile to life and love. I suggest that the one only becomes the other because of free acts in the created order, so that God is now confronted by a nothingness and a death which is experienced as alienating and strange. Otherwise the pain of God would be simply all God's own work, God's making God's self suffer, which (as we have already seen) would be no suffering at all. Nor would God's experience of death be anything like ours, and divine empathy with us would be a charade.

But this observation leads on to a further question. In what sense can God experience death and still be God? How can God suffer death and not be dead? This question can only be answered out of a doctrine of God as Trinity.

Death in the Triune God

In July 1995 the Ludwig Museum of Modern Art in Budapest presented a piece of installation art by Dimitrij Progov, entitled 'God is Dead. A known event which happened this time in Budapest'. In a long, white room the walls were solemnly hung with twelve black drapes from ceiling to floor; behind each drape at ceiling height was an eye weeping red blood, streams of red and black paint dripping down the wall on to the floor. The impression of suffering was immense, aptly installed in a city which has known continual suffering. Though this piece of art was thirty years after the 'God is Dead' movement in theology, it seemed to offer the same assertion: God is dead, in the sense of being irrelevant to a suffering world; God is absent from our consciousness; we are living at the time of God's funeral.[33] A powerful reply has, in my view, been offered to this challenge by theologians who have proposed that God is not dead precisely because God suffers death.[34] That is, God is not irrelevant to this world marked by death because God shares in the experience of death in sympathy with us. God endures death but is not dead: all that is dead or cancelled out is a certain metaphysical concept of an invulnerable God. But what sense can we make of such a statement? How can God suffer death and not go out of existence? Two kinds of answer might be offered to this question, each based in the human experience of confronting and approaching death.

First, Jürgen Moltmann appeals to what he considers to be the self-evident fact that we never experience our own death.[35] We experience the *death* of others in the grief of bereavement, but in our own case what we experience is our *dying*. Moltmann makes this observation while reflecting on the event of the cross of Jesus where Christian believers find God's encounter with death most fully disclosed, and so distinguishes by analogy between 'death' and 'dying' in God. His idea is that when Christ dies on the cross, God the Father suffers 'death', in the sense of the experience of the death of the Son or bereavement, but the Father does not suffer 'dying'. The Son suffers 'dying', but not 'death', since no one who dies can know the event of his or her own death. In this way, the loss of the Son by the Father can be distinguished from the loss of the Father by the Son, while our own forsakenness in life can be taken into the space of abandonment between the Father and the Son. So Moltmann concludes that the death of Jesus is *in* God, but not *of* God; it is not the 'death of God' because, although God the Father suffers death, it is not his own death but that of the Son.[36]

I can only applaud the insight of Moltmann that death is something that happens in the midst of the relationships that make up God's triune life. But Moltmann's distinction between death and dying has problems. Moltmann denies that he is talking about the death 'of' God because the *Father* does not suffer dying; he suffers the experience of the death of the *Son*. But this looks like a case of the swiftness of the theologian's hand deceiving the eye of the reader. If God is really participating in the event of the cross, is not God as much in the *dying* of the Son as in the bereavement of the Father? Moltmann himself speaks of the cross as an event 'between God and God'.[37] If God is communion, a perichoresis of relationships, we must be speaking of the death 'of' God. Otherwise we end up with one God who suffers with us (the Son) and one who inflicts the suffering (the Father). Then it almost looks as if God the Father rejects the Son in order to provide us with someone who can sympathise with us in our predicament.

Another problem with dividing up 'dying' and 'death' between Son and Father in God is that this is based by analogy on a certain view of human experience; it is assumed (though Moltmann does not directly argue the point) that we cannot gain experience of death from knowledge of our own being but only from the grief at the death of others. Now it is true, of course, that we do not experience ourselves *as being dead*; we cannot literally suffer our own bereavement. But unless we take Freud's view that our unconscious can never envisage our own death, then while we are alive we do experience our own death in anticipation. We discover about death from experiencing the running out of time; we experience death as the final deadline, the last boundary in the face of which we feel time passing. We feel the death of others as an offence against love because they no longer have time for us, and we can no longer spend time on them; but in our own being too we experience the same sense of loss of time in face of death. The anticipation of death is acute in those who are dying, but not yet dead, as we have seen. Psychotherapists who have explored the experience of dying identify the depression that often comes as one of the stages of moving towards death as a kind of grief at our own death, similar to bereavement.[38] This grief has to be worked through for acceptance to come. As Beverley Raphael points out, such grief is especially intense in those who have survived a tragedy in which others have died; survivors often endure a lifelong grief over their own death, a kind of mourning of 'the loss of innocence about death'.[39] I intend to return to the question of the *appropriateness* of grief in the face of death; here I want to make the point that grief comes before as well as after death.

Pastoral experience of the care of the dying thus raises basic questions about any sharp distinction between the experience of 'dying' (the Son's) and the experience of 'death' (the Father's) in God. There is one further problem too. I have been suggesting that it is not alone in the cross of Jesus that God enters with empathy into the suffering of the world. God has always been taking the painful journey of forgiveness into the experience of created beings (Chapter 6). We must surely affirm the same thing of God's experience of death. God has always been exposing the divine life to the strange annihilating nothingness that emerges from creation because of the freedom God gives it. I do want to affirm that the cross is more than a *disclosure* of this journey of pain; it is the *furthest* point to which a God of love can go – that is, to the uttermost depth of alienation and estrangement. But it is not the first time that God has faced death. Moltmann's definition that the Father experiences death in the sense of bereavement, that is, the loss of the Son in this particular event, isolates death in God to the cross. It seems to be only in this one event of history that we can speak of God's experience of death.

A second account of 'death in God' might draw a different conclusion from the human phenomenon of approaching death. Rather than contrasting dying with death, we might pay attention to the condition of being in a 'threshold' situation or 'no man's land' in which there is a complex experience of transition from life to death. We have seen that in human experience this process takes the form of a tension between denial and acceptance, but we might find another kind of conflict in God which is more appropriate to God's encounter with non-being. Here Eberhard Jüngel proposes that God 'exists in the struggle between possibility and nothingness', and so maintains that we can speak of a 'perishability' (*Vergangenheit*) of God like the perishability we ourselves experience in the face of death.[40] There is a 'passing away' (*Vergangenheit*) in God's own self, a movement which has been denied by metaphysical accounts of God as absolute and immutable essence. While in the past perishability was understood as distinguishing finite beings from God, Jüngel suggests that unless we can think of God as sharing in some way in this perishability, in our age we cannot think of God at all.[41]

Our experience of 'perishability', or the passing away of the present moment into the past, is often a negative one. We experience it as a 'tendency towards nothingness', a kind of swirling 'undertow' towards annihilation in the currents of life, and this can be accentuated in the period when we anticipate an imminent death. As time runs out, death becomes a simile for this destructive nothingness. (It has, we might say, become 'another death'.) Jüngel points out, however, that there is a positive and even creative side to perishing. The true tendency of perishing is towards the opening of possibilities; even what is past does not have to disappear into nothingness, but can be remembered and repeated in new ways. 'That which is positive about perishing is the possibility.'[42] The tendency towards nothing, or towards the 'absolutely impossible', is merely parasitic on the tendency towards the possible, or the capability of becoming. 'Perishing', then, is a struggle between possibility and nothingness, or between being and non-being. God, by creating out of nothing, exists in this struggle. Indeed, affirms Jüngel, there is only such a struggle at all *because* God exists.

Jüngel affirms that in God the tendency towards the impossible is always being overcome by the movement towards the possible.

This victory is disclosed in the death and resurrection of Jesus, so that:

> In the event of the death of Jesus, the being of God and the being of death so strike against each other, that the being of one puts into question the being of the other . . . this reciprocal putting of each into question ends with the rising of Jesus from the dead.[43]

Jüngel thus speaks of God's overcoming of the negative side of perishability in terms of God's taking nothingness into God's own self, of drawing it into God's history and 'giving it a place' within God's own being. God is 'that one who can bear and does bear in his being the annihilating power of nothingness, even the negation of death, without being annihilated by it'.[44] Once it is taken into God's being it is given a new function. Instead of being destructive it defines God's own deity, showing God to be the one who overcomes death. It has become a phenomenon that belongs to God, God's own nothingness, God's own death. In contrast to Moltmann's reluctance to speak of the death 'of' God, Jüngel affirms that death has become 'the death of the living God'. He offers here the illustration of being stung by a wasp: as we take the sting of a wasp with its poison into ourselves and carry it within us, as we absorb the sting and it becomes part of us, so God uses death to define the divine being.[45] Above all God does this in the death of Jesus, choosing to be defined as God in a dead man; in this crucified man God shows who God is, a God of sacrificial love.

How then can we say that God experiences death but is not dead? Moltmann suggests that we should exempt God the Father from the experience of dying and understand his suffering as a kind of bereavement. Jüngel traces out a second approach, that God has experienced both death and dying, but has made death into God's servant by taking it into God's self. So, to speak of God's suffering 'death and dying' is to speak metaphorically of God's exposure to the non-being, the negation we ourselves feel in the experience of 'perishing'. Unlike us, God is never overcome by this, and while experiencing it universally in sympathy with all humankind, endures one moment of the most intense conflict. In identification with one dead man, Jesus Christ, who was most intimately bound up in relationship with God, the being of God goes furthest into the valley of the shadow of death and yet is not consumed.

Although Jüngel himself does not refer to the human 'threshold' experience of dying, the complex period of transition in the face of death, reflection on this will lead us to affirm his basic approach. God too is involved in a process of being 'on the boundary', and in the tensions and struggles that take place there. But I suggest that we must not lose sight of God's taking into God's self the *movement* towards nothingness; it is the movement, the tendency, the 'undertow' which is aggressive non-being. At times Jüngel, like Moltmann, speaks as if the problem were the 'nothing' from which God created, or even the very fact of death in itself, and as if it is these that must be conquered in God's being.[46] What is annihilating is surely the *slipping back* towards this nothing, away from the 'something' of the creative Good. It is this that makes death into 'another death'. Following our dynamic concept of God as an event of relationships, we may say that God gives a place to this movement of 'slipping towards nothing' within the movements of the divine life, and so transforms it into a movement towards the possible. This is participatory and not objectifying talk about God.

The doctrine of the Trinity thus offers a means of thinking of this experience of nothingness as entering into God. 'Trinity' expresses the nature of God as communion, as a web of dynamic relationships, a dance of love and joy between movements of being. It cannot be observed, but is known only by participation. The negative movement of perishing is, accordingly, a separation entering into the heart of God's own relationships. The dance of perichoresis can be disturbed; the measures can be broken; a gap can open up between the movements of the dance. This would be a kind of death, since death threatens our relationships with others. The story of the cross of Jesus, with its cry of forsakenness, tells us that God has taken the most desolate kind of death into God's self in identification and empathy. But if the dance is to absorb this interruption, to weave this very brokenness into the dance and make death serve it, transforming the movement to nothingness into a movement to possibility, we have to think carefully about the nature of the breach. If we follow Moltmann's view that the Father only suffers bereavement and not dying, then we make too wide a division between one person who suffers the dying and another who suffers the death. There is even the danger that we might think of the brokenness as the Father rejecting the Son, or God's 'casting out' God.[47]

Rather, we might follow an insight about the nature of persons that we have explored in previous chapters, that we only become really close to someone when we experience the other as different from us. As our encounter with someone deepens, we become more and more aware of the uniqueness of the Other. Only in awareness of this difference from ourselves can the relationship take on a new depth of nearness. If God's being is in relationships, then the 'persons' are in the deepest communion just because they are different from each other, because there is real otherness.[48] We can, then, with Hans Urs von Balthasar, take a further step and think of the Father's very begetting of the Son as an act of self-emptying, of *kenosis*. Von Balthasar dares to say that the Father 'destitutes' and 'strips' God's self in bringing forth the Son, and the Son and the Spirit continually empty themselves also in communion with the Father in self-giving love.[49]

Now, if the dance of perichoresis already has this gulf at its heart, we can begin to understand how God in extravagant love allows death itself to enter that space. In free will, God allows God's own *otherness* to become a painful *alienation*. Von Balthasar puts it like this:

> God as the gulf of absolute love contains in advance, eternally, all the modalities of love, of compassion, and even of a 'separation' motivated by love and founded on the infinite distinctions between the [persons] – modalities that may

manifest themselves in the course of a history of salvation involving sinful humankind.[50]

In the difference between the persons, in the distances between the movements of love, there is room to take in the painful experience of relationlessness in death.[51] God can enter with empathy into the human experience of the breaking of relations because the triune life is existence in relationships which have an otherness about them. It is not that God abandons God, that one person of the Trinity expels another. Rather, God is willing to experience God's own relationships in a new way in the face of death. God is willing to allow otherness to become alienation, to take a journey into the unknown, into 'no man's land'. This is a risk for God, sharing the risk of creation. What it might mean for the divine life cannot be predicted ahead of its happening, any more than can any journey of forgiving love. God is open to the strangeness of a new, dark movement in the dance of love. God encounters death, and uses it to define deity, in victory over death as the living God.

We can then dare to say that God experiences death *and* dying, in the sense of perishing and relationlessness, but is not dead. God's experience of death is always in the mode of triumph won through pain.

Grief in Victory over Death

The human experience of trembling on the 'threshold' of death, a period in which there is an ambivalent mix of acceptance and denial, can thus help us to think about God's own encounter with death, and to shape our doctrine of God's triune life. At the same time, through hearing the story of the death of Jesus as remembered and narrated in the community of faith, we become aware that those making this journey are actually participating in God's own 'passing away', and this will have an effect upon our response to people's grief or our own experience of it – whether it be in anticipation of death or in bereavement after it.

In grief before death an element of denial is appropriate, arising from the ambiguous nature of death, and echoing God's protest against what death has become. Denial, however, is the negative side of hope, as we have seen, and so those who accompany the dying may help them gradually to transfer hope to new objects, to move 'from a hope that is becoming unrealistic to one that has more promise for sustaining the person through the crisis of approaching death'.[52] Participating in the 'perishing' of God which is a movement towards possibility, hope may be refocused on 'being' rather than 'doing', and so on relationships with others and with God.[53] This hope will include 'quite simply, the promise that the person will not be left to face death alone'.[54]

In the grief that follows the death of another, hope in God does not replace the proper need for mourning, and the biblical view of death that we have explored shows why this should be. When hope in a meaningful life after death developed in Israel towards the end of the Old Testament period, between the fourth and second centuries BC,[55] there could be no thought of an immortal soul surviving the end of the body. The *nephesh* or vitality leaks away, and has no capacity for an independent existence. Because of the strong Hebraic understanding of the psychosomatic unity of human life, if there were to be life beyond death it must take the form of a new creation of the whole person by God. In this view, death is final as far as human beings are concerned: it puts an end to everything. Any hope beyond death must lie in God and not in us. The Creator must act in the face of death to overcome it, to make the whole person anew. This is the point of the biblical symbol of the 'resurrection of the body': not a literal reviving of the body with recomposition of its present atoms, but a re-creation of everything that makes us human, as something at least equivalent to being embodied.

This is the hope that the New Testament expresses in the resurrection of Jesus Christ; this is the victory God has won for us against the death which has become an enemy. The New Testament understanding of resurrection is not merely, then, about the survival of the individual. It is not about having a survival capsule ('the soul') that outlives the body, but about a new creation. It is a hope for the entire created cosmos, that it will be raised to a new level of being, and persons will be renewed within this context. Moreover, there is a clue in the resurrection of Jesus that this new creation will be marked by a greater degree of interpersonal existence, a greater participation of each person in the other, a richer dance of life. While the resurrection body of Christ is not simply exhausted into the church without remainder, the followers of Jesus may be said in a sense to be his 'Body', so that the risen Jesus leads a life of deeper participation in others than was possible during his earthly life.

Now, in the light of this form of hope for the conquest of death, we can see why the experience of grief is not only proper but essential. Death has a finality. It *does* put an end to the old creation, all that is familiar to us. It is not a mere flimsy door through which the soul strides and which can be smiled at. In the face of death we have to trust God to overcome an enemy to life and to re-create, to make again from nothingness. We may trust God that new creation will fulfil all our hopes, but it is a real future that we cannot predict or map, not just an extension of the present; we step out into the unknown. So there is a real loss of the familiar, a loss of the way that relationships have been felt and experienced within *this* creation. We may trust God to remake our relationships with those whom we love, but it will not be just the same, a mere repetition. The dance moves on into new and richer measures, into a deeper interweaving of persons. It is right, then, to feel grief for the loss of the old, even though it will be taken up into the new. It is not a lack of faith to feel the awful sense of separation, that is so often expressed in bereavement in a period of 'searching' for the one who has died.[56] There is loss in the very heart of gain. Indeed, in this experience we enter into the life of God who also takes a strange journey in the facing of death.

But being aware of our participation in God should enable us to 'complete' the process of mourning in a healthy way. Psychotherapists have suggested that a key to completing the grief process is the 'internalising' of the lost person, so that he or she ceases to be an object 'out there' to be searched for, and instead (as Lily Pincus expresses it) 'becomes part of the bereaved, a part which can be integrated with his own personality and enriches it'.[57] We need not here explore the way that success or failure to achieve this integration may be linked to childhood experiences.[58] The point is that sharing in the life of a God who has internalised the countless multitude of human experiences of death means that we do not have to complete our grief as isolated individuals. As we become more deeply aware – through the story, the music and the prayers of a community – of our part in the God who has taken 'perishing' into God's self, so we are enabled to become part of each other, on the way to resurrection.

Those who care for people facing death will always be seeking to help them find their own blend of acceptance and denial. There is a proper resistance to death as an enemy, and a proper acceptance of the death which marks a good limit to life. There can be no rules here, but only an increasing harmony with the God who makes even death into a servant.

NOTES

1. 'The Questionnaire: Ivor Cutler', *Guardian Weekend*, 5 February 2000.
2. Sigmund Freud, 'Thoughts on War and Death' in *Complete Psychological Works*, Vol. 14 (London: Hogarth Press, 1957), 289.
3. See Colin Murray-Parkes, *Bereavement: Studies of Grief in Adult Life* (London: Tavistock Publications, 1972), 150–3; John Hinton, *Dying*, 2nd edn (Harmondsworth: Penguin Books, 1972), 94–9, 105.
4. Eberhard Jüngel, *Death: The Riddle and the Mystery*, trans. I. and U. Nicol (Edinburgh: St Andrew Press, 1975), 6–7.
5. For an account of this, see Hinton, *Dying*, 102–3, 128–31.
6. Elisabeth Kübler-Ross, *On Death and Dying* (London: Routledge, 1985 [1970]), 12–13.
7. Dylan Thomas, *Collected Poems 1934–1952* (London: Dent, 1967), 116.
8. Richard Lamerton, *Care of the Dying*, revised edn (Harmondsworth: Penguin Books, 1980), 121, 124.
9. Hinton, *Dying*, 136–9.

10. Kübler-Ross, *On Death and Dying*, 101–5.
11. Shakespeare, *Macbeth*, V.5.26–8.
12. Ursula Le Guin, *The Farthest Shore* (London: Gollancz, 1973), 189.
13. Oscar Wilde, *Poems in Prose*, in *Collins Complete Works of Oscar Wilde* (Glasgow: HarperCollins, 1999), 901.
14. Martin Heidegger, *Being and Time*, trans. J. Macquarrie and E. Robinson (Oxford: Blackwell, 1962), 280–90; Paul Tillich, *Systematic Theology* (London: Nisbet & Co., 1968), Vol. 1, 207ff.; John Macquarrie, *Principles of Christian Theology*, revised edn (London: SCM Press, 1977), 78–80, 264–6.
15. Kübler-Ross, *On Death and Dying*, 123.
16. Ibid.
17. Ibid., 41.
18. Hinton, *Dying*, 101. Also, on the cultivation of hope see Lawrence LeShan, *Cancer as a Turning Point* (Bath: Gateway Books, 1990), 157ff.
19. See Hinton, *Dying*, 134–6.
20. Lamerton, *Care of the Dying*, 163–5, 168.
21. Beverley Raphael, *The Anatomy of Bereavement: A Handbook for the Caring Professions* (London: Hutchinson, 1985), 26–7.
22. Heidegger, *Being and Time*, 233–5.
23. Raphael, *The Anatomy of Bereavement*, 26; Lamerton, *Care of the Dying*, 173–5.
24. See, e.g. Anselm, *Cur Deus Homo* 2.2.
25. This accords with the exegesis of G. Von Rad, *Genesis: A Commentary*, trans. J. Marks (London: SCM Press, 1963), 91–4.
26. Shakespeare, *King Lear*, V.2.9.
27. Karl Rahner, *On the Theology of Death*, trans. C. Henkey (London: Burns & Oates/ Freiburg: Herder, 1961), 45.
28. Irenaeus, *Adversus Haereses* 4.38.
29. A. R. Peacocke, *Creation and the World of Science* (Oxford: Clarendon Press, 1979), 165.
30. Plato, *Parmenides* 160c–162a. Cf. Plotinus, *The Enneads* 1.8.3.
31. Augustine, *De Civitate Dei* 12.7–8; *De Libero Arbitrio* 3.1.2.
32. Jürgen Moltmann, *God in Creation*, trans. M. Kohl (London: SCM Press, 1985), 91. My italics.
33. Representatives of the movement in the 1960s were: Gabriel Vahanian, *The Death of God: The Culture of our Post-Christian Era* (New York: George Braziller, 1961); William Hamilton, *The New Essence of Christianity* (New York, Association Press, 1961); Thomas J. J. Altizer, *The Gospel of Christian Atheism* (London: Collins, 1967).
34. E.g. Eberhard Jüngel, 'Vom Tod des lebendigen Gottes: Ein Plakat', repr. in *Unterwegs zur Sache* (Munich: Chr. Kaiser, 1972), 105–25; *God as the Mystery of the World*, trans. D. Guder (Edinburgh: T. & T. Clark, 1983), 43–63, 94–104; Hans Küng, *The Incarnation of God*, trans. J. R. Stephenson

(Edinburgh: T. & T. Clark, 1987), 538–58; Jürgen Moltmann, *The Crucified God*, trans. R. A. Wilson and J. Bowden (London: SCM Press, 1974), 200–16.

35. Moltmann, *The Crucified God*, 243.
36. Ibid., 207, 217, 243ff. Cf. Moltmann, *The Future of Creation*, trans. M. Kohl (London: SCM Press, 1979), 64–79.
37. Ibid., 244.
38. Kübler-Ross, *On Death and Dying*, 77.
39. Raphael, *The Anatomy of Bereavement*, 347.
40. Jüngel, *God as the Mystery of the World*, 217–19.
41. Ibid., 199–204.
42. Ibid., 213.
43. Jüngel, 'Vom Tod des lebendigen Gottes', 121.
44. Jüngel, *God as the Mystery of the World*, 219.
45. Jüngel, *Death: The Riddle and the Mystery*, 112.
46. E.g. Jüngel, *God as the Mystery of the World*, 222: 'nothingness and its representative, death'.
47. In his book *The Crucified God*, 241, Moltmann quotes the phrase 'the first person of the Trinity casts out and annihilates the second' from a New Testament scholar, Wiard Popkes, in the context of affirming the 'delivering up' of the Son; also see *The Future of Creation*, 73. Later he denies approving these exact words: see *The Way of Jesus Christ*, trans. M. Kohl (London: SCM Press, 1990), 175–6.
48. Aquinas, *Summa Theologiae*, 1a.28.3, 30.4, 31.2, argues that there is real 'otherness' between the persons, but not alienation. Further, see Karl Rahner, *The Trinity*, 104ff.
49. Hans Urs von Balthasar, *Mysterium Paschale*, trans. A. Nichols (Edinburgh: T. & T. Clark, 1990), viii; *Theo-Drama: Theological Dramatic Theory*, Vol. IV. 326–8.
50. Von Balthasar, *Mysterium Paschale*, ix.
51. See above, Ch. 5, pp. 184–6.
52. *Mud and Stars: Report of a Working Party on The Impact of Hospice Experience on the Church's Ministry of Healing* (Oxford: Sobell Publications, 1991), 4.
53. Ibid., 143.
54. Ibid., 4.
55. The earliest evidence is Isaiah 26:19, then Daniel 12:2f. See Robert Martin-Achard, *From Death to Life: A Study of the Development of the Doctrine of the Resurrection in the Old Testament*, trans. J. Penney Smith (London: Oliver & Boyd, 1960), 130–46.
56. See John Bowlby, *Attachment and Loss, Volume 3: Loss* (Harmondsworth: Penguin Books, 1981), 86–93.
57. Lily Pincus, *Death and the Family: The Importance of Mourning* (London: Faber & Faber, 1976), 124.
58. See Melanie Klein, 'Mourning and its Relation to Manic-depressive

States', in *Love, Guilt and Reparation, and Other Works 1921–1945* (London: Virago, 1991), 352–5.

8

The Spirit of God
and Spiritual Gifts

'And in the Holy Spirit'. This abrupt statement of belief is *all* that the bishops gathered at Nicaea in AD 325 had to say about the Holy Spirit in their new creed. Nearly three centuries of church life after the day of Pentecost, the Holy Spirit appears as an appendix, or even a footnote. It is some explanation that the delegates were following existing baptismal creeds, and that the person of the Holy Spirit had not as yet become the same kind of storm-centre of controversy as had the Son. But even quite early commentators were embarrassed by such minimalism in the early creeds.[1] Nor would I be doing any better with this study if the Holy Spirit were indeed making a dramatic entrance for the first time in this penultimate chapter. In fact, while we have already explored ways in which talk about the Holy Spirit illuminates aspects of pastoral experience, in this chapter we shall be teasing out what the very elusiveness of this talk might mean for a doctrine of God.

The Anonymous Spirit

It *is* difficult to speak about the Holy Spirit, as the history of Christian doctrine bears witness. In line with the terse footnote of Nicaea, the Spirit appears as God incognito, God anonymous. The particular role of the Spirit in Christian experience and thinking appears hard to define or isolate. It seems that the label 'Holy Spirit' is often used to say things about our relationship to God or about God's activity that could as easily have been said about God the Father or the Son without mentioning the Spirit at all. As an example of this we might turn to the rite for the Ordination of Priests in *The Alternative Service Book 1980* of the Church of England (*ASB*). In choosing this example of language about the Spirit, I do not of course mean to imply that only ordained ministers receive pastoral gifts.

In his 'Declaration' near the beginning of the ordination service, the bishop urges that: 'Because you cannot bear the weight of this ministry in your own strength but only by the grace and the power of God, pray earnestly for his Holy Spirit.'[2] Here is an appeal to the Spirit as the source of power, and the church fathers reflected this biblical idea when they expanded and revised the Nicene Creed at Constantinople in AD 381: 'The Holy Spirit . . . the Lord and giver of life'.[3] But then in the act of ordination itself, the bishop prays: 'Almighty Father, give to these your servants grace and power . . .'[4] The *Father* himself is now being envisaged as the wellspring of power and energy.

Further in his Declaration, the bishop goes on to expand the idea of the Spirit's power by urging: 'Pray that he will each day enlarge and enlighten your understanding of the Scriptures.' Here is another motif for the work of the Spirit, the enlightener of minds and hearts, especially in connection with the writing and reading of Scripture; similarly the fathers at Constantinople affirmed: 'who spoke through the prophets'. But then in the prayers before the ordination, it is the 'Lord' or 'Holy God' who is asked to 'Enlighten your ministers with knowledge and understanding'; while the prayer begins with a petition addressed to the Trinity, from the concluding prayer it would appear that this 'Lord' is again the Father, since he is said to 'hear those who pray in the name of your Son . . .'[5]

We may take one more example from this rite. Before the prayers, there is to be sung the ancient hymn to the Holy Spirit, *Veni Creator*, with its significant line for ordination, 'Who dost thy sevenfold gifts impart'. Here is another traditional motif for the work of the Spirit, the giver of gifts or *charismata* (as in 1 Cor. 12:4–11). But then in the act of ordination, the bishop prays by recalling words from Ephesians 4:7–16 about the gifts of the ascended *Christ*, praising God that Christ has 'given his gifts abundantly . . . to equip your people for the work of ministry'. It is the Son who is now being celebrated as the gift-giver, but this announcement is immediately followed by the words, 'Send down the Holy Spirit upon your servant for the office and work of a priest in your Church'.

So in this Anglican rite of ordination, God the Father is invoked as the source of power and illumination, and the Son is praised as the source of gifts for ministry. What does it *add* to attribute power, enlightenment and gifts to the Spirit as well? What extra dimension, what new insight into the nature of God does the appeal to the Spirit give us? When John Wesley felt his heart 'strangely warmed' in the Aldersgate Street Chapel, he described this as the impact of *Christ* on his life.[6] Yet this experience was surely one of power, illumination and gifting, which gave impetus to his whole succeeding ministry.

Christians through the ages have found the idea of the Holy Spirit curiously hard to pin down. For the Apostle Paul there seems to be a shifting identity between the Risen Christ who is *present in* the Spirit, the 'Spirit of Christ', and the 'Spirit of God'. As George Hendry comments: 'The relation between the Spirit and Christ appears in [a] dialectical pattern of identity and distinction.'[7] What then does Paul mean when he declares in 2 Corinthians 3:17, 'Now the Lord is the Spirit'? Despite his confident tone, it seems an experimental, even playful, assertion. It was not surprising that when the church fathers came to say more about the Holy Spirit at the Council of Constantinople in AD 381 than they had previously managed at Nicaea, they modelled their thought on the conclusions they had already come to about the Son of God. The Son, they affirmed, is begotten from the Father and *homoousios* ('of one substance') with the Father; so also the Holy Spirit 'proceeds' from the Father and 'together with the Father and the Son is worshipped and glorified'. In the discussions around the making of the creed, the Cappadocian Fathers in general cautiously affirmed *homoousion* of the Spirit also, and Gregory of Nazianzus boldly asserted it.[8] But then, this led to the many later theological disputes on what the difference might be between 'being begotten' and 'proceeding', to talk of the 'two processions' and their relation to each other.[9]

Having worked out the model of the Fatherly begetter and the Filial begotten, the theologians of the fourth century thus portrayed the Spirit as a pale shadow of the Son. While progressing beyond the tendency of earlier theologians to subordinate the Spirit to the Son 'in third rank' or as 'the prophetic spirit' or as 'the grace of God',[10] the Spirit now duplicates the Son in fainter outline. The lingering of the Old English phrase 'Holy Ghost' evokes in modern English the notion of something vague, insubstantial and unreal. My aim, however, is to show that the anonymous face of the Spirit takes us instead into the most solid kind of reality.

Spirit as the Breath of Life (Ruach)

The word 'spirit' when applied to God is a metaphor. As used in Christian speech its origin is in the Old Testament, translating the Hebrew word *ruach* which means either 'breath' or 'wind'; it is a picture of air in movement, and this is also true of the Greek and Latin equivalents, *pneuma* and *spiritus*. Since moving air is invisible in itself (though its effects are not), it aptly evokes the anonymous character of the Spirit. Experiencing the mystery of God's activity among them, and searching for words, people exclaimed, 'it's like the wind', or 'it's like the breath in our bodies'.[11] If this ancient metaphor has gone dead on us, I suggest it might be revived by a modern image from medical science.

Some while ago a piece appeared in the *Guardian* newspaper, about 'celebrating 20 years on a respirator'. The writer − Ann Armstrong − was a polio sufferer, and she was reflecting on her experience of living for the past twenty years on the machine which made it possible for her to breathe at all. She writes wistfully about the time before her illness struck her when, she says, 'I possessed a much more efficient breathing machine of my own . . . a treasure chest . . . my own heart and lungs which had helped me to introduce myself to the world with my first yell.' Today, she writes,

> Even with the puff from my mechanical respirator I cannot
> make such a powerful shout now. In consequence I am
> always softly spoken and those around me can have no idea
> of the intensity of my passion or the commotion I should
> like to make at times.[12]

In Ann's story we catch something of her longing to breathe in deeply, to live with vitality, to communicate with the energy of that first 'yell' of birth. Instead she has only a puff of breath. And those of us who do have our own equipment for breathing, lungs all intact, can *still* feel a lack of energy, not simply in physical terms but at the psychical level of our being. We can feel 'winded' or 'breathless' − in our emotions, our minds, our spirits. We experience a lack that we may well express as a need to 'take a deep breath', to be filled with the breath of life. It was this kind of human experience that led people long ago in ancient Israel to speak about the 'Breath' of God, or the 'Spirit' of God. It was an image that enabled them to express the inexpressible, the action of God in human life and in the natural world. Reading their accounts, we find that the image had two dimensions.

First they were saying it was like the gentle moving of breath in our bodies, mysterious and fascinating. Our breath is close to us, intimate and yet not under our total control, stirring inwardly within us and promoting a sense of fullness of being and life. In

Hebraic thinking, physical life could not be separated out from moods and dispositions, and so *ruach* also expresses 'the whole range of [human] emotional, intellectual and volitional life'.[13] The writer of Genesis (2:7) affirms: 'The Lord God breathed into the man's nostrils the breath (*ruach*) of life and he became a living personality (*nephesh*).'[14] While the religious thinkers of ancient Israel, here and elsewhere, do not simply identify our bodily breath with the divine Spirit, they discern the closest analogy between them, finding the Spirit to be *like* human breath in its mysterious, immanent movement. The same kind of gentle breathing was also experienced in the kindly western winds of Palestine, the cool winds which heal the parching of the midday sun, refreshing and revitalising. With the cool winds blowing against their faces and their bodies, people could breathe again freely after the stifling heat; it was as if they came alive again once more.[15] This was a situation in which they could say: 'God's action with us is like *ruach*, like breath.'

But there was also a contrasting aspect of wind which they knew, the storm-wind with its awesome strength, blowing down between the hills of Palestine. The blast and gust of the gale showed up the weakness of human life: 'The grass withers [says the prophet], the flower fades, when the *ruach* of the Lord blows upon it' (Isa. 40:7). This is the wind, say the psalm-writers, that makes the oaks whirl, that strips the cedars, that shakes the forests, that drives the dust and chaff before it and whips up the waves of the sea.[16] So the activity of God among humankind could be experienced like that – overwhelming, subduing, seizing hold of human beings and mastering them. This is the Spirit that catches people up in its onward momentum, like a wind sweeping up leaves into its path, or propelling a sail on its course. When people saw a prophet suddenly prompted to utter powerful, insightful words that did not seem to be his, or when people saw a leader like Samson inspired to do impressive acts, they saw the moving of 'the Spirit'.[17] We notice that Ann in her account expresses the wish to have the breath to make a real 'commotion'.

So to speak of God as Spirit was to express God's astonishing aliveness, to name God as a living presence that could be experienced like two kinds of 'breath'. There is the gentle breath that moves deeply within our being, and there is the majesty of the strong wind, catching us up into its path; so there are two dimensions of Spirit – the Spirit within, and the Spirit beyond us. These correspond to Rudolph Otto's twofold description of the Holy as Mystery which is both 'fascinating and tremendous', or as 'attractive and awesome'.[18] Both aspects are mysterious, for this breath is not under our control, whether stirring deep within us, or catching us up from beyond.

Some biblical texts weave these ideas together, so that the image of being filled with the Spirit (like breath within us) is inseparable from the image of being taken into the flow of the Spirit (like wind beyond us); indeed, one interprets the other. It is as if the experience of being 'filled' with Spirit stems from participating in the realm of the Spirit. In his famous vision of the valley of the dry bones (Ezek. 37), the prophet Ezekiel is addressing a nation in the depths of depression. The Israelites are exiles in a foreign country; they have lost their homes, their occupations, their religious institutions, their monarchy, and above all – it seems to them – their God whom they locate in the shattered capital city. They feel weak, at the very lowest ebb. They feel just like a heap of dried-up bones lying on the open ground, bleaching white in the heat of the midday sun. And then Yahweh speaks his promise: he will come like the wind which is also breath (v. 9); he will give them life so that they will stand on their feet once more, not as a heap of broken human wreckage, but a great army, ready for action. This is not a picture of the resurrection of the individual beyond death, but the revival of a whole nation within history. God will breathe within it; and the four winds of the earth will blow, raising it up as dried leaves are whirled up from the ground by the force of the gale. The coming of the Spirit here is like breath within *and* breath beyond, stirring deep *and* taking people into its flow.

In the Fourth Gospel, there is the same combination of images.

The mysterious activity of the Spirit is portrayed as wind blowing through the world; but the hint is given that this is also breath in the body which is born from taking its first breath of air, an allusion confirmed by a similar text from Ecclesiastes:

> The wind blows where it wills; you hear the sound of it, but you do not know where it comes from, or where it is going. So with everyone who is born from spirit. (John 3:8 *NEB*)

> As you do not know how the breath comes to the bones in the womb of a woman with child, so you do not know the work of God who makes everything. (Ecclesiastes 11:5)

I have been referring so far to a biblical *analogy* between our experience of breath and wind and our experience of God as Spirit. But the examples show that the metaphor also points to something else. As Ian Ramsey proposes,[19] it seems from the Hebrew Scriptures that the experiences of drawing breath and of feeling the movement of the wind were actually the occasions which *gave rise* to these images of divine action. They were situations of disclosure or revelation, in which it became appropriate to speak of God's presence and activity as 'spirit', and so to 'license discourse about mystery and transcendence'.[20] Correspondingly, such language cannot be appreciated as abstract doctrine, but must be grounded in situations in experience. This insight fits in with my claim throughout this study that language about God is not observational but participatory. It arises from our participation in the life of God, enabled by God's own participation in the life of the world. The Spirit is Creator Spirit; that is, talk about God as Spirit is fitting because we encounter God as sustaining a creation in which life is experienced in breath and wind, while God is not to be simply identified with these events.

It may be pointed out, however, that the biblical images of spirit we have been exploring are not attached to 'the Holy Spirit' in the developed trinitarian sense of a third hypostasis within the being of God. They are about *God as Spirit*, about the activity of God in the world. The Old Testament *does* have a concept of the 'extended personality' of God,[21] so that God is present through such personifications as the divine word, name, wisdom and spirit. This may be seen as a witness to the experience of God as complex and not simple reality, even perhaps as a hint that the being of God is relational. But more argument is needed to justify the transference of these biblical images of 'Spirit' to the person of the Holy Spirit in the Christian doctrine of the Trinity. I hope to provide this as the chapter proceeds.

The Spirit: Self-Effacing in God and Us

'Wind' or 'breath' may be an image of anonymity when associated with God, but we need to ask *why* the Holy Spirit appears to be the anonymous face of God. We can, I suggest, detect two reasons, which are themselves closely connected with the image of *ruach*.

In the first place, the New Testament records the experience of early Christians that the Holy Spirit points away from the Spirit's own self towards God as Father and Christ as Son. In the memorable phrase of John Taylor, the Spirit is the 'Go-Between God', arousing awareness of Others. The Spirit awakens in us a consciousness of Christ, and alerts us to the 'Father' whom this Son is representing. In the language of the Fourth Gospel, this is an action of *glorifying* the Son and the Father (Jn 16:12–15). Jürgen Moltmann has drawn the important conclusion here that it is because the Spirit glorifies both Father and Son, and glorifies each through the other, that the Spirit also *unifies* them.[22] The action of glorifying is an anonymous one, apparently suppressing the subject who glorifies, but it brings about the union of God, the making of an even closer communion between the persons. Union in God is thus an eschatological concept; it is not only the origin, as unity, of the dance of perichoresis, not only the opening steps; as unification, it is the climax.

But if we go one step further and ask *how* the Spirit glorifies the Son and the Father, it is through the bringing of many human sons and daughters to glory. By glorifying creation, by transforming it by gifts and energies, the Spirit brings glory to God. It has thus been the insight of theologians like Moltmann and Pannenberg[23] that the unifying of creation through the Spirit actually effects the union of Father and Son. The work of the Spirit is eschatological for the world and for God, and for the world as it is *in* God. Precisely in glorifying and uniting creation in God, the Spirit glorifies and unites God in God's self. We might then, with Moltmann, speak of an 'eschatological Trinity' as well as an 'economic Trinity'.[24] God as Trinity has a real future. In the 'economic' Trinity, there is a movement of sending: the Father sends out the Son in the power of the Spirit. In the eschatological Trinity there is a reverse movement of glorifying: the Spirit glorifies the Father through the response of the Son. In the first movement God goes out into the world; in the second, God carries the world back into God's self.

We have already in past chapters explored the implications of these divine journeys for the suffering of God and the self-fulfilling of God. If we are ever inclined to miss noticing them, the biblical picture of the Spirit as wind, as air in movement, alerts us to *all* the threefold movements of the God who is on a costly voyage of love into the world. Thus it is not *alone* the Spirit who is 'catching up and incorporating the created realm into the life of God', as Sarah Coakley seeks to characterise the distinctness of the Spirit.[25] But the *particular* character of the movement of the Spirit, its anonymity in witnessing to Father and Son, certainly makes us aware that these movements of love and desire have a future orientation. We can lean into the wind beyond us and be carried into the heart of God, into the centre of the dance; participating in the glorifying of God, we are also carried towards the future.

The Spirit appears anonymous, then, first because the Spirit glorifies the Father and Son. But the image of breath *within* us, complementary to the wind which is *beyond* us, gives us a second clue: it indicates how very close the Spirit is to us, as close as the breath in our bodies. The Spirit is the 'breath of life' and life is so much part of us that we cannot stand back and look at it objectively.[26] The image of breath makes clear that the Spirit is so bound up with our lives that we find it hard to separate the Spirit out from ourselves. While the Spirit of God is not exactly the same as our spirit, the same words (*ruach*, *pneuma*) are used in Old and New Testaments for the two realities. In the Hebrew Scriptures, there is an overlap, even a blurring between the two, because God as '*ruach* and not flesh' continually sustains 'the *ruach* of all flesh';[27] this seems to be why the divine *ruach* can be operative directly in human persons. The Apostle Paul even makes the astonishing comment that God knows what is the mind of the Spirit because God searches the minds of people in whom the Spirit is present (Rom. 8:27).

The Orthodox theologian Vladimir Lossky makes the daring suggestion here that the Spirit is not only self-effacing before the Father and the Son, but 'the Holy Spirit effaces himself, as Person, before the created persons to whom he appropriates grace'. Commenting on the text of Paul that the Spirit cries 'Abba, Father' in our hearts (Rom. 8:14), he concludes that 'He mysteriously identifies himself with human persons while remaining incommunicable. He substitutes Himself, so to speak, for ourselves.'[28] H. Wheeler Robinson had earlier made a similar suggestion by speaking of the 'kenosis of the Spirit' in a humble accepting of human life as the medium of presence and activity.[29]

Now, I do not think we should conclude from all this with Karl Barth that the Spirit is to be defined as 'subjective revelation' where Christ as Son is the 'objective revelation' of the Father.[30] It is not the Spirit alone who engages with human persons and draws them into the divine life. Nor is it the Spirit alone who makes past events of salvation present in the life of the believer, communicating for example the benefits of the cross to our present experience. The Spirit is often appealed to like this, as a kind of practical application of salvation, a means of subjective appropriation, a filler of gaps in time and space. Often (though not in Barth), the assumption behind such a theory is that the Father and the Son are somehow absent from the world. Perhaps a dispensational scheme is in mind in which the Father has always been absent in absolute transcendence, and so sent the Son as a representative, and now the Son has also disappeared from the scene with his resurrection and ascension, leaving the Spirit in his place. It might just be possible to construct such a scenario from Luke's portrayal of the sequence of ascension and Pentecost (Acts 1: 4–11), but it does not fit with the Johannine picture in which Jesus promises that with the coming of the Spirit 'the Father and I will make our home with you' (Jn 14:18–24) or Paul's complementary affirmations that we are 'in Christ' as we are 'in the Spirit' (Rom. 8:1–17). The doctrine of God I have been presenting in these chapters is one in which the whole triune life of God is open to the world, and in which we are drawn into communion with the relationships within God – into the inter-weaving movements of being which are like the relations between Father, Son and Spirit. Participation in God overcomes the split between objective and subjective which has been an unhelpful part of our consciousness since the Enlightenment.

A Distinct Movement in God

The anonymity of the Holy Spirit is thus an eschatological self-effacement in God, and a self-effacement in human life which enables our participation in God. We are already unfolding here some of the distinct character of the movement in God that we call 'Holy Spirit', but at this point we should notice that 'wind' or 'breath' is only one of the range of pictures for the Spirit that appear in Scripture, though the most prominent one. All the images of Spirit strongly evoke movement.

There is, for instance, fire. Like wind it can be a gentle and warming movement, but like wind it can also be a violent force, like the fire in a volcanic eruption: 'The bloodstains of Jerusalem' will be removed 'by a Spirit of burning' (Isa. 4:4). There is oil, the gentle trickling down of oil for anointing: 'The Spirit of the Lord God is upon me because the Lord has anointed me' (Isa. 61:1). There is water: 'I will pour water upon the thirsty land, and streams upon the dry ground; I will pour my Spirit upon your descendants, and my blessing on your offspring' (Isa. 44:3). And there is the movement of wings through the air, wings brooding over the waters of chaos in the creation story of Genesis 1: 'And the Spirit of God hovered over the surface of the water' (*REB*).

These metaphors for the Spirit come to a focus and profusion in the New Testament, with the coming of Christ whose ministry in the Gospels is portrayed as being empowered by the Spirit. His healings, exorcisms and authoritative teaching are all traced to the energies of the Spirit, as they are equally grounded in his heightened awareness of God as Father.[31] These two aspects – anointing with the Spirit and sonship – come together in the baptism of Jesus, when the Spirit is described as descending like a dove, and the heavenly voice declares Jesus to be God's 'beloved Son'.[32] Here the moving of the Spirit is depicted through the images of running water, and of hovering wings like the those of the Spirit upon the dark waters in the Genesis story. The latter image is also recalled earlier in Luke's story of the Spirit's coming upon Mary at the conception of Jesus, 'overshadowing' her (Lk. 1:35). Jesus gives the Spirit to his disciples like breath (Jn 2:22), and the disciples at Pentecost experience the Spirit like wind and fire (Acts 2:2–3). Paul speaks of believers being immersed into Spirit like being plunged into water: 'For in the one Spirit we were all baptized into one body' (1 Cor. 12:13 *NRSV*).

These metaphors – blowing wind, pulsing breath, trickling oil, raging fire, pouring water, beating wings and (we may add) the outstreaming of light[33] – may appear to be impersonal. I suggest, however, that they are impressionistic images that are needed to evoke dimensions of personal relationships of which we are normally not aware. They awaken a sensitivity to deep and hidden areas of personal being which can only be described through such metaphors. They are archetypal symbols which cause us to go underground, deep beneath the surface of life; they awaken an awareness of areas that we sometimes call intuitive, at the level of mood or sympathy rather than logical argument. They allow us to notice the way that the Spirit moves in human community, moving between people and building bridges of awareness and empathy.

Such images for the Spirit thus enable us to talk about our relationship with God and with each other. But they also enable us to talk about the relationships *within* God. When we are tempted to reduce the relationship of 'Father' and 'Son' to a human kind of family relationship, like that between two finite individuals, talk of the Spirit challenges us. The one who is breath and fire and water cannot be reduced to the anthropomorphic. This Spirit cannot be anything other than movement. Further, if we ever thought that the movements of love in God that we call Father and Son were actually male in gender, we cannot so classify the Spirit. I do not mean that Spirit is feminine (like a token female on a divine committee), but that the great images for Spirit break open all gender-typing, with the result that we are open to noticing feminine characteristics in God alongside male ones. Again, if we are tempted to reduce God to a static kind of being, existing in a simultaneous eternity, we cannot exclude futurity from the Spirit whose images are full of dynamism and whose self-effacement (as we have seen) is bound up with a future unifying of God.

The images of the Spirit thus constantly open up our sense of God. They enable not only talk about God but participation in God, and they awaken us not only to encounter with God but to the nature of God. It would correspond to our *experience* of Spirit that Holy Spirit should be the movement within God that is constantly opening up the relationship of Father and Son to new depths of personality and to new fulfilment in the future. *All* the relations in God are movements of being, but we may discern a distinct movement that is always opening up the others, so that another image for the Spirit might be 'the disturber'.

Spirit of God and Holy Spirit

We might be confirmed in this understanding of the Spirit as 'the opener' or 'the disturber' by reflecting on another aspect of the difficulty we find in establishing the distinct identity and role of the Holy Spirit. It seems especially problematic to distinguish the 'Holy Spirit' as a 'person' (*hypostasis*) from the whole being of God as Spirit. When the Jesus of the Fourth Gospel affirms that 'God is Spirit, and those who worship him must worship in spirit and in truth' (Jn 4:24), he is echoing the use of *ruach* in the Hebrew Scriptures that we have already explored. When the church doctrine of the Trinity develops the incipient diversity in God represented by the personification of divine Spirit, it seems that the word 'Spirit' is now being used in an ambiguous and confusing way. God is Spirit, yet the Holy Spirit proceeds from the Father.

The Western tradition of the Trinity, following Augustine, has attempted to make this ambiguity into a positive advantage by conceiving the Spirit as the bond of love between Father and Son.[34] The affirmation that the Spirit proceeds 'also from the Son' (*filioque*)[35] emphasises the symmetry of the relation and, in effect, this identifies the Spirit with the essence of God.[36] In modern times, the best expression of this makes the bond an active *movement* of binding and not just a passive link in a chain; so Karl Barth describes the Holy Spirit as the 'common act' of the Father and Son, their mutual act of communion and self-giving. The Spirit *is* the very reciprocity of Father and Son.[37] But the obvious problem with this Western approach is that the Spirit does not appear to have a distinct identity, being either the common factor between Father and Son, or simply the divine nature. A separate hypostasis of the Holy Spirit can easily be dispensed with altogether, such as in the proposal of G. W. H. Lampe that we use language of Holy Spirit as 'a way of speaking about God in his activity and relationship with ourselves, interchangeable with "Word" language'.[38]

By contrast, the Eastern approach which insists that the Spirit proceeds from the Father alone, through the Son, makes clear the distinct identity of the Spirit as a *hypostasis* or person. But then the question arises, why only three? Why should there not be a multiplicity of hypostases which proceed from the Father? What about, for example, the claims of the Wisdom of God, the female

Holy Sophia, who seems to have been suppressed in early centuries in favour of the Logos of God who had a more masculine profile?[39] Why should there not be at least a quaternity of Father, Word, Spirit and Wisdom?

A valuable attempt to answer this question was made in the West, by a writer who broke somewhat away from the Western tradition of the Spirit as the bond of love. Richard of St Victor proposed that if God is love, there must be a plurality of persons in God for love to be actualised. But if there are only two, love will be self-enclosed. In the most fervent kind of love, observes Richard, you wish there to be another person who could be loved equally by the one whom you love supremely and by whom you are loved supremely: 'When a third is loved concordantly and socially by two, the affection of the two flows together in the kindling of a third love.'[40] Perhaps we might add the analogy of love between husband and wife which is opened up and fulfilled by love for a child.

The way that a third person opens up what could be a narrow and claustrophobic relationship has been explored in modern times by the playwright Harold Pinter, in such plays as *The Dumbwaiter* and *The Caretaker*. This is what Pinter had to say about these plays and others:

> Two people in a room – I am dealing a good deal of the time with this image of two people in a room. The curtain goes up on the stage, and I see it as a very potent question: What is going to happen to these two people in the room? Is someone going to open the door and come in?[41]

The room represents security, the status quo, traditional ways of thinking, a narrow space of life. Something dramatic will happen when the Third Person enters. The two will be forced to search themselves and each other more deeply, to ask questions they have never asked of each other before, when the Third Person comes in.[42] They may even be asked to take the leap of courage to leave the room and go outside. So in our human experience the Holy Spirit is the Third Person who comes in, who opens up relationships, who makes us look more deeply at ourselves, at others and our society around us. When the Third Person comes, it is to disturb – and through disturbing, to make a new fellowship. Two are never complete without the Third. And if this is true of *our* experience of the Spirit, it must surely also correspond to the fellowship of the Spirit in the communion of God's life. The Spirit is the disturber, the opener, the third over against the two.

But neither Richard nor our theological appropriation of Pinter really answer the question: why only a third? There must be *at least* a third to open up the two, but why stop at three? I suggest that the strength of the Western idea of the Spirit as the bond of love or the mutual act of loving does answer the question, 'why three?' There are two, and the reciprocity of the two. And yet this under-plays the distinct identity of the Spirit. By contrast, the Eastern view of the Spirit as proceeding only from the Father retains identity, and may be developed into the image of the Third who opens up the relationship of the other two. But with the Eastern approach it is not clear why there must be only three, and so I believe it is possible to combine the strength of both these visions of God.

When we speak of the 'Spirit of God', or 'God as Spirit', we mean the being of God in communion, the divine essence, the mutual relating of persons. The Spirit is the fire of love glowing through the divine movements of love that we usually name 'Father' and 'Son', uniting them in their difference and shining forth from them. But when we use the name 'Holy Spirit', we mean that through the initiative of the Father, this common life now stands over against Father and Son as a disturbing element, a movement of being that is always opening up the relationships of Father and Son to new depths and a new future. This is the same life and love, but constantly renewing itself.

This may be what Pannenberg intends when he comments that:

> The Spirit comes forth as a separate hypostasis as he comes
> over against the Son and the Father as the divine essence,

common to both, which actually unites them and also attests and maintains their unity in the face of their distinction.[43]

But he seems to lose the otherness of the Spirit by envisaging that the Spirit in 'coming forth' is still only playing the role of the common divine essence. Pannenberg tries to hold together the Spirit as separate person and divine essence by an analogy with field theory in modern physics. The Spirit, he urges, is both the force field of God's fellowship and one form or manifestation of the field.[44] But surely, when the Spirit 'comes forth over against . . .' it must be as a *disturbing* presence in the field.

Spiritual Gifts and Nature

In a moment I want to consider the role of the Spirit as opener and disturber in pastoral practice. But we cannot do this without considering first the idea of 'spiritual gifts', which have already appeared in our opening quotations from the *ASB* rite for ordination. The New Testament word is *charismata*, but unfortunately this term is frequently drawn into a distinction between two separate realms that are named 'the supernatural' and 'the natural'. Spiritual gifts are often contrasted with natural gifts, and so a kind of spiritual élitism develops, as well as an escapism from the natural world. Usually, more spectacular phenomena like spiritual healing, prophecy, deliverance from evil powers and speaking in tongues are classified as 'spiritual' or 'supernatural' gifts, and activities like hospitality, generous giving, acts of kindness and efficient administration are dismissed as 'merely natural gifts', despite the fact that they appear in a list of *charismata* in the New Testament (Rom. 12:7–13). Spiritual gifts are seen as being 'supernatural' in the sense of direct intervention by God, acting unilaterally and setting the realm of nature on one side.

In contrast, our thought in this volume has been about a God who always works in co-operation with the created world, influencing and persuading rather than coercing. This is a vision of grace *through* nature; if the word 'supernatural' is ever used for an act of grace, it must never be divorced from the natural. As Sallie McFague has wittily proposed, we should therefore speak of 'Super, Natural Christians' in the sense of being those who are 'excessively, superlatively concerned with nature and its well-being'.[45] This approach is now supported by our understanding of the Holy Spirit as a *movement* of the being of God. In the New Testament spiritual gifts are not possessions of the believer, but something which the Spirit does; they are acts of the Spirit's giving, happenings in which the Spirit acts to manifest grace. As James Dunn puts it neatly: 'The exercise of a spiritual gift is itself the charisma.'[46] There must then be a place in the world *where* the Spirit acts, an area in nature where the Spirit moves, like a field or a town through which the wind blows. As we have seen, the image of wind or breath makes no sense unless there are natural contexts where this language comes alive.

As the listing of such gifts as hospitality alongside such gifts as healing should tell us, there is always a base in nature for *charismata*, always a natural foundation for all spiritual gifts.[47] This can readily be seen in such gifts as teaching, preaching and pastoral care, but it is no less true of the more unusual phenomena that are often called charismatic. For example, I have already suggested (in Chapter 4) that in so-called 'spiritual healing' God can use hidden and mysterious processes in nature; after all, inexplicable remissions and recoveries take place quite outside any religious faith. To take another example of a high-profile *charisma*, one might speak of 'prophecy' where a word is spoken which exactly matches a situation, a word of insight is uttered which 'hits the spot'. It is a word in season, which might be heard by individuals as applying to them, or spoken into a Christian community corporately, or into the wider society. But we can again discern a quite natural foundation here, that we sometimes describe as a 'hunch' or a 'sixth sense'. We can relate to others in ways that are more a matter of mood or sympathy than surface communication, and some people are quite skilled at picking up these signals and having intuitive perceptions about what might be wrong with a situation. The Spirit might breathe through such a natural intuition and make it into a *charisma*, a prophetic word. Again, ecstatic 'visions' might well be brain events, triggered by such factors as stress, migraines or chemical changes, in which images of memory are released from the substrate of the temporal lobe. But, as the psychologist Oliver Sacks judges, this 'does not detract in the least from their . . . spiritual signifi-cance', or prevent their becoming 'portals to the beyond or the unknown'.[48]

I have taken these examples to make clear that no *charismata* should be put into a category of the 'purely supernatural'. We will, however, be far more likely to encounter what Jürgen Moltmann calls the 'everyday *charismata* of the lived life'. Through the calling of faith, he stresses, every individual's potentialities and natural powers are 'charismatically quickened and put at the service of the liberating kingdom of God'.[49] Nevertheless, to insist that all *charismata* have a natural foundation does not mean that this always has to be there beforehand, ahead of the gifting. Given the sense of *charismata* as actions performed, the Spirit may inspire new kinds of gifts which are not already present as corresponding natural capacities; the point is that, wherever this happens, they will then also have a basis in nature. To meet the needs of a changing culture, individuals may be endowed with *new* abilities, not only for the service of the church in worship and life within its walls, but for sharing in the mission of God in the world. That is, people will receive new gifts of healing, reconciliation and prophetic insight which will be appropriate for such contexts as the competition of the money-markets, the repetitive boredom of the factory, the lonely world of cyberspace-working, and the internal stresses of homes which take forms beyond the nuclear family.

All these gifts will be *charismata*, as the Spirit seizes hold of different areas of our lives and personalities, making them play-grounds for charismatic activity, places where the wind blows.

Spiritual Gifts and the Holy Spirit

Although I have written about the role of the Holy Spirit in spiritual gifts, it might be said that they could just as well be related to the work of God as a whole, God whose whole being is Spirit. Why should we relate the *charismata* to the person of the Holy Spirit in particular? As the *ASB* rite for ordination reminds us, it is the gifts of the *Christ* which are being celebrated in Ephesians 4. The *charismata* should be seen as the taking up of natural faculties into the perichoretic life of God, into interweaving movements of love and justice. Thus nature is graced. It hardly seems, then, that the bestowing of spiritual gifts answers our initial question about what might be the *particular* role of the Holy Spirit in the work of God in the world.

I suggest that it is not the *charismata* themselves that display the work of the Holy Spirit, but the dimension *within* them that is always opening situations up to new possibilities. This is what John Taylor calls the wild, 'Dionysiac' element of the Spirit.[50] As nature participates in the movement of the Spirit, it is opened up to new depths and a new future, in surprising and unpredictable ways. Perhaps this is why 'fellowship' is assigned to the Spirit in a well-known New Testament blessing (2 Cor. 13:14). Although 'fellowship' must belong to the whole life of the triune God which is open to our participation (1 Jn 1:3–7), there is an aspect of a *charisma* that goes beneath the surface of life, into regions that we might call intuitive. There is a whole level of interaction between persons that happens too deep for words, and we have already seen that we need spirit-language to evoke this.

In his book *The Go-Between God*, John Taylor takes one of the symbols for our experience of Spirit, that of the New Testament picture of being 'baptised' in Spirit, as if immersed in water. Imaginatively he explores the range of this image by drawing attention to the experience of people who swim underwater, and who speak of the startling closeness that is felt when two swimmers meet and clasp each other in an almost weightless embrace.[51] Such, he suggests, is the interaction that is possible beneath the surface of life;

we can touch and affect one another at the deepest level, with an openness of sympathy and intuition. Sometimes we transmit not words but moods to each other ('the atmosphere was so charged you could light a torch with it', we might say). Sometimes we communicate through bodily, non-verbal signals without being aware we are doing it. People who are especially skilled at picking up these signs become good counsellors and advisors. Unlike Taylor, I have been affirming that the whole triune life of God should be called 'Go-Between God', not just the the Spirit, since we encounter other created persons in the midst of the divine dance; but Taylor is surely right to detect a particular role for the Spirit as the bridge of communication, the spark of electric charge, between people at hidden, non-conceptual levels of experience. The wild, untamed quality of the Spirit in the *charismata* is felt in the sudden breaking down of barriers between what we usually hold apart as the conscious and the unconscious.

There is also something wild and disturbing about the Spirit in unexpectedly opening up the intercourse between the present, the past and the future. The traditional association of the Spirit with the *charismata* of illumination and enlightenment points to the bringing of the past *word* into the present, both from Scripture and church tradition. It is, of course, not only the Spirit who acts to illumine the mind, as the *ASB* rite of ordination has reminded us. The poem which stands as a Prologue to the Fourth Gospel affirms that it is the eternal Word, identified with Christ, who 'enlightens everyone who comes into the world'. As we are taken into the dance of the Trinity, we discover the distinctive movement of the Logos, continually summing up the patterns of the universe into a coherence that can be grasped: 'in him all things hold together' (Col. 1:17). But as we share in the distinctive movement of the Spirit within the dance, we are able to take new creative steps with the word, receiving the tradition and being able to take creative leaps of interpretation for the present day. This meaning may not be exactly what the writers themselves intended as they witnessed to the Word in their time, and there may often seem to be something uncontrolled about it. But in this re-creation of meaning today in the impulse of the Spirit, all must take part, not only the scholar. In Latin America, it is the poor and unlearned, the peasants and factory-workers in the base communities who have seen the meaning of the New Testament text for their society in a way that the priests have failed to do.[52]

At the same time, as we engage in the particular movement of love in God that is Spirit and that always has a dynamic tendency towards the future, we can dream the dreams of a future Kingdom of peace and justice. This is what Harvey Cox has called 'political fantasy' which is 'not content to dream up interesting twists within existing societal patterns'.[53] The vision of the new creation, fed by the stories and symbols of past tradition, makes us discontented with the status quo of the present; these dreams are therefore not escapist, since they offer the motivation to challenge decaying and oppressive structures in society and church.

A further disturbing element of the *charismata* is their amazing diversity and exuberant variety. This is both characteristic of the 'wildness' of the Spirit, and also stems from the rooting of charismata in nature, since the diversity of gifts will reflect the diversity of personalities and circumstances. Christian ministers may react in several ways to try and control this embarrassing plenitude of gifts. The liberation theologian José Comblin writes from his experience of the church in Brazil that the clergy are good at taming the *charismata* of the laity by organising them. People manifest gifts of teaching, healing and caring and these are chanelled within huge administrative machines to carry out works of education, health and assistance to the needy. The result of this organisation is that people lose the sense of their charism, and that the charisms that do not fit in with ecclesiastical plans can be 'selected out'. Comblin observes that 'Like all bureaucracies, the clergy tend to simplify, to rationalize, to cut down diversity.'[54]

A second way of exercising control looks at first more charismatic than bureaucratic, and therefore may be the more dangerous. This is where one person's *charisma* becomes dominant, usually the *charisma* of the pastor or priest, and everyone else's gifts are subordinated to serve it. Someone with a gift for healing, for instance, turns the whole church into a healing centre. Someone with a gift for communicating the gospel of Christ in the youth culture of today insists that everyone should adopt this style of culture under his personal direction. The latter example is not invented, but is what seems to have happened at the now notorious 'Nine O'Clock Service' in Sheffield, which had attempted to re-mint worship in a 'disco' style. The disillusioned worship leaders who gave interviews on the BBC TV *Everyman* programme in October 1995 insisted that the problems had not begun with the later sexual abuse of women by the priest in charge, which had hit the headlines. It had, they said, been 'an abuse of religious power' from the beginning, as everyone had to conform to the vision of the leader, good though it may have been at first.

It is perhaps because of insecurity that Christian ministers seek to control and suppress the *charismata* of others, to reduce the diversity to their own plans. But the call of Christ to an office of pastoral oversight should make pastors confident enough to give power – in a secular sense – away. True spiritual power is the power of increasing the faith of others, guiding their prayer, stimulating their service and making liturgy a sacred drama through which people can live in the glory of the new creation. The greatest power is that of persuasion and influence. So Jesus in the Fourth Gospel says of the Spirit: 'He will convince the world.' This is the Spirit in whom and by whom we live, 'who with the Father and Son is to be worshipped and glorified, world without end'.

NOTES
1. See J. N. D. Kelly, *Early Christian Creeds*, third edn (London: Longman, 1972), 152–3.
2. *The Alternative Service Book 1980. Services Authorized for Use in the Church of England* (Oxford: Oxford University Press/Mowbray, 1980), 357.
3. See Kelly, *Early Christian Creeds*, 338–44.
4. *Alternative Service Book*, 362.

5. Ibid., 361.
6. *The Journal of John Wesley*, abridged Christopher Idle (Tring: Lion Publishing, 1986), 46 (entry for 21 May).
7. George Hendry, *The Holy Spirit in Christian Theology*, revised edn (London: SCM Press, 1965), 24.
8. Gregory Nazianzen, *Orationes* 31.10; 34.11. Cf. Gregory of Nyssa, *De Oratione Dominica* 3; more cautiously, Basil, *Epistolae* 159.2.
9. E.g. Augustine, *De Trinitate* 5.12; 15.29; Aquinas, *Summa Theologiae* 1a. 27.2–5; Duns Scotus, *Opus Oxoniense* 1, 2, q.1, n.18.
10. See Justin Martyr, *Apologia I* 13.3, 60.6f., 64.1ff.; Origen, *In Iohannem* 2.10.75, 77; Hippolytus, *Contra Noetum* 14.
11. The double meaning of *ruach* as 'breath' and 'wind' made it a richer concept theologically than the other word for breath, *nᵉshamah*.
12. Article, 'Polio victim Ann Armstrong celebrates twenty years of survival at home on a respirator', *The Guardian*, 6 September 1977.
13. Aubrey R. Johnson, *The Vitality of the Individual in the Thought of Ancient Israel* (Cardiff: University of Wales Press, 1964), 30–2.
14. For *nephesh* or vitality (hence also standing for the complete personality) see above, pp. 231–2.
15. For this description, see Ian Ramsey, *Models for Divine Activity* (London: SCM Press, 1973), 6.
16. E.g. Psalms 18:10–15; 29:5–9; 82:13–18; 147:18; 107:25.
17. E.g. Judges 15:14–16; 1 Samuel 10:10, 16:13; 1 Kings 18:12; 2 Chronicles 15:1; Isaiah 11:2.
18. Rudolph Otto, *The Idea of the Holy*, trans. J. W. Harvey (London: Oxford University Press, 1925), 42; cf. 13–18, 31–9.
19. Ramsey, *Models for Divine Activity*, 7–9.
20. Ibid., 8.
21. Aubrey R. Johnson, *The One and the Many in the Israelite Conception of God* (Cardiff: University of Wales Press, 1942), 19–24.
22. Jürgen Moltmann, *The Church in the Power of the Spirit*, trans. M. Kohl (London: SCM Press, 1977), 58–62.
23. Moltmann, ibid., 63–5; Wolfhart Pannenberg, *Systematic Theology*, Vol. 1, trans. G. W. Bromiley (Grand Rapids, Mich.: Eerdmans, 1991), 444–6.
24. Moltmann, *The Church in the Power of the Spirit*, 63. On the meaning of 'economic Trinity', see above p. 6.
25. Sarah Coakley, 'Why Three? Some Further Reflections on the Origins of the Doctrine of the Trinity' in Sarah Coakley and David Pailin (eds), *The Making and Remaking of Christian Doctrine: Essays in Honour of Maurice Wiles* (Oxford: Clarendon Press, 1993), 36–7.
26. See Jürgen Moltmann, *The Spirit of Life*, trans. M. Kohl (London: SCM Press, 1992), 157.
27. Johnson, *The Vitality of the Individual in the Thought of Ancient Israel*, 32.

28. Vladimir Lossky, *The Mystical Theology of the Eastern Church* (Cambridge: James Clarke & Co., 1957), 172.

29. H. Wheeler Robinson, *The Christian Experience of the Holy Spirit* (London: Nisbet, 1928), 83, 87.

30. Karl Barth, *Church Dogmatics*, trans. and ed. G. W. Bromiley and T. F. Torrance (Edinburgh: T. & T. Clark, 1936–77), I/1, 449–53.

31. See, for instance, Mark 3:11, 5:7. James D. G. Dunn, *Jesus and the Spirit* (London: SCM Press, 1975), 5–7, attributes both these aspects to the consciousness of the historical Jesus.

32. Mark 1:10–11; Matthew 3:16–17; Luke 3:22.

33. 2 Corinthians 3:7–8, 17–18; cf. 4:6.

34. Augustine, *De Trinitate* 5.12; 15.27–31. See in modern theology Eberhard Jüngel, *God as the Mystery of the World*, trans. D. Guder (Edinburgh: T. & T. Clark, 1983), 327–8; Barth, *Church Dogmatics*, IV/2, 757f.

35. For discussion, see above, pp. 77, 80.

36. See Pannenberg, *Systematic Theology*, Vol. 1, 427–8.

37. Barth, *Church Dogmatics*, I/1, 469–70.

38. G. W. H. Lampe, *God as Spirit* (Oxford: Oxford University Press, 1977), 219. Lampe, of course, is also dispensing with a separate hypostasis of a pre-existent Son.

39. See Joan C. Engelsman, *The Feminine Dimension of the Divine* (Philadelphia, PA: Westminster Press, 1979), 74–120.

40. Richard of St Victor, *De Trinitate* 3.11, 19, translated in Edmund J. Fortman, *The Triune God: A Historical Study of the Doctrine of the Trinity* (London: Hutchinson, 1972), 193. Richard Swinburne re-uses Richard's argument in 'Could there be more than one God?', *Faith and Philosophy* 5 (1988), 225–41.

41. Harold Pinter, BBC interview with Hallam Tennyson (7 August 1960), cited in Martin Esslin, *The Theatre of the Absurd* (Garden City: Doubleday, 1961), 199.

42. David L. Miller, *The Three Faces of God: Traces of the Trinity in Literature and Life* (Philadelphia, PA: Fortress Press, 1986), 117–27, similarly finds a hint of the Trinity in the configuration of relationships in Pinter's plays, but without any development of the concept of the Spirit.

43. Pannenberg, *Systematic Theology*, Vol. 1, 429.

44. Ibid., 382–4, 430.

45. Sallie McFague, *Super, Natural Christians: How We Should Love Nature* (London: SCM Press, 1997), 6.

46. Dunn, *Jesus and the Spirit*, 254.

47. Cf. D. L. Gelpi, *Charism and Sacrament* (London: SPCK, 1977), 107ff.

48. Oliver Sacks, *The Man Who Mistook His Wife for a Hat* (London: Picador, 1986), 122.

49. Moltmann, *The Spirit of Life*, 183.

50. John V. Taylor, *The Go-Between God: The Holy Spirit and the Christian Mission* (London: SCM, 1972), 50–2.
51. Ibid., 44.
52. See Christopher Rowland and Mark Corner, *Liberating Exegesis* (Louisville, KY: Westminster/John Knox Press, 1989), 38–46.
53. Harvey Cox, *The Feast of Fools* (New York: Harper & Row, 1969), 82. So also Jürgen Moltmann, *The Future of Creation*, trans. M. Kohl (London: SCM Press, 1979), 55–7.
54. José Comblin, *The Holy Spirit and Liberation*, trans. P. Burns (London: Burns & Oates, 1989), 113.

9

The Incarnate God and the
Sacramental Life

Persons and Bodies

There have been several recent books on the dangers as well as the
benefits of the internet, that electronic spider's web linking millions
of computers throughout the world. In one book, the author interviews a number of people who have 'virtual relationships' with
other net-users. These are people who meet, talk and even – it
seems – find love in cyberspace. What fascinated the author was
the way that these relationships were not just a matter of words (or
rather duodecimal digits), but seem to have taken over the whole
person, including the body. This was despite the fact that the
internet was supposed to offer a reality that was purely mental, free
from the limits of the body. Although one net-user gave the author
permission to communicate with his 'virtual partner', he became
increasingly agitated, abruptly took the keyboard back, and could
hardly type because his hands were shaking so much. He felt that
this had been an intrusion on an intimate relationship. Other people
the author talked to felt strongly that they were being unfaithful to
their married partners by having such relationships, and that they
had – virtually – committed adultery. His conclusion was that the
cyberspace personality had taken on a 'surprising substance'.[1]

This modern (postmodern?) phenomenon confirms that encounters between persons always involve the body. Words that are spoken are also embodied in looks, gestures and other bodily language. There is no such thing as a purely mental communication. Even between two net-users who only meet in virtual space there is bodily communication. Of course, there is the use of the fingers to type and eyes to monitor the screen, but beyond this there is a commitment of the whole body to the interchange in a way that cannot be entirely rationally analysed. Those who have a 'virtual' social life know, or feel, that it still happens in some way through the body.

This raises a key issue for the way that we know God. Does it make any sense to speak of a 'personal encounter' with God, if God does not have a body? In this book I have been giving an account of an engagement with a personal God in various pastoral contexts. To be sure, I have not been writing about an 'I–Thou' encounter with either *one* personal being or *three* personal beings, but about participating in a flow of personal relationships in God which are like 'movements between' an I and a Thou. Nevertheless, this is a personal way of talking about encounter with God. Can we use such language at all if God is Spirit, without a body? John Macquarrie proposes that we cannot, and so urges that when it comes to God, talk about encounter with 'Being that lets-be' is more adequate than talk about personal relationships.[2] I suggest we do not attempt to meet this challenge by arguing that there *can* be disembodied personal meetings; the limiting case of the internet adulterers would be against us. We should rather take a different path altogether, to assert that *God indeed does have a body.*

Of course, all talk about God must be analogy, and so has an element of the 'unlike' as well as the 'like' about it. I am not suggesting that God has a body in the same way that we are embodied, but that God commits God's own self to body – or rather, to bodies – as a meeting place with us. The divine Word will not be spoken without physical mediation. God takes on bodies in order to draw us into the triune relationships in God. This conviction is at the heart of the Christian tradition. Christian belief is about the incarnation of the divine Logos in flesh and blood; it is about physical sacraments which connect us here and now with the Word-made-body; it affirms that the bodies of men and women make up the body of Christ in the church, and that eternal life can only be conceived as the resurrection of the body in the image of Christ's body of glory. Christianity is a religion of the body and so it is highly surprising, as Sallie McFague notes, that it has so often disparaged the body, and especially been offended by the bodies of women.[3] There is a Western intellectual tradition (stemming from Plato and Aristotle[4]) in which a polarity of mind and body is associated with the difference between male and female. While men have been identified with reason, women have been defined as bodies embedded in 'mere' nature, and so regarded as inferior to mind. Feminist theologians such as McFague and Grace Jantzen[5] diagnose a consequent 'deep sickness' in our culture, which is an inability to love the body of the earth and a corresponding hatred of our own bodies. To the healing of this sickness I want to return.

For the moment I want to explore two ideas that belong to the belief that God is committed to bodies. First I want to examine what it might mean to call the whole universe the 'body of God', or to take what is often called a 'sacramental view of the world'. If the world is in some sense God's body, then personal encounter with God is possible in its many and varied places. As Gerard Manley Hopkins exclaims:

> The world is charged with the grandeur of God.
> It will flame out, like shining from shook foil;
> It gathers to a greatness, like the ooze of oil
> Crushed . . .[6]

Second, I want to consider what it might mean to call a Christian pastor a 'living sacrament', and here I include with ordained ministers all those who are commissioned to care for others – doctors, nurses, social workers and others who through their circumstances have become 'carers' as a way of life. These two enquiries are interlinked, as I hope we shall see; but clearly, we will not get very far unless we first consider what the word 'sacrament' implies.

Sacrament and Divine Presence

Theological debates about the sacraments in Christian history have tended to focus on notions of 'substance'. With regard to the eucharist, does the earthly substance of bread and wine become the *substantia* of God, despite its outward appearance and qualities ('accidents')? Does the substance of the water in baptism become a holy substance, something different from ordinary water, that has the virtue of cleansing from sin?

Throughout this study I have been urging that, in our doctrine of God, we should make a shift in thought from substance language which is static, to dynamic ideas of movement and relationship. God *happens*, in an interweaving flow of relationships like those between a father and a son, opened up and deepened by the currents of the Spirit. This would lead us to an understanding of the sacraments as pieces of earthly stuff that are meeting places with this God who exists in ecstatic movements of love. They are doors into the dance of perichoresis in God. If we use the time-honoured phrase of the *Book of Common Prayer* that the sacraments are 'outward and visible signs of an inward and spiritual grace', then we shall not think of the 'grace' as a kind of substance or divine fluid, but as God's gracious coming and dwelling with us. They are signs which enable us to participate in the drama of death and resurrection which is happpening in the heart of God. We share in death as we share in the broken body of the bread and in the extravagantly poured out wine, and as we are covered with the threat of hostile waters. We share in life as we come out from under the waters (whether immersed in them or affused by them), to take our place in the new community of the body of Christ, and to be filled with the new wine of the Spirit.

When Augustine used the word *signum* of the sacraments he

meant more than a visual aid. Through the Word of God, the outer material sign could *convey* (without being confused with) the *virtus sacramenti* or the grace in the sacrament.[7] We may adopt the useful definition of Paul Tillich here, and say that these signs are 'symbols' in the sense of enabling us to 'participate in the reality' to which they point,[8] and that the grace is in this very act of participation. Such an understanding of the eucharist and baptism as sacred drama is in fact common in modern sacramental theology, whether Protestant, Orthodox or Catholic. The agreed statement of Anglican and Roman churches on the eucharist speaks of the presence of Christ in the 'whole action' of the rite, not isolated in the elements.[9]

This idea of participation does full justice to the commitment of God to bodies, and to the real presence of the triune God in and through the sacraments. It takes substance seriously, but not in the sense of identifying divine and human substances with each other. After all, there *is* no such God-substance to be identified. The earthly substance, the material stuff, is a means of being drawn into the movements of the divine life. So there is a kind of 'transvaluation' of the worldly object. This understanding of sacrament also enables us to extend the sacramental principle beyond the two sacraments of Reformation faith (or the seven sacraments of Trent). Working from the focal point of eucharist and baptism we can also find a sacramental encounter with God in the gathering of disciples of Christ. Paul surely intends this when he uses the phrase 'body of Christ' in an overlapping way of the resurrection body of Christ, the communion bread, and the church. They are all 'body of Christ', not in an absolute identification but because in both bread *and* fellowship we can encounter the risen Christ. As the Reformer Zwingli perceived in commenting on 1 Corinthians 10.17, 'We eat bread so that we are made into one bread . . . What we become by this eating . . . is the body of Christ.'[10]

Correspondingly, the understanding of the 'church meeting' in the English nonconformist tradition among Baptist and Congregational (now mainly United Reformed) churches has been highly sacramental, even when church members would be surprised to hear it described like this. In this meeting, members of the church gather together to find the mind of Christ. They vote on issues, not to impose a majority view but to find the purpose of the risen Lord for their life and mission. Because Christ is embodied among them through the meeting of their bodies, they expect to be able to discern his mind for them. In the seventeenth century it was common practice for members to hold the church meeting either immediately before or after the Lord's Supper. So the church book, which recorded the names of the members, the church covenant and all the decisions taken in the church meeting, was kept in a drawer in the bench behind the Lord's table, or in the 'table pew'. Here is a symbol of the sacramental significance of the coming together of human bodies into the body of Christ – table and church book together.

But the extension of sacrament reaches beyond the bodies of believers into the whole body of the world. From the focus of the Lord's table, we can discern the presence of God at every meal table, and in the whole process of sustaining life in our complex ecosystem. Every living creature and plant at whatever level of creation needs food and nourishment in order to survive and grow. We may find here the presence of the generous God who was found at the meal-table of Jesus when he ate with outcasts and sinners during his ministry, and when he shared table-fellowship with his disciples after his resurrection. From the focus of baptism we can find God in the many occasions in the world where water is involved: in the experience of the breaking of waters in birth, in moments of refreshment, when passing over a boundary river, in the washing away of what is unclean, and in facing the hostile force of great floods.[11] The particular moment of encounter with God through the elements of eucharist and baptism can thus awaken us to the God who can be met through the many bodies of the world. Discerning the body of Christ in the breaking of the bread enables us to discern him through the broken bodies of the prisoners, the thirsty and the hungry.

In this reflection on sacraments, the direction of thought has been from the particular to the universal. I have been following the thought of Teilhard de Chardin, who speaks of 'prolongations' and 'extensions' of the eucharist. He writes, 'From the particular cosmic element into which he has entered, the Word goes forth to subdue and to draw into himself all the rest.'[12] So, when Teilhard was on a geological field trip in the bitter-cold mountains of Northern China in 1923, he wrote a piece called *Mass on the World*, and begins:

> Since once again, Lord – though this time not in the forests
> of the Aisne but in the steppes of Asia – I have neither
> bread, nor wine, nor altar, I will raise myself beyond these
> symbols, up to the pure majesty of the real itself; I, your
> priest, will make the whole earth my altar and on it will offer
> all the labours and sufferings of the world . . .
>
> I will place on my paten, O God, the harvest to be won
> by this renewal of labour. Into my chalice I shall pour all
> the sap which is to be pressed out this day from the earth's
> fruits . . .[13]

For Teilhard, this is not merely a playful simile. He believes he is *actually* celebrating the mass: 'Do you now therefore, speaking through my lips, pronounce over this earthly travail your twofold efficacious word . . . This is my Body . . . This is my Blood.'[14] But he can make this universal celebration, *only because* bread and wine are consecrated in the eucharist of the church.

In another piece called *Christ in the World of Matter*, written in 1916 in the trenches of the First World War where he served as a stretcher-bearer, Teilhard tells the stories of three visions. The person recounting the visions is supposedly a close friend, but it is clearly Teilhard talking about himself. First he contemplates a picture of Christ, and sees the outlines of the portrait dissolving away, so that (he says) 'it was as though the planes which marked off the figure of Christ from the world surrounding it were melting into a single vibrant surface whereon all demarcations vanished'.[15] Similarly he sees a piece of communion bread displayed in a monstrance, and watches its surface spread out like an aureole of light from a lamp, until 'through the mysterious expansion of the host the whole world had become incandescent, had itself become like a single giant host'.[16] The third vision I will return to in a moment, but it is clear that Teilhard sees the particular expanding or extending into the universal.

There is of course an alternative way of conceiving the world as a sacrament, that is to begin with the *universal* body of the cosmos and then consider the particular sacraments of the church as being windows into the larger scene, paradigms of the whole. The universal will not then be dependent upon any particular instance. Bread and wine can be sacraments of grace because the entire ecosystem which sustains life with its many and varied bodies is *already* a sacrament of the presence of God. This is the path of thought taken by Sallie McFague in her book *The Body of God*. The difference between these two approaches has a significant effect on our doctrine of God; but we can only see what the difference really is by considering the ways in which a a sacramental idea of the world might be related to the Christian idea of God's incarnation.

The World as God's Body: Incarnation in Christ as Paradigm?

When Sallie McFague speaks of the world as God's body, it is clear that she regards this as a metaphor, not a literal description. She draws upon the classic story of God's self-disclosure to Moses in Exodus 33:23 when God declares that Moses may see his back (or his backside) but not his face, and so proposes that *all the bodies* of the world are the 'backside' of God; they are visible signs of the divine radiance, but only show the *reflected* glory of the divine face which remains invisible.[17] Moreover, she proposes that the metaphor is incomplete if we simply refer to the world as the body of God; this body is filled with spirit or breath. God as the *spirit* of the world indicates that God relates to the world as an agent, acting with purpose and intentions; God as the *body* of the world indicates the organic relationship of God to the world. McFague concludes that the total metaphor is God as 'the embodied spirit of the universe', or God as the 'inspirited body of the universe';[18] the divine breath liberates, heals and fulfils all created bodies.

Sally McFague thus considers the universe to be the body of God in the sense that *all bodies* are God's body. The basis of the metaphor is in the universal, not in one particular body, such as the body of Jesus of Nazareth or even its historical extension in the church. God is incarnate in the whole cosmos, and Jesus is a paradigm of what we find everywhere. The sacramental presence of God is in all bodies, insists McFague, in 'the bodies of the sun and moon, trees and rivers, animals and people';[19] but we find this presence erupting or breaking through in special ways which give clues to the meaning of the whole. For Christians, one such break-through is in Christ. The story of Jesus enables us to understand the shape and the scope of God's body, because Jesus shows us that the direction of creation is towards inclusive love for all, and especially love for the outcast and the vulnerable. McFague argues that we could never have deduced this shape of the body from the story of evolution; it is a perspective we read back into the world from having faith in the presence of God in the paradigmatic story of Jesus. To speak of 'the cosmic Christ' thus means a 'Christic perspective' for understanding the cosmos.[20]

So we begin from perceiving the universe as the inspirited body of God. Looking at the particular body of Christ we then understand the whole body better; especially we see that the health of the body depends upon caring for the weak, the vulnerable and the oppressed – and for McFague this especially means caring for ravaged nature and the animals who are the 'new poor' in our modern age.

It is important to understand *why* McFague insists on beginning with the whole cosmos, and not with the particular body of Christ. She has, we may judge, legitimate concerns. She worries that beginning with the particular will result in the imposing of one kind of body as the measure and standard for all – namely the male, human body. Diversity will be lost. Moreover, she thinks that other bodies will not be given intrinsic value as holy in themselves, valued for what they are as the body of God. They will be treated only instrumentally, as a means to the end of the life of the body of the church. The unity of the whole cosmos, she emphasises, does not come from expressing the life of one particular, ideal, body; it comes from the common creation story which all bodies share, their one ultimate origin, which modern science tells us is the 'Big Bang' and consequent expansion of the universe. It comes from the organic interconnections of many bodies which is the character of creation.[21]

We should not miss the point, however, that for McFague all bodies are the body of God only in a 'backside' sense. Equally, talk of God as the 'spirit' of the world is 'backside' language. There is no dualism here in which the spirit might be the real essence of God in contrast to the body. God as spirit *and* body, or the 'embodied spirit' of the universe is a metaphor for the final reality of God which remains totally hidden. But while spirit is not transcendent in opposition to the immanence of body, there *is* nevertheless an absolute transcendence – the invisible face of God.[22] Here we may detect that McFague stands in the tradition of negative theology which, from the writings of Gregory of Nyssa onwards, has found in the story of Moses' two encounters with Yahweh on Sinai (Exod. 20:19–21; 33:19–23) the traces of an ineffable God.[23]

Here too we may discern both an affinity with process theology and a difference from it. Process thought also employs the mind–body model of the relation of God to the world; 'body' is an analogy for the world-related and world-dependent aspect of God, containing and being enhanced by all the organic relations of the universe. As Charles Hartshorne expresses this vision:

> In sum, then, God's volition is related to the world as though every object in it were to him a nerve muscle . . . God has no separate sense organs or muscles because all parts of the world body directly perform both functions for him.[24]

Unlike McFague, this is not merely 'backside' talk; it refers, though using analogy, to *all there is* of the world–immanent aspect of God. But, like McFague, the process theologians insist that God is 'more than the cosmos', and that 'the all which is in God [is] yet not all of God'.[25] The 'more' is another aspect of God, a world–independent absoluteness, an unchanging character which is not affected by the cosmic body but remains as a reservoir of possibilities.

Grace Jantzen rightly objects that this is just another form of dualism, and is not really analogous to the wholeness of a person with her body. She is driven by similar motivations to McFague, but proposes a third model of the world–as–God's–body which she is resolute in calling pantheism. The only way to overcome the dualisms and polarisations which have subjugated women to men, and especially the dualism of mind and body, is to regard the world as the body of God in the same sense that we are related to our bodies as persons. That is, just as 'the body is my body–self, yet I am not reducible to its physiological processes',[26] so there is no aspect or hidden reality of God apart from the world, and yet God is not reducible to its physical processes. She regards such pantheism as a 'feminine symbolic', and argues that it preserves the particularity and rich variety of all bodies in the world, where a dualistic view of God and the world just narrows diversity into a strict range of polar opposites – such as mind/body, one/many, form/chaos, light/darkness, male/female.[27]

Both McFague and Jantzen thus begin with the universal in thinking of the world as the body of God, intending thereby to overcome the ethos of male domination and patriarchy that has gripped our Western culture. As Jantzen puts it, the life of Jesus manifests the 'flourishing' that has its origin in the interconnections of the whole community of the world.[28]

The World as God's Body: Incarnation in Christ as the Key

Feminist theologians such as McFague and Jantzen offer powerful arguments for making our starting point in *all* bodies in the universe.

Any doctrine of God which fosters domination of one group by another must be unmasked and undermined. But their approach is not unlike that of Maurice Wiles in his vision of God's action in the world, which 'gives purpose to the whole'.[29] It reflects a modern discomfort with a particularity of divine action or incarnation. Here I want to defend the opposite movement, from the particular to the universal. This is rooted in taking seriously the nature of the presence of God as *participation*, which I have been developing throughout this book. We are summoned to *participate* in God, who with great humility participates in our lives. Thus the whole world is God's body in the sense that the eucharistic bread and the church meeting are the body of Christ: they are a place of meeting, and a point of being drawn into the life of God.

But I have also been arguing in this study that in the life of *one human son* God achieved a unique depth of participation, and received a unique human response. We may say that the eternal movement of love in God that is like a son relating to a father, or like a child to a parent, was totally identified with this human sonship. In this case, and only here, they were exactly the same. Here and only here the divine and human 'yes' to the Father were one voice. If we have this understanding of incarnation in Christ, then the church sacraments will depend upon Christ, and the cosmic sacraments upon baptism and eucharist.

The designation of Jesus as the 'cosmic Christ'[30] does not, then, just mean that he offers a particular perspective upon the whole sacramental universe. It means that the 'yes' in God, like the 'yes' of a child to a father or mother, can now never be separated from the 'yes' of Jesus of Nazareth. So when we say 'Amen' to the Father as we meet God in all creation, we are leaning upon the particular human response of Jesus, the Jesus of the wilderness beyond Jordan, of Gethsemane and Golgotha, interweaving inseparably with the ecstatic response of eternal sonship. Meeting God through bodies, we are always dependent upon the particular body of Christ.

This particularity at the heart of a sacramental universe does not, I believe, undermine our attention to the manifold particulars of the world. It does not prevent us from affirming all things as they truly are, and being full of wonder at what Duns Scotus called their 'thisness'.[31] It did not, for example, inhibit the poet Gerard Manley Hopkins, who celebrates the unique expressiveness of every created thing. In one poem, for instance, he rejoices in the different ways that kingfishers and dragonflies catch the light, and in the quite different sounds of stones falling into water, strings being plucked, bells rung. Everything has its intrinsic reality and value, its 'being indoors' or 'inscape', in his special terminology:

> As kingfishers catch fire, dragonflies draw flame;
>> As tumbled over rim in roundy wells
>> Stones ring; each tucked string tells, each hung bell's
> Bow swung finds tongue to fling out broad its name;
> Each mortal thing does one thing and the same;
>> Deals out that being indoors each one dwells;
>> Selves – goes its self; *myself* it speaks and spells,
> Crying, *What I do is me; for that I came.*

Yet in the same breath, in the same sonnet, Hopkins can attribute this unique identity of all things to the presence of Christ, indwelling all inscapes, responding through them to the Father:

> For Christ plays in ten thousand places,
>> Lovely in limbs, and lovely in eyes not his
>> To the Father through the features of men's faces.[32]

I suggest that this particularity of the Christ-response is not just *compatible* with all creation as the body of God, but actually preserves the diversity of the many and varied bodies through which we encounter God. If this event, which has all the contingency of time and space, of the dusty roads of Galilee, the sweat of crowds and the blood of executions, is normative for the embodiment of God, then we can never escape the particular. Attention to the details of this particular body in its actual context will make us alert to bodies in all their diversity. It will stop us *absorbing* all things into God and so losing their differences from each other. It will enable us to keep hold of an idea of participation, in which the participants are not confused with each other.

Beginning from a universal cosmic body may mean everything gets swallowed up into an undifferentiated oneness. This is especially the problem with pantheism ('everything as God'), which Jantzen overtly espouses. She maintains that the difference and uniqueness of every entity in the world, its 'otherness' of race, gender, age and ability, arise simply from its particular body and embodied experience. Rightly, she judges that this diversity is lost when all things are grounded in a single divine 'mind',[33] but there seems to be a comparable problem when the world is conceived as the body of God without remainder. She attempts to avoid absorption into a divine whole by declining to make definite statements about the objective reality of God: the female divine – the world as God's body – is a 'projection' of earthed female subjectivity, and in this way it functions as the horizon and enabling of our 'flourishing'. Feminine symbols for the divine have the effect of de-stabilising masculine images, and this can occur within either an anti-realist or a ('chastened') realist position; we need not, urges Jantzen, ask 'questions of truth or objective reference too insistently or too soon'.[34] It seems, then, that she hopes to prevent loss of diversity by leaving the reality of God as an open question. What matters at this moment is the effect of the symbol of the world as the body of God on our understanding of the world and on the flourishing of the divine in our own bodies.

Sallie McFague has a different strategy for avoiding absorption into God. She reminds us that 'it is the back and not the face of God that we are allowed to see', so that it is the ineffable face of God that keeps us from a pantheism in which 'God is embodied necessarily and totally'.[35] She claims that her vision is thus panentheistic ('everything in God'), in which God is 'embodied but not necessarily or totally'. Thus she certainly uses the metaphor of God's body in the sense of the *presence* of God in the world: 'God is

mediated, expressed, in and through embodiment.' This accords
with my proposal that the world is a sacrament in the sense of being
a place of encounter with God. But her talk of an 'embodied
spirit' and an 'inspirited body' means that where divine presence is
concerned – whatever reservations she has about a hidden or absent
'face' of God – God is equated with the world. Her vision of the
world as God's body means that God is not met only *in* and *through*
all suffering and mistreated bodies in the world, but *as* these bodies.
She quotes with approval[36] the verse of a young boy:

> Goodnight God
> I hope that you are having
> a good time being the world

My own proposal is that 'pan-entheism' as the participating of
everything in God is a sharing in interweaving movements of
relational love. This makes clear that God is not separable from the
world; it affirms the reality (but not observability) of God; and it
prevents us from simply identifying God and the world. We are
drawn into the life of the triune God through bodies, in all their
diversity and otherness. Beginning with one particular body, that
of Christ, we are awakened to the particularity of all bodies; noticing
his maleness, for instance, we are also enabled to recognise and fully
affirm femaleness. Indeed, as Caroline Bynum proposes, medieval
religious art shows that different gender characteristics could be
incorporated into the one body of Jesus.[37]

The power of the particular to prevent absorption into either
God or the world as a whole is illustrated in the third vision related
by Teilhard de Chardin in 1916. The third is a little different from
the first two, in which the boundaries between Christ and the
world simply dissolve. Here he speaks of carrying the communion
wafer in a portable pyx or container in his breast pocket, while in
the trenches. He cannot bear to have the sacrament so close and
yet not to partake of it; the thin gilded walls of the pyx are an
unbearable barrier: 'how could Christ be at once so close to my

heart and so far from it, so closely united to my body and so remote from my soul?'[38] So he celebrates mass and eats the wafer, but now finds something extraordinary:

> But now it seemed to me that in the depths of being, though the bread I had just eaten had become flesh of my flesh, nevertheless it remained outside of me . . . Still the host seemed to be always ahead of me . . . its centre was receding from me as it drew me on . . .[39]

Each time he thought he had grasped the surface of the host in his vision, he found that what he was holding was 'not the host at all, but one or other of the thousand entities which make up our lives: a suffering, a joy, a task, a friend to have or console'. So the result of the breaking down of the barrier between the communion bread and all the bodies of the world was:

> . . . [a] feeling of rapture produced in me by this revelation of the *universe placed between Christ and myself* like a magnificent prey . . . From the host which I held in my fingers I was separated *by the full extent and the density of the years* which still remained to me, to be lived and to be divinized . . .[40]

The word 'prey' in this account is unfortunate, perhaps betraying the tendency of the scientist at this stage to visualise the world as an object to be examined and mastered. Nevertheless, we can hear the witness of his vision that as the barriers between Christ and the world dissolve, Christ remains out ahead of the world, enabling us to see and value 'the thousand entities that make up our lives'. This vision was to be unpacked later in Teilhard's philosophy of the world as developing in an evolutionary way towards the omega point, the final breaking of consciousness through on to a new level of unity in God. In Christ this breakthrough has already happened, in the middle of time, and so Christ is not just a paradigm of the whole process; reflecting as he does the omega point back into the centre of the process, he affects and promotes the forward movement of the whole towards the end.[41]

Much less sublime, but also about the importance of the particular, is the novel by Anthony Burgess called *Earthly Powers*.
Among other targets the story lampoons the results of attempts to
modernise and secularise all the rituals of the church, as a reforming
pope is impatient with the 'mystery', the 'hocus pocus' of the
particular symbols of bread and wine. One edict of the Vatican
therefore allows the replacement of bread and wine by other
elements; in what is called the African Eucharist it is replaced by
the much more 'culturally relevant' meal of pig's flesh and blood.
The result is inevitable: a slipping from the use of animal flesh to
human flesh and a convenient way of disposing of one's enemies.[42]

This is an outrageous satire, but the shock-value must not be
despised. The very particularity of bread and wine enables us to
find God present in and through other table fellowship; if the
particularity is lost, so may be the awareness of the universal presence
of the God of love, and the 'discerning of the body' (I Cor. 11:29) –
all bodies.

The Pastor as Sacrament

It is only in the context of a truly sacramental theology of the
world as God's body that we can begin to understand the claim of
Austen Farrer that the Christian minister is 'a walking sacrament'.[43]
It is this to which I now want to turn. Like other professional carers
– doctors, nurses, social workers – in the Christian minister there
is a blurring of the line between person and function, between
being and doing. The sort of person that any pastor seems to *be*
will affect the way that she or he will be able to help others. So
also the vocation to Christian ministry is a call to a *way of being*,
not just to the exercise of skills or the carrying out of a set of
functions. Those who are 'personal service professionals' (a name
offered by Paul Halmos)[44] are symbolisers of value. They point
beyond themselves to some value, such as concern for health and
welfare, or the benefits of education, and they are expected to
embody these values in their lives. Christian pastors (of all kinds)

are therefore sacraments of the transcendent grace of love and forgiveness, and the kind of persons they are will be bound up with the things they do. They are 'living symbols'[45] of the sacrificial and persuasive love of Christ.

This conclusion is often resisted out of a proper anxiety that pastors may be 'put on the pedestal' of an unreachable ideal. In reaction, a pastor may develop a totally functional view of ministry, as if all that matters is the task performed. Yet disaster looms if the link between doing and being is neglected. If a pastor is with people for God at the critical points of sorrow and joy in life, her personality is bound to be shaped by this and in turn to shape the quality of her presence there. And people in fact want someone as their pastor who is open to the mystery of God in the midst of these events and is able to be that for them. Of course, it is *also* disastrous if a pastor succumbs to fostering the expectation that she is going to be the ideal Christian. The whole point of a sacrament is that it is a piece of weak, created and fallible stuff in itself, but is a doorway into the life of the triune God. Precisely in its frailty the sacrament symbolises an ultimate value. It can *embody* an ideal without *being* an ideal; the roughest and coarsest piece of bread can symbolise the body. This is not an argument for *ex opere operato* grace, but grace which is always greater than its communicator.

Moreover, we have seen that sacraments are always to be placed in the context of the sacramental life of the whole community. As Alastair Campbell points out, pastoral care must be shared by the whole people, in the *diakonia* of the whole body.[46] He argues for the need to break the exclusive link between ordained ministry and pastoral care, and among other reasons it is because otherwise there emerges the unrealistic, heroic ideal of the perfect professional. The one who is 'paid to care' will *represent* and *symbolise* the transcendent dimensions of acceptance and forgiving love, but he or she will reach 'burn-out' if the activity of caring and the values it expresses are not shared by all. As Elaine Graham emphasises, pastoral practice is the 'purposeful presence' of the community of faith in the world, and the values that give shape to its actions are carried by the story of faith which the community as a whole inherits and lives by.[47]

With these qualifications, then, we may regard the pastor as a living sacrament, *embodying* the accepting and healing love of God. Following our definition of sacrament, she embodies the presence of God in the sense that *in her body there is a place of encounter*, an interface, with the movements of God's life of love. In my chapter on the practice of forgiveness, I suggested that it was essential for the word of absolution to be embodied in flesh and blood, and now I want to extend this to the embodiment of all care for others. Sacramental care is physical care, involving the body. What might this mean in practice?

In the first place, it means *being there*, occupying a shared bodily space with another even though this close proximity may be uncomfortable. It means staying alongside even if the emotions or the senses of the body revolt against being there. This may well make possible the kinds of non-verbal communication described in the previous chapter as being gifts of the Spirit. It will certainly mean costly presence.

Second, it means that the person offering care in God's name will explore the way that beliefs about God are actually embodied in his or her experience. Christian pastors are to examine their own bodily life – their use of the senses and their physical relationships – from the perspective of God's purposes for life. This is a creative step beyond the merely academic joining together of theology and the behavioural sciences; it involves a journey of imagination and self-understanding. It will certainly include being freed from any anxieties about accepting our own bodies and sexuality.

Third, it *may* mean expressing care for others through touch. Love as we know it is communicated through bodies, and physical contact may be one of the most helpful as well as one of the most potentially destructive aspects of pastoral ministry. Alastair Campbell at one point tells the story of a woman named Stella, who had known several traumatic losses, including husband, parents and friends. These experiences, noted her minister, made the physical presence of others both enticing and threatening to her. Campbell concludes, 'Without touching [her] she cannot be helped . . .'[48]

Yet there are acute dangers with physical contact in Christian ministry. As far as children are concerned, because they are specially vulnerable, extreme caution should be exercised for their sake, and the constraints of child-care legislation against inappropriate and intrusive touching make this clear.[49] Physical expressions of concern and comfort for fellow-adults can also lead to sexual self-indulgence, or to other kinds of exploitation which feed the power of the pastor rather than being truly liberating. Consent can often be assumed rather than sought.

There is a vivid illustration of the abuse of what purports to be caring touch in Jean-Paul Sartre's play, *Lucifer and the Lord*, set in sixteenth-century Europe. A former military leader of extreme cruelty, Goetz, vows to become the best person in the world; from being God's most vicious enemy he will become his most devout follower. In one scene, the now 'saintly' Goetz, is in company with Tetzel the seller of indulgences, when he meets a leper:

GOETZ: If the Church loves without revulsion or recoil the most despicable of her sons, why do you hesitate to embrace him? [*Tetzel shakes his head.*] Jesus would have taken him in His arms. I love him better than you. [*Pause. He goes to the leper.*]

THE LEPER [*between his teeth*]: Here comes another to pull the trick of the leper's kiss.

GOETZ: Come here, my brother.

THE LEPER: I thought so! [*He goes to Goetz unwillingly.*] If it's a matter of your salvation, I cannot refuse, but do it quickly. You're all the same; you'd think the Lord had given me leprosy expressly to give you a chance to earn your place in heaven. [*As Goetz approaches him*] Not on the mouth! [*Goetz kisses him on the mouth.*] Pah! [*He wipes his lips.*][50]

The surprise of this scene is that we expect the leper to be grateful for the physical embrace given him, just because he is a leper and an outcast. But we see that it is one thing to touch a leper, and another to make the kind of contact that does not demean and manipulate, but arouses a true response of love.

There is probably less danger of abuse where touch is ritualised. There are many opportunities for this in the liturgy: the laying on of hands in confirmation, ordination or for healing; the use of anointing oil; laying of hands on the heads of children for blessing at the eucharist, or at services of the blessing of newborn infants; marking with the sign of a cross in water at infant baptism, or with ashes in Lent; holding and immersing a candidate in water in the baptism of adults; the offering of bread and wine; the ritual washing of feet; the grasping of the hand in the offering of peace at the eucharist or in receiving into church membership. Even this kind of ritual touch can be intrusive, of course, and the person offering it must take care that those receiving it have truly given their permission to be touched. But such moments in worship, in the midst of the whole body of the people, can focus and heighten the more general and continual commitment to bodily presence with another, to 'being there'.

If we are to be at ease in 'being there' for others, and if we are to learn what is appropriate and non-intrusive physical contact in the context of caring, then (as I have already suggested), we need to come to terms with our own bodily life. Ordained Christian ministers in particular have to make difficult decisions about what is an appropriate use of the body in caring for others. If we are doctors and nurses, then physical contact in examining, treating and even washing patients is part of our proper functions and this can be infused with grace to make it truly sacramental, or what Alastair Campbell calls 'graceful care'.[51] Social workers are given precise instructions in their training about when physical contact might (rarely) be appropriate in a client relationship. Though Christian ministers must learn guidelines in this area, relationships with others are not so clearly defined as with 'clients' in social work, and this is why they must know themselves and their weaknesses clearly. A good place to begin is to ask themselves *why* they want to touch someone, and to listen carefully to the answer that emerges from deep within. Hopefully, such a process of self-exploration is built into any process of pastoral formation. It is part of the risk of a sacramental life that is committed to the value of bodies.

The World as the Body of the Trinity

A sacramental lifestyle is based upon the commitment of God's whole triune self to bodies. While we have largely concentrated on sacrament as 'the body of *Christ*', we have also been thinking of sacrament as a doorway into the perichoresis of *three* persons in God, as an invitation into the divine dance. If the whole world is sacramental, and is a place of encounter with God, we must surely speak of the universe as the body of the Trinity. We must see not only the 'Son' but the three persons or three movements of love in God as committed to the body, though not in the same way.

Indeed, in Christian history the practice of the sacraments seems to have been the place where talk of God as Trinity seemed to arise most naturally. According to the end of Matthew's Gospel, the early church baptised in the name of the Father, and of the Son, and of the Holy Spirit (Mt. 28:19). The oldest eucharistic liturgies are trinitarian in expression.[52] Older still is the triune grace at the end of 1 Corinthians (13:13), that many New Testament scholars think would have led into a celebration of the Lord's supper. It seems that as water, bread and wine became places where the presence of the risen Christ was experienced in a more intense way, the whole interweaving personal life of God was known and celebrated.

When the sense of encounter and interface is lost from sacrament, and thought moves more towards 'identity of substance', an awareness of the presence of the whole triune God also seems to be lost. For instance, Sallie McFague's understanding of the world as God's body leads to a concept of Trinity in which the first person is the invisible face, or the 'mystery'; the second person is the visible body, or the sheer 'mud' of the world; the third person is the breath in the body which mediates 'the mystery and the mud'.[53] The invisible face of God is thus *radical* transcendence, beyond all forms of expression. Like other theologians we have taken note of already, McFague uses the language of Trinity to preserve an absolute and mysterious Otherness in the first person, while allowing interaction with the world through the second and third. However, this kind of division between an immanent Son and Spirit and a transcendent Father locates God's suffering with the many bodies of the world only in one dimension of God, at God's 'back' rather than before the divine 'face' (to use McFague's terminology).

Rather, we should envisage sacraments drawing us deeper into the heart of the interweaving flow of relationships in God. The key is participation, so that God is always open to make room for the world, while remaining an event of relationship in God's own self. God has a body, in so far as finite bodies are in God, and so movements of love and justice in God are expressed through bodies.

The 'fatherly' (or 'motherly') movement in God is expressed, for instance, by the constant coming into being and sustaining of bodies. As there is a movement of love which is like an eternal bringing forth of a Logos-Son, so there is a continual creating of bodily realities which in their otherness from God are echoes or ripples of the otherness of the Son, and some of which as persons are even *images* of the Son. Everything is interconnected and interdependent because it has its origin in this ecstatic overflowing of this maternal Father's love. Whenever we affirm the worth of bodies and give them respect and justice, giving of ourselves to sustain them in being, we are sharing in this distinctive movement in God.

Here we may agree with those theologians, like Duns Scotus in the Middle Ages or Karl Barth in our age, who envision God as eternally intending this divine creative movement to reach its goal in the deepest possible incarnation of God in one particular human body, irrespective of the need to deal with sin in the world.[54] Such is the extravagant generosity of divine love, that it will not be satisfied with anything less than identification with a finite body. This particularity is eternally there in God. Even before its actualisation in the sonship of Jesus of Nazareth, the movement of love in

God which is like the response of a son to a father, or a child to a parent, was destined to be identical with one embodied life, in order to draw all bodies into deeper fellowship in God. Thus at all moments in the story of the universe we lean on the movement from the particular to the universal, as we participate in God. There is always a particular 'yes' in which human daughters and sons make their 'yes' to the creative love of God.

No less than the Father and the Son, the Spirit is also committed to bodies, as the breath which blows through the many places of the world, opening up surprising depths in relationship and hope in the future. So the Trinity is not only in the world, but the world will increasingly become what it is in the Trinity. It will, as Leonardo Boff puts it, increasingly *be* the body of the Trinity, 'showing forth, in the limited form of creation, the full possibility of the communion of the divine Three'.[55]

Sharing, with God's hope, in these threefold movements of God will mean taking bodies as seriously as God does, and this means paying attention to people as they actually are, rather than resorting easily to generalisations. It is, as Alastair Campbell points out, always painful for professional carers to face up to particular cases rather than classifying them under general headings ('the inadequate mother', 'the senile demented', the 'oppressed minority', and so on).[56] But if we notice what is particular about others, and are alert to what is unexpected there, we will see people's value as images of God, as playgrounds for the Spirit. This will lead to our having hope for them, to believing that change is possible and that they are not fated to repeat past patterns of self-destruction.

In 1996 Dundee City Council planned to create a residential unit for four families who had been evicted from their council houses because of their violence, drug abuse and vandalism. These anti-social families would have to learn to live together, and would be helped to confront their disruptive past through intensive counselling by a team of seven social workers who would actually live in the project with them. The unit itself would be situated in the middle of an ordinary housing estate. This project had all the marks of incarnation, in which some would be called to be 'sacramental' for others. The neighbours, however, found this painful. One said, 'I and other decent people will stop at nothing to defend our homes and way of life.' Another said,

> The social workers say these people want to change . . . Well, they've had a hundred chances before and what have they done? They've made others' lives a living hell and we will be next . . . these families have no hope of getting back into the community because nobody [here] wants them.[57]

Before we quickly dismiss the neighbours, classifying them under a generalisation like 'demagogue fascists', as did the leader of the City Council, we should feel through their reaction the real pain of facing the particular. This is the kind of cost to be carried by those who are willing to be 'living sacraments'. The sacramental life is one that is open to the presence of God, and can open a door for others into eternal movements of love and justice that are there ahead of us, and before us, and embracing us. This openness can be felt like the invitation to a dance, but sometimes like the raw edges of a wound.

This is participation in God. This is theology.

NOTES

1. Mark Slouka, *War of the Worlds: Cyberspace and the Hi-tech Assault on Reality* (London: Abacus, 1996), 52–5.
2. John Macquarrie, *Principles of Christian Theology*, revised edn (London: SCM Press, 1977), 93.
3. Sallie McFague, *The Body of God: An Ecological Theology* (London: SCM Press, 1993), 14–17, 35–8.
4. See Plato, *Timaeus* 42B–D; *Phaedrus* 246–9; Aristotle, *Politics* I.6.
5. McFague, *The Body of God*, 16; Grace Jantzen, *Becoming Divine: Towards a Feminist Philosophy of Religion* (Manchester: Manchester University Press, 1998), 31–2, 137–9; Rosemary Radford Ruether, *Sexism and God-Talk: Towards a Feminist Theology* (London: SCM Press, 1983), 72–92.
6. Gerard Manley Hopkins, 'God's Grandeur' in *Poems of Gerard Manley Hopkins*, ed. W. H. Gardner and N. H. Mackenzie (Oxford: Oxford University Press, 1967), 66.

7. Augustine, *In Johannem* 80.3.
8. Paul Tillich, *Systematic Theology* (London: Nisbet & Co., 1968), Vol. 2, 10.
9. *An Agreed Statement on Eucharistic Doctrine* (Windsor, 1971), Anglican–Roman Catholic International Commission (London: SPCK, 1972), 5.
10. Zwingli, *Letter to Matthew Alber*, 16 November 1524, trans. in H. Wayne Pipkin, *Huldrych Zwingli: Writings*, Vol. 2 (Allison Park, PA: Pickwick, 1984), 141.
11. See Paul S. Fiddes, 'Baptism and Creation' in *Reflections on the Water* (Oxford: Regent's Park College and Macon, GA: Smyth & Helwys Publishing, 1996), 49–57.
12. From Pierre Teilhard de Chardin, *Le Prêtre* (1917) in *Hymn of the Universe*, trans. S. Bartholomew (London: Collins, 1965), 14.
13. Teilhard, *Hymn of the Universe*, 19.
14. Ibid., 23.
15. Ibid., 43.
16. Ibid, 48.
17. McFague, *The Body of God*, 133–4.
18. Ibid., 144, 149–50.
19. Ibid., 134.
20. Ibid., 162–70.
21. Ibid., 35–46.
22. Ibid., 131–3, 150.
23. E.g. Gregory of Nyssa, *De Vita Moysis* 2.162–4 (Exodus 20); Denys the Areopagite, *Mystical Theology* 1000C–1001A.
24. Charles Hartshorne, *Man's Vision of God: And the Logic of Theism* (Hamden: Archon Books, 1964 [1941]), 185.
25. Ibid., 204, 347.
26. Jantzen, *Becoming Divine*, 265.
27. Ibid., 266–8.
28. Ibid., 165–6.
29. See above, Ch. 4, pp. 126–30.
30. The idea, but not the term, is presented in Colossians 1:16–17.
31. See above, pp. 81–3, and note 52 on p. 110.
32. Hopkins, 'As kingfishers catch fire', *Poems*, 90.
33. Jantzen, *Becoming Divine*, 273–4.
34. Ibid., 191–2, 275.
35. McFague, *The Body of God*, 150.
36. Ibid., 130.
37. Caroline Walker Bynum, 'The Body of Christ in the Later Middle Ages' in *Fragmentation and Redemption* (New York: Zone Books, 1992), 92–6.
38. Teilhard, *Hymn of the Universe*, 51.
39. Ibid., 51–2.
40. Ibid., 53.

41. Teilhard de Chardin, *The Phenomenon of Man*, trans. B. Wall (London: Collins, 1959), 257–64, 294–9.
42. Anthony Burgess, *Earthly Powers* (London: Hutchinson, 1980), 342–3, 627–9.
43. Austin Farrer, *A Celebration of Faith* (London: Hodder & Stoughton, 1970), 110.
44. Paul Halmos, *The Personal Service Society* (London: Constable, 1970).
45. See Alastair Campbell, *Paid to Care? The Limits of Professionalism in Pastoral Care* (London: SPCK, 1985), 24.
46. Ibid., 24–34, 58–60.
47. Elaine Graham, *Transforming Practice: Pastoral Theology in an Age of Uncertainty* (London: Mowbray, 1996), 114–18, 199–201, 208–10.
48. Campbell, *Paid to Care?*, 65.
49. In the UK the Children Act, 1989, was followed by the Home Office Code of Practice, *Safe from Harm* (London: Home Office, 1993).
50. Jean-Paul Sartre, *The Respectable Prostitute [and] Lucifer and the Lord*, trans. K. Black (Harmondsworth: Penguin, 1965), 128–9.
51. Alastair Campbell, *Moderated Love: A Theology of Professional Care* (London: SPCK, 1984), 107–11. On 'expressive touch' or 'caring touch', see also Norman Autton, *Touch: An Exploration* (London: Darton, Longman & Todd, 1989).
52. E.g. Hippolytus, *Tradition of the Apostles* 4.4; for texts, see Gregory Dix, *The Shape of the Liturgy* (London: Dacre Press, 1945), 158, 164.
53. McFague, *The Body of God*, 161–2.
54. So Duns Scotus, *Opus Oxoniense (Ordinatio)* 3, d.7, q.3; See Karl Barth, *Church Dogmatics*, trans. and ed. G. W. Bromiley and T. F. Torrance (Edinburgh: T. & T. Clark, 1936–77), II/2, 101–4, 115–21; Leonardo Boff, *Trinity and Society*, trans. P. Burns (London: Burns & Oates, 1988), 186–8; Wolfhart Pannenberg, *Systematic Theology*, Vol. 2, trans. G. Bromiley (Edinburgh: T. & T. Clark, 1994), 63–5.
55. Boff, *Trinity and Society*, 231.
56. Campbell, *Moderated Love*, 91.
57. Article, 'Ghetto from Hell', *The Observer*, 27 October 1996.

INDEX